BEYOND CYBERSECURITY

BEYOND CYBERSECURITY

PROTECTING YOUR DIGITAL BUSINESS

James M. Kaplan
Tucker Bailey
Chris Rezek
Derek O'Halloran
Alan Marcus

WILEY

Contents

Foreword

We live in a remarkable age of technology innovation. The speed with which we are able to communicate, collaborate, and transform our businesses and organizations is truly astounding. Yet the risk created by our increasing dependence on those technology advancements is equally astounding. The economic, operational, and reputational risks of technology are well known to anyone who has paid even passing attention to the almost daily security breach headlines.

In their research, so effectively laid out in this book, the authors explain why there is so much cyber insecurity today, how it has become such an intractable problem, why it could get worse, and what organizations, industries, and governments must do now to start to address the problem. Importantly, James Kaplan, Tucker Bailey, Chris Rezek, Derek O'Halloran, and Alan Marcus go beyond elucidating today's risks and how to mitigate them, and extrapolate the downstream economic consequences if organizations don't change their fundamental approach to cybersecurity.

During the course of the authors' work, I had an opportunity to preview their methodology and early results. So much of what they were seeing in organizations around the globe mirrored what I had been seeing and hearing from RSA's customers. As the authors subsequently presented their early findings to national representatives of countries from Europe, Asia, and the Americas at the 2014 RSA Conferences, it was clear that their findings resonated globally and reflected a universal experience. At these sessions, I was encouraged to see such an improved understanding of the need for all nations to cooperate to solve this problem.

It is clear from the research that the advent of cloud, mobile, and social media technologies combined with contemporary digital business practices has so expanded and distorted the attack surface of organizations that it is no longer possible to use the perimeter as an effective defense method. The perimeter that used to serve as a barrier between organizations and the external world has been perforated to the point that even a Swiss cheese metaphor is too charitable. The perimeter has become fragmented, ephemeral, dynamic, and contextual. As such, the security programs and controls on which we have relied are being overwhelmed. A new security model is called for and the authors of this book are recommending a multitiered approach based on the concept of digital resilience—an approach that has been adopted by leading companies around the world and has rapidly become conventional wisdom.

Digital resilience is not just a theory. It is a strategy, yes, but it is also a framework of policies, processes, and controls that promise real security in our increasingly insecure world. It starts with a thorough understanding of risk and the need to view digital risk through the lens of an organization's business objectives, priorities, and critical assets. It's about creating a culture of security among business leaders so that digital business decisions are made with security in mind and not just as an afterthought. It's about being prepared for attacks from any source, including insiders, and having the visibility, analytical tools, and dynamic controls necessary to respond rapidly and with agility to the inevitable intrusions. Most of all, digital resilience is about bringing all of these elements together in a coherent whole to create true defense in depth.

But our organizations are not islands. It's hard for them to succeed on their own. The authors acknowledge the need for an ecosystem of governments, regulators, vendors, and industry groups in which organizations work together and create policy that will protect the collective whole.

For many, the topic of cybersecurity continues to be unfathomable. A lack of organizational maturity, fear, and a sense of hopelessness permeate many organizations. As the authors explain in their analysis of the economic consequences of continued cyber insecurity, the impact of this lack of clarity goes beyond the current challenges we face, since the adoption of innovative, potentially transformative technologies is being hampered by fear and uncertainty around cyber risks. But, as two-time Nobel Laureate Marie Curie said, "Nothing in life is to be feared. It is only to be understood. We must understand more so that we may fear less."

The authors do an exceptional job of creating that understanding in this book and are to be commended for providing the research and analysis necessary to distill such a clear and compelling path to a secure future.

I believe this book can be of enormous help to security practitioners and IT executives, not only to benchmark themselves against real-world successes, but as a tool to explain to senior management the importance and relevance of cybersecurity to their organizations' future and very viability.

Every politician and regulator should use this book as a guide for developing thoughtful, effective policy and practical regulation that can support the private sector in its efforts.

And, finally, for executives and boards of directors, it can be a valuable guide for their fiduciary understanding of a problem that all organizations face and will only grow in import in the future. I am frequently invited to speak to boards of directors about their cybersecurity situations and outlook, and, while I frequently draw upon my own experience and the experiences of our customers around the world in those conversations, I'm thankful to be able now to share the excellent insight and perspective of this book as well.

Arthur W. Coviello, Jr.
Executive Chairman
RSA, The Security Division of EMC

Preface

Progress for the world economy depends on tens of trillions of dollars in value being created from digitization over the next decade. Institutions are moving from having pockets of automation to using pervasive connectivity, massive analytics, and low-cost scalable technology platforms to achieve fundamentally different levels of customer intimacy, operational agility, and decision-making insight. In banking, this means opening accounts and approving mortgages in minutes rather than days or weeks. In insurance, better underwriting and fairer pricing based on massive analytics. In airlines and hotels, it means more transparency and less hassle for travelers.

When "everything is digital," private, public, and civil institutions become more dependent on information systems. In such a hyperconnected world, online and mobile capabilities increase these institutions' vulnerability to attack by sophisticated cyber-criminals, political "hacktivists," nation-states, and even their own employees. As a result, the success of continued digitization hinges on consumers and companies trusting that financial records, patient data, and intellectual property will remain confidential, valid, and available when required in the face of increasingly determined cyber-attacks.

Protecting institutions from cyber-attacks is therefore critical to continued economic development, which led the World Economic Forum and McKinsey to collaborate to raise the visibility of cybersecurity among C-suite executives at the Forum's 2014 Annual Meeting in Davos.

We agreed that two outputs would be critical: a fact-based point of view on the broad strategic and economic of implications of cyber-attacks, and a plan for what the full set of players in the cybersecurity ecosystem should do to achieve digital resilience, with a strong focus on how senior executives could address this as a business rather than a technology issue.

Based on interviews, surveys, and working sessions involving executives at several hundred institutions, our research yielded four findings.

First, without dramatic changes both in the way institutions protect themselves and in the external support they receive, the risk of cyber-attack will reduce trust and confidence in the digital economy—reducing the value created by $3 trillion in 2020. To counter this, the world's institutions will have to achieve a state of digital resilience. Only then will they be able to capture the value of a hyperconnected world despite the risk of operational disruption, intellectual property loss, public embarrassment, and fraud that cyber-attacks create.

Second, although there is a high degree of consensus on the practices required for digital resilience, companies are not putting them in place fast enough. Digital resilience requires companies to integrate cybersecurity deeply within their business processes and information technology (IT) environment. Unfortunately, to date, most companies continue to treat cybersecurity as a control function, which causes increasing friction between the need to protect their valuable information assets and digital processes on the one hand and the need to extract value from technology investments on the other. Even the largest and best-funded institutions design their cybersecurity programs backwards, starting with technology controls rather than business risks, and failing to drive the broader organizational and business process change required.

Third, in order for companies to achieve digital resilience, they will need to improve the collaboration between their cybersecurity team and the business, increase the entire IT organization's focus on resiliency, and dramatically upgrade the skills and capabilities of the cybersecurity function. Only the CEO and the rest of the senior management team can drive organizational change of this scale.

Finally, although nobody can protect companies from cyber-attacks but themselves, regulators, law enforcement, defense/security agencies, technology vendors, and industry associations will all have important roles to play in creating an ecosystem that enables digital resilience. Although there is much less consensus on how the broader digital ecosystem should evolve than on the actions individual companies should take, increased collaboration across the public, private, and not-for-profit sectors will be critical.

SETTING THE CONTEXT FOR DIGITAL RESILIENCE

Thinking about digital resilience requires an understanding of cyber-attacks and cybersecurity and how they fit into the digital ecosystem.

Cyber-attacks: Risks across the Business Model

In an increasingly digitized economy, all the world's important institutions depend on "information assets," structured and unstructured information such as customer data, intellectual property, and business plans, as well as on online processes that include everything from customer servicing to vendor payments. Cyber-attacks compromise information assets to further attackers' personal, economic, political, or national-strategic objectives. While the popular press has focused on a few examples of cyber-attacks, typically theft of intellectual property and credit card information, companies have to take a broader range of potential risks into account (Table P.1).

TABLE P.1   **Companies Face a Wide Range of Cybersecurity Risks**

Type of Risk	Actor	Attack
Competitive disadvantage	Foreign competitor	Steals sensitive business plans to gain economic advantage
	Foreign intelligence agency	Steals intellectual property for reasons of national advantage
	Employee leaving for new company	Takes customer account information with her as she leaves to work for a competitor
Regulatory and legal exposure	Cyber-crime organization	Steals customer data to use later to undertake identity theft or medical fraud
Reputational damage	Employee	Releases sensitive documents to the public because he disagrees with company policies
	Hacktivist	Exfiltrates and releases confidential management discussions publicly because it disagrees with company policies

(continue)

Type of Risk	Actor	Attack
Fraud and theft	Cyber-crime organization	Corrupts an online financial transaction to undertake fraud
	Cyber-crime organization	Threatens to destroy important information assets unless it receives a ransom
Business disruption	Terrorist organization	Changes data required for critical business processes to harm a country or organization it despises
	Insider	Destroys corporate data because he suspects he will be fired
	Hacktivist	Disrupts business processes (like online customer service) to draw attention to a cause

Cybersecurity: How Companies Have Protected Themselves

Cybersecurity[1] is the business function of protecting an institution from the damage caused by cyber-attacks in the face of constraints such as other business objectives, resource limitations, and compliance requirements. It has three facets: risk management, influencing, and delivery.

Cybersecurity is first and foremost a *risk management function*— there is no way to prevent all cyber-attacks from happening. As one chief information security officer (CISO) puts it, "My job isn't to reduce risk. My job is to enable the business to take intelligent risks."

If a company launches a new mobile servicing platform for customers, it is taking a risk—the mobile platform creates a new way for attackers to get at company data. But it is also seeking a return: it hopes the platform will improve revenues per customer. As a risk manager, the CISO helps business leaders make intelligent decisions about the risk of cyber-attack by answering questions such as:

- What are the risks associated with a new mobile platform? Does the business return justify the incremental risks?
- How can the mobile platform be designed to yield the best possible customer experience (and therefore business impact) at the lowest risk of losing data to a cyber-attack?

---

[1] Different institutions may use the terms *cybersecurity, information security,* and *IT security* to refer to the same activities. For the purposes of this book, we consider the terms to be interchangeable.

Cybersecurity is also an *influencing function*. The decisions CISOs make in tandem with business leaders on the right mix of risk and return lead to far-ranging actions across different parts of the organization: procurement teams have to negotiate security requirements into contracts; managers must limit the distribution of sensitive documents; developers have to design secure applications and write secure code. Cybersecurity necessarily involves a wide variety of stakeholders, some of whom need to be guided by compliance, some by less rigid and more persuasive measures.

Finally, cybersecurity is a *delivery function* that includes managing both technologies such as firewalls, intrusion detection, malware detection, and identity and access management, and also activities that are focused primarily on protecting information assets and online processes such as compiling and analyzing threat intelligence and conducting forensic analysis.

Naturally, cybersecurity as a business function is not the same as cybersecurity as an organization. A company may decide to consolidate all or most risk management, influencing, and delivery activities into a single cybersecurity group or distribute them among several organizations.

The Digital Ecosystem: Companies Cannot Protect Themselves Alone

Although institutions must protect themselves, they do so in the context of a broader digital ecosystem (Figure P.1), which includes:

- *Business customers.* Given the need to connect corporate networks to ease collaboration, business customers are a source of risk and vulnerability for many companies. Attackers may use a customer's IT environment as a way into a supplier's network. Equally, business customers worry about how their suppliers protect data. Both situations can create stringent security expectations and requirements for many companies.

- *Retail customers.* Consumers are not yet as sensitized to the risk of cyber-attacks as businesses, but their expectations about how companies should protect their data are starting to influence their buying decisions.

- *Business suppliers.* Suppliers such as law firms, accounting firms, banks, and business process outsourcing providers will handle

FIGURE P.1   **Companies Face a Wide Range of Cybersecurity Risks**

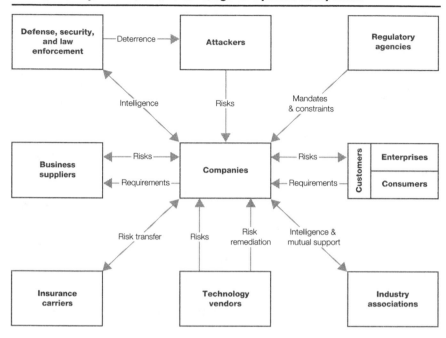

a company's most sensitive data at some point. In addition, like business customers, suppliers can provide an entry point for attackers, given the interconnection of corporate networks.

- *Technology suppliers.* Vendors are a source of both risk and risk remediation. Any technology a company buys may have security flaws that create vulnerabilities attackers can exploit. However, technology vendors also offer products and services that enable companies to reduce risk by eliminating vulnerabilities, analyzing cyber-attacks, and otherwise protecting their corporate technology environments.

- *Government agencies.* The public sector—in the form of different types of agencies or ministries in each jurisdiction—plays multiple roles that affect the cybersecurity environment. It investigates attacks and prosecutes attackers. It regulates private companies, sometimes requiring specific protections or retaining the right to approve a company's cybersecurity strategy. It may also adjust civil law, provide subsidies, perform research, share intelligence, disseminate know-how, or provide capabilities with the objective of reducing the economic damage from cyber-attacks.

- *Civil society groups*. There is a huge range of civil society groups that participate in the digital ecosystem, from industry associations to standards-setting bodies and advocacy groups.
- *Insurers*. Cyber-insurance is in its early days, but even today carriers can enable companies to transfer some risks related to cyber-attacks in return for cash premiums.

What Do We Mean by Digital Resilience?

Senior executives sometimes ask chief information officers (CIOs) and CISOs when cybersecurity will be solved—when the risk of cyber-attack will go away and they can stop worrying about it. Sometimes they draw an analogy with commercial aviation. At the dawn of the jet age, there were some horrifying crashes. Now, while airlines continue to pay obsessive attention to safety, the cab ride to the airport is typically the most dangerous part of air travel.

Indeed, driving may be a better analogy for cybersecurity. A vastly wider group of people undertakes a vastly wider set of activities using a vastly wider range of vehicles than is the case with commercial aviation. As a society, we could choose to reduce automotive fatalities to almost zero by increasing the driving age to 30 and reducing the speed limit to 25 miles per hour, but that would have a devastating impact on the value of personal transportation.

Or take financial risk. A banking CEO would never ask when she can stop worrying about market and credit risk. She understands that her institution is in the business of accepting these risks in exchange for economic returns. Therefore, her business depends on understanding market, credit, and other risks and managing them appropriately in the context of potential returns.

Given increasing digitization, rapid technology innovation, and attackers that may be beyond the reach of law enforcement, the world economy cannot expect to eliminate the prospect of cyber-attacks anytime soon. Companies and economies can, however, aspire to achieve a state of digital resilience in which:

- Companies understand the risks of cyber-attacks and can make business decisions where the returns justify the incremental risks.

- Companies have confidence that the risks of cyber-attack are manageable, rather than strategic—they do not put the company's competitive position or very existence at risk.
- Consumers and business have confidence in the online economy— the risks to information assets and of online fraud are not a brake to the growth of digital commerce.
- The risk of cyber-attack does not prevent companies from continuing to take advantage of technology innovation.

It is in this context that the World Economic Forum and McKinsey & Company have collaborated to understand how to help both companies and countries reach their aspirations.

BACKGROUND AND APPROACH

"Risk and Responsibility in a Hyperconnected World" has been a theme for the World Economic Forum since 2011. Since the middle of 2012, the Forum has worked with nearly 100 companies to sign the "Principles for Cyber-Resilience." Adhering to these principles commits companies to recognize that all parties have a role in fostering a resilient digital economy and to develop a practical and effective implementation program. It also encourages executive-level awareness and leadership of cyber-risk management and, where appropriate, it encourages suppliers and customers to develop a similar level of awareness and commitment.[2]

For the Forum's 2014 meeting in Davos, it asked McKinsey to help it increase C-suite executives' level of engagement with cyber-attacks, cybersecurity, and digital resilience across industries, including not only technology and telecommunications, but also financial services, manufacturing, consumer goods, transportation, energy, and the public sector.

Jointly, McKinsey and the Forum decided that the most useful outputs of this project would be a fact-based point of view on the broad strategic and economic implications of cyber-attacks; and a plan for what the full set of players in the cybersecurity ecosystem should do to achieve digital resilience, with a strong focus on how senior executives could address this as a business rather than a technology issue.

We began collecting data in the late spring of 2013, developed and validated our hypotheses through the summer and fall, and shared our findings at the Forum's Annual Meeting in Davos in January 2014.

[2] World Economic Forum, "Partnering for Cyber Resilience," March 2012.

The Fact Base   Interviews with more than 180 CIOs, CISOs, chief technology officers (CTOs), chief risk officers (CROs), business unit executives, regulators, investors, policymakers, and technology vendors provided input into how all the different participants in the ecosystem thought about the overall cybersecurity environment. In addition, surveys of nearly 100 enterprise technology users gave us a clear understanding of business risks, the threat environment, and the potential impact of a range of actions. Finally, more than 60 Global 500 institutions participated in a detailed survey on their cybersecurity risk management practices (Table P.2).

Scenarios and Economic Impact   Based on insights gleaned in the interviews, we identified more than 20 drivers of how the cybersecurity environment could evolve over the next five to seven years and synthesized those into two macro-level drivers: intensity of threat and quality of response. From there, we derived three future state scenarios: muddling into the future, digital backlash, and digital resilience. Based on

TABLE P.2   **Our Research Was Based on Extensive Surveys and Workshops**

Sources of Input	
Interviews with 180+ industry leaders	CIOs, CISOs, CTOs, CROs, and business unit executives in financial services, insurance, health care, high-tech/telecom, media, industrial, and public sectors
	Policymakers, regulators, and members of the defense and intelligence communities
	Across the Americas; Europe, Middle East, and Africa (EMEA); and Asia
Survey of nearly 100 technology executives	Covered: • Most important business risks • Business implications of risk of cyber-attacks • Perspectives on external environment • Actions for improving resilience
Cyber-Risk Maturity Survey results from 60+ companies	Assessment of cybersecurity risk management capabilities based on 180 best practices
	Included financial services, health care, insurance, and other participants from the Americas, EMEA, and Asia
Validation in range of forums	Tested at events involving more than 500 executives, policymakers, academics, and other thought leaders: • World Economic Forum events in Geneva; Washington, D.C.; New York; Davos; Baku; Brussels; and Dalian, China • McKinsey convened forums for CISOs in the banking and health care industries

input from the interviews and surveys, we estimated how each scenario would affect the adoption of a range of important technology innovations such as cloud computing, enterprise mobility, and the Internet of Things—and what impact this would have on value creation.

Critical Actions to Achieve Digital Resilience   Again, based on the interviews and surveys, we highlighted the most important actions for each participant in the cybersecurity ecosystem, with a particular focus on the actions individual companies would have to take across all their business functions to protect themselves.

Once we defined the scenarios, assessed the economic impact, and identified the critical actions, we reviewed these interim findings with dozens of CIOs, CISOs, policymakers, and other relevant executives. These reviews took place at working sessions in Silicon Valley, Geneva, and Washington, D.C.; at executive roundtables convened by McKinsey; and at the World Economic Forum's Annual Meeting of New Champions in Dalian, China.

We summarized our findings in a high-level report published on January 26, 2014[3] and discussed the results in a spirited private session with more than 80 senior executives and policymakers at the Forum's meeting in Davos. There is already strong evidence that this effort is starting to achieve its objectives. *CSO* magazine explained that our estimate of a $3 trillion impact is "getting everyone's attention because it looks not only at direct losses, but also at unrealized value creation as businesses and individuals avoid 'digitization'—or the adoption of technology."[4]

Since presenting the findings, both McKinsey and the Forum have worked on what it will take to get to digital resilience. Based on its work supporting leading institutions in developing cybersecurity strategies and implementing cybersecurity programs, McKinsey has further validated and fleshed out the actions that individual institutions should take to protect themselves. Meanwhile, the Forum has conducted dozens of working sessions involving hundreds of companies to build support for collaboration among all participants in the ecosystem to get from cybersecurity to digital resilience in this world where $3 trillion is at stake.

[3] World Economic Forum, in collaboration with McKinsey & Company, "Risk and Responsibility in a Hyperconnected World," January 2014.
[4] Bragdon, Bob, "When Leadership Gets on Board," *CSO*, June 19th, 2014. www.csoonline .com/article/2365152/security-leadership/when-leadership-gets-on-board.html.

Executive Summary

The theft of information assets and the intentional disruption of online processes are among the most important business risks facing major institutions. If companies, governments, and other organizations continue to address this issue in the way that they have, the risk of cyber-attacks could slow the pace of technology innovation with as much as $3 trillion in lost economic value in 2020.

Companies, with the support of a broader ecosystem, must instead build cybersecurity into their business and information technology (IT) processes in order to achieve digital resilience.

At its heart, this book addresses three questions:

1. What is the risk of cyber-attacks, and how could their impact evolve over the next few years?
2. How can companies achieve digital resilience and protect themselves from attacks while still creating value from technology investments and innovation?
3. What practical steps should business and public-sector leaders be taking to facilitate this progress toward digital resilience?

$3 TRILLION AT RISK

Companies are losing ground to cyber-attackers. Nearly 80 percent of technology executives said that they cannot keep up with attackers' increasing sophistication and many said they are seeing attack strategies filter down from nation-states to a wide range of criminals and hacktivists, who have much more destructive ambitions.

Although companies are spending tens, and sometimes hundreds of millions of dollars protecting themselves, they lack the facts and processes to make effective decisions about cybersecurity. Of more than 60 institutions whose practices we surveyed in detail, a third had only a "nascent" level of cybersecurity maturity, while the next 60 percent were still "developing." Very few were "mature" and not a single one was "robust." Many institutions simply appear to be throwing money at the problem, but larger expenditures have not translated into greater maturity.

The controls required to protect against cyber-attacks are already having a negative impact on business. For example, security concerns are delaying the rollout of more advanced mobile functionality in companies by an average of six months, and are even more dramatically limiting the extent to which companies are using public cloud services. For nearly three quarters of companies, security controls reduce frontline productivity by slowing employees' ability to share information, and even though direct cybersecurity spend is relatively small, the indirect costs can be substantial: some CIOs told us that security requirements drove as much as 20 to 30 percent of their overall activity.

The cybersecurity environment could evolve in many different ways over the next five to seven years. However, if attackers continue to increase their advantage over defenders, the result could be a cyber-backlash that decelerates digitization. In this scenario, a relatively small number of destructive attacks would reduce trust in the economy, causing governments to impose new regulations and institutions to slow the pace of technology innovation. The world would capture less of the $8 trillion to $18 trillion we predict can be generated by 2020 from technological innovations such as big data and mobility—the ultimate impact could be as much as $3 trillion in lost productivity and growth.

Companies, governments, and society at large must strive for digital resilience in order to realize the full potential value of innovation. This means cybersecurity must move up the corporate and political agenda.

The first section of this book deals with this issue. Chapter 1 demonstrates why concerns about cyber-attacks are already affecting companies' ability to derive value from technology investments. Chapter 2 lays out the potential scenarios that describe how the cybersecurity environment could evolve over the next five to seven years and explains in more detail why we believe that $3 trillion is at risk.

DIGITAL RESILIENCE PROTECTS THE BUSINESS AND ENABLES INNOVATION

As recently as seven or eight years ago, cybersecurity was not a priority for many companies. Even large and sophisticated IT organizations spent relatively little protecting themselves from attack and had little insight into the business risks caused by technology vulnerabilities. What protections existed were focused on defending the perimeter of the corporate network, and IT security organizations' role was to manage tools such as remote access and antivirus software. Managers and frontline employees faced few consequences for violating security policies, and insecure application code and infrastructure configurations were pervasive.

Since then, most technology executives tell us that they have made significant progress in establishing cybersecurity as a control function. There are now true cybersecurity organizations with significant budgets and headed by chief information security officers (CISOs). They have locked down desktops and laptops to prevent end users from unwittingly introducing vulnerabilities into the environment; they have introduced architecture standards; and they review processes to identify and remediate security flaws in new applications.

Establishing cybersecurity as a control function was a necessary step that dramatically reduced risk for a great many institutions, but it is less and less tenable as the threat of cyber-attacks continue to rise (Figure E.1). It places the responsibility for security primarily with the cybersecurity team. It is backward-looking and tries to protect against yesterday's attacks. It depends on manual interventions and checks and double checks, and has limited scalability. It seeks to inspect security in, just as old-school manufacturing processes futilely sought to inspect quality in. Most importantly, it increases the tension between cybersecurity and the innovation and flexibility craved by the business.

FIGURE E.1 **Existing Cybersecurity Models Become Less Tenable as Threats Increase**

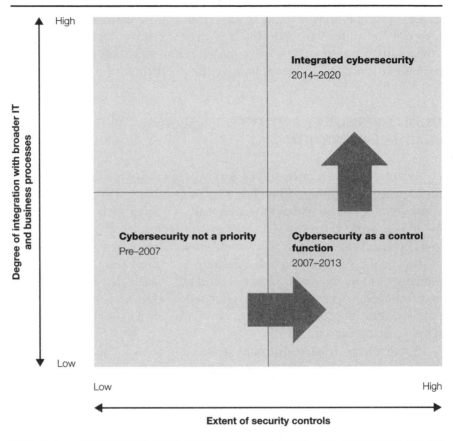

To achieve digital resilience, companies need to undergo fundamental organizational changes, including integrating cybersecurity with business processes and changing how they manage IT. Specifically, there are seven hallmarks of digital resilience:

1. *Prioritize information assets based on business risks.* Most institutions lack insight into what information assets need protecting and which are the highest priority. Cybersecurity teams must work with business leaders to understand business risks across the entire value chain and then prioritize the underlying information assets accordingly.

2. *Provide differentiated protection for the most important assets.* Few companies have any systematic way of aligning the level of protection they give to information assets with the importance of those assets to the business. Putting in place differentiated controls (e.g., encryption or multifactor authentication) ensures that institutions are directing the most appropriate resources to protecting the information assets that matter most.

3. *Integrate cybersecurity into enterprise-wide risk management and governance processes.* Cybersecurity is intertwined with almost all of an institution's major business processes. Companies must create much tighter connections between the cybersecurity team and each critical business function—product development, marketing and sales, supply chain, corporate affairs, human resources (HR), and risk management—in order to make the appropriate trade-offs between protecting information assets and operating key business processes efficiently and effectively.

4. *Enlist frontline personnel to protect the information assets they use.* Users are often the biggest vulnerability an institution has— they click on links they should not, choose insecure passwords, and e-mail sensitive files to broad distribution lists. Institutions need to segment users based on the assets they need to access, and help each group understand the business risks associated with their everyday actions.

5. *Integrate cybersecurity into the technology environment.* Almost every part of the broader technology environment affects an institution's ability to protect itself—from application development practices to policies for replacing outdated hardware. Institutions must move from a crude "bolt-on security" mentality and instead train their entire staff to incorporate it into technology projects from day one.

6. *Deploy active defenses to engage attackers.* There is a massive amount of information available about potential attacks—both from external intelligence sources and from an institution's own technology environment. Companies will need to develop the capabilities to aggregate and analyze the most relevant information, proactively engage with attackers, and tune defenses accordingly.

7. *Test continuously to improve incident response across business functions.* An inadequate response to a breach—not only by the

technology team, but also from marketing, public affairs, or customer service functions—can be as damaging as the breach itself. Institutions should run cross-functional "cyber-war games" to improve their ability to respond effectively in real time.

There are three important points about this list:

1. Technology executives believe that these actions collectively could be game changing in terms of digital resilience.
2. Only two are primarily cybersecurity levers; the remainder require broader IT or business process change.
3. Companies are not making progress on these levers fast enough. On average, technology executives gave their companies C to C– grades on their efforts so far.

The seven levers are discussed in Chapters 3 through 7. Chapter 3 looks at how to prioritize business risks and put in place different levels of protection for the most important information assets. Chapter 4 provides a perspective on how to incorporate cybersecurity considerations into business decision making and how frontline users can help protect information assets. Chapter 5 shows how cybersecurity must be built into the broader IT environment. Chapter 6 describes integrating intelligence, analytics, and operations into active defenses that can respond quickly to emerging threats. Chapter 7 covers the use of war gaming to build incident response skills across business functions.

BUSINESS LEADERS MUST DRIVE CHANGE

Cybersecurity has several characteristics that make it tough for large, complicated institutions to address in an integrated way. Cybersecurity is pervasive—it touches just about every business process, which means that many cybersecurity decisions have a far-reaching market and strategic impact, requiring senior management engagement. Conversely, getting the right level of senior engagement is also tough: the language is arcane, cybersecurity teams often lack the skills to interact with senior executives, and few tools exist to quantify cybersecurity risk or mitigation.

Too many companies put programs in place that avoid these inherent challenges rather than address them. They conduct mechanistic assessments that may not unearth the real issues. They fail to consider the full range of risk reduction mechanisms. They approach the task of achieving digital resilience as a technology program focused on compensating controls rather than as a business strategy and operations program with significant technology implications. Perhaps worst of all, they neglect to engage senior business leaders effectively.

An effective cybersecurity program that will make rapid and sustained progress toward digital resilience must be designed from the start around three principles:

1. Collaborative engagement between the cybersecurity team and their business partners to prioritize risks, make intelligent trade-offs, and, where appropriate, change business processes and behaviors rather than implement technology solutions to manage risks.

2. A focus on resiliency in the broader IT organization, to facilitate the convergence of security, efficiency, and agility—and to make sure that IT managers design technology platforms from the very beginning to be resilient and secure.

3. A dramatic upgrade of the skills and capabilities of the cybersecurity team so its managers can understand business risks, collaborate effectively with business partners, navigate a rapidly changing technology environment, influence application and infrastructure environments, and implement active defense tactics.

This implies an ambitious agenda, and companies may be inclined to walk before they run. Unfortunately, attackers will not patiently wait for cautious companies to improve their cybersecurity capabilities in this incremental manner—companies must act in a proactive and determined fashion now.

THE BROADER ECOSYSTEM MUST ENABLE DIGITAL RESILIENCE

While companies must upgrade their own capabilities, technology executives told us that individual institutions could not be left to fend for themselves and that governments, private institutions, and civil society should work together to build a resilient digital ecosystem.

There was a wide range of views about the value and feasibility of the specific actions governments could take, but a set of potential aspirations did emerge. Countries should create national cybersecurity strategies that have clear lines of accountability among public-sector agencies and provide support and assistance to the public and civil sectors. Law enforcement, prosecutorial, and judicial functions should increase their familiarity with and expertise in cybersecurity issues so that they can better combat cyber-crime. Finally, countries should prioritize cybersecurity issues in bilateral exchanges in order to create transparency into motivations, constraints, and objectives for actions in this field.

Equally critically, industry associations and voluntary groups will have to enable companies to share intelligence, disseminate best practices, align on how to address challenging issues, and eventually create shared utilities to provide important cybersecurity functions.

At the same time, financial institutions and insurance companies could support progress by creating markets for pricing the risk of cyber-attacks.

The final two chapters of the book discuss how leaders can advance the cause of digital resilience. Chapter 8 describes how companies can design and launch a cybersecurity program that will sustain progress. Chapter 9 addresses the role played by the broader set of players in the digital ecosystem—including regulators, vendors, and others—in facilitating the path to digital resilience.

• • •

Sustaining the pace of innovation and growth in the global economy in the face of determined cyber-attacks will require dramatic change. Companies must make the transition from managing cybersecurity as a control function to implementing the practices required to protect information assets into their business processes and their entire IT environment. In addition, regulators, technology vendors, and law enforcement must collaborate with companies to create an ecosystem that facilitates digital resilience. Changes of this scale and complexity cannot be achieved without the active engagement and participation of the most senior business leaders and policymakers.

1

Cyber-attacks Jeopardize Companies' Pace of Innovation

All business investments require trade-offs between risk and reward. Does the interest rate on a new bond issue adequately compensate for the risk of default? Are the potential revenues from entering a new emerging market greater than the risk that the investments will be confiscated by a new regime? Does the value of oil extracted via deep-water, offshore drilling outweigh the chance of a catastrophic accident? Tough questions must be answered by weighing up the business imperatives against a calculation of the risk—and the greater the risk, the harder it is to make the case for investment.

Technology investments are no different. They, too, have always been a trade-off between risk and return. However, for enterprise technology, increased global connectivity is raising the stakes on both side of the equation. The commercial rewards from tapping into this connectivity are enormous, but the more tightly we are connected, the more vulnerabilities exist that attackers can exploit and the more damage they can do once inside. Therefore, when a manufacturer invests in a new product life-cycle management system, it is making a bet that the system will not enable the theft of valuable intellectual property. When a retailer invests in mobile commerce, it is betting that cyber-fraud won't critically damage profitability. When a bank invests in customer analytics, it is betting that the sensitive data it analyzes won't be stolen by cyber-criminals. The odds on all those bets appear to be shifting away from the institutions and toward cyber-attackers. They could swing decisively their way in the near future given most companies' siloed and reactive approach to cybersecurity.

Our interviews with business leaders, chief information officers (CIOs), chief technology officers (CTOs), and chief information security officers (CISOs) indicate that concerns about cyber-attacks are already affecting large institutions' interest in and ability to create value from technology investment and innovation. Potential losses, both direct and indirect, reduce the expected economic benefits of technology investments, as do the high cost and lengthy time frame required to build the defense mechanisms that can protect the organization against a growing range of attackers. In short, the models companies use to protect themselves from cyber-attack are limiting their ability to extract additional value from technology.

RISK OF CYBER-ATTACKS REDUCES THE VALUE OF TECHNOLOGY FOR BUSINESS

Concern about cyber-attacks is already having a noticeable impact on business along three dimensions: lower frontline productivity, fewer resources for information technology (IT) initiatives that create value, and—critically—the slower implementation of technological innovations.

Lower Frontline Productivity

Compared to even a few years ago, companies have many more security controls in place that limit how employees can use technology. They prevent users from installing applications on their desktops. They turn off USB ports and block access to consumer cloud services such as Dropbox. They prohibit executives from taking their laptops to certain countries or require that the laptop be reimaged on return. Layers of security controls can even make turning on a desktop or laptop a prolonged and frustrating process at some companies.

Cybersecurity teams may have good reason to implement these measures. Unknown applications can contain malware that antivirus programs can't detect. USB ports can be a source of infection, and both USB ports and consumer web services can be a mechanism for inappropriately copying sensitive data.

Employees, however, can see such measures as draconian. Worse, they can directly affect productivity and morale. The salesperson can't hand a USB stick with a video about a new product to a potential customer. The executive traveling overseas has to spend time copying her contacts onto another disposable phone before the visit and is unable to access Skype from her laptop to speak to her husband back home while away.

Security controls also limit frontline experimentation, which has been the source of so much of the value users derive from IT. In the 1980s, the first bankers who started using Lotus 1-2-3 to construct pro-forma models didn't have approval from corporate IT. Twenty years later, IT had no idea that small groups of executives had started using Blackberries to communicate with one another. Today, such innovations would be an explicit violation of most large companies' information security policies.

As a result of these factors, 9 out of 10 technology executives say cybersecurity controls have at least a moderate impact on end-user productivity; in the high-tech sector, 60 percent say the impact on productivity is a major pain point. A senior technology executive at a large bank said that if the CEO realized how many hours were lost as employees struggled with security controls, "he would hang us all." The CISO for a high-tech firm said he was convinced that the security controls he had to put in place contributed to talented engineers leaving the company.

Unfortunately, in many cases, restrictive security controls do not even solve the initial problem. They can lead users to circumvent corporate IT entirely, ironically increasing the risk dramatically. For example, at one securities firm, many bankers became so frustrated by long boot-up times and other controls that they stopped traveling with their IT-issued laptops. Instead, they just bought cheap laptops with no security controls and used free web-based e-mail services to communicate with each other.

Even government employees find workarounds. In a 2010 survey of U.S. federal officials, just under two thirds said security restrictions prevented them from getting information from some websites or using applications related to their jobs. The solution: using a nonagency device to access the information they need. In fact, more than half said they accessed information from home instead of from the office to get around the security controls.[1]

---

[1] Rashid, Fahmida Y., "Cyber-security Hurts Federal Government Productivity, Survey Says," *eWeek*, September 30, 2010. www.eweek.com/c/a/Security/CyberSecurity-Cutting-Federal-Government-Productivity-Survey-744792.

Less Money for IT Initiatives that Create Value

Direct cybersecurity expenditures are small compared to overall IT budgets and business revenues, but cybersecurity still diverts resources away from IT projects that create value because of the downstream effects it has on other IT functions such as application development and infrastructure.

It is hard to get a handle on how much companies spend protecting themselves from cyber-attacks. Some security-related functions, such as firewall management and identity and access management (I&AM), may be located in security budgets or may be found elsewhere in IT. This, as well as differences in security posture, means that there is a large range in how much companies spend on their cybersecurity function. Most commonly, cybersecurity organizations represent between 2 and 6 percent of an IT function's budget, though we know of some companies that dedicate as much as 8 or 9 percent—typically those with stringent requirements or that are in the middle of large programs to improve their security capabilities (Figure 1.1).

Although cybersecurity is growing more quickly than other areas of enterprise IT, direct cybersecurity expenditures do not appear to be that big an issue for most companies. While some of the largest banks and telecommunications firms can spend several hundred million dollars

FIGURE 1.1 **Cybersecurity's Share of the Overall IT Budget Can Vary Widely—Even within One Sector**

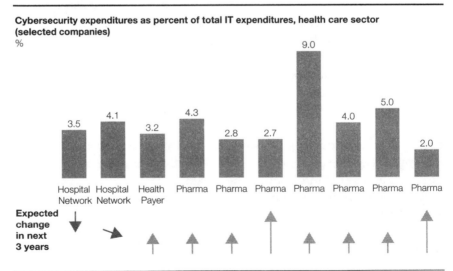

Cybersecurity expenditures as percent of total IT expenditures, health care sector (selected companies)

on cybersecurity, many other large companies spend much smaller amounts. For example, a $25 billion manufacturing company that devotes 2 percent of revenues to IT and 5 percent of that IT spend to cybersecurity would be spending just $25 million—a financial nit. Of the $2.1 trillion in global enterprise IT spend, only about $90 billion falls the into cybersecurity budget, of which three quarters goes to hardware, software, and services, and the other quarter on internal labor (Figure 1.2).

Many technology executives believe that they already spend enough to protect their companies. Slightly more than half of those we interviewed said their company spent about the right amount on cybersecurity, while only about a third said that their company spent significantly too little. Some CISOs told us that they received whatever budget they asked for. For them, the constraint is the lack of available talent rather than money. Cisco estimates that the gap between security roles that need filling globally and the talent available may be as high

FIGURE 1.2 **Cybersecurity Spend Is Less than $100 Billion of Total Business IT Spend of $2 Trillion**

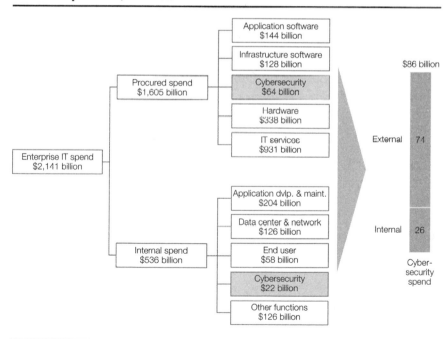

Note: Excludes telecommunications services.
Source: Gartner, Computer Economics, McKinsey & Company

FIGURE 1.3   **Half of Technology Executives Believe They Spend Enough on Cybersecurity**

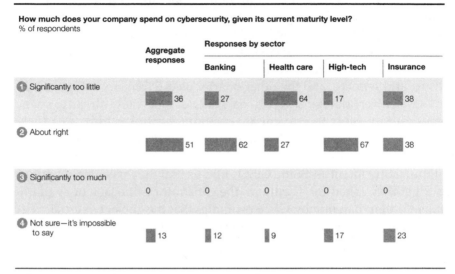

How much does your company spend on cybersecurity, given its current maturity level?
% of respondents

	Aggregate responses	Responses by sector			
		Banking	Health care	High-tech	Insurance
① Significantly too little	36	27	64	17	38
② About right	51	62	27	67	38
③ Significantly too much	0	0	0	0	0
④ Not sure—it's impossible to say	13	12	9	17	23

as 1 million professionals.[2] Almost all CISOs told us they could get approval for more head count but cannot hire quickly enough to fill the slots that they have.

CISOs' perceptions of their budgets did vary significantly by sector. More than 60 percent of financial services and high-tech companies said they had big enough cybersecurity budgets. But less than 40 percent of insurance companies and only about a quarter of health care companies felt the same. Nearly two thirds of health care technology executives say their company's cybersecurity budgets are significantly too small (Figure 1.3).

Cybersecurity's cost increases dramatically when it includes the indirect security activity undertaken outside the security organization itself. Not only do many organizations perform some security-related functions outside IT security, but many actions the security organization takes create unfunded mandates for application development, infrastructure, and the broader business groups. Developers spend months or years rearchitecting applications to meet security standards; network teams spend tens of millions of dollars reconfiguring networks to make them more secure; system administrators devote countless hours to applying security patches across tens of thousands

[2] *Cisco 2014 Annual Security Report*, January 2014.

of servers; and after years of infrastructure optimization, many IT departments can provision a server in hours or days, but then spend three or four weeks doing the security-related configuration, with all the cost that implies.

We asked CIOs, CTOs, and CISOs to estimate how much of the nonsecurity IT budget is actually spent on security. Quite frankly, many had no clue but were sure it was large. Many of those that offered a figure said it could be 25 to 30 percent of the budget, which would imply that the combination of direct and indirect security activity is consuming a third of IT budgets.

In a world where business aspirations for technology innovation bump up against constrained IT budgets, where business leaders complain bitterly about the cost of developing and running applications, and where there are pitched battles about which projects IT can afford to do each year, this means security requirements are diverting significant resources away from IT that creates value.

Slower Adoption of New Technologies

CIOs and CTOs have a crowded innovation agenda. Senior executives, customers, and ultimately shareholders expect them to roll out new capabilities in areas including cloud computing, big data, e-commerce, the Internet of Things, mobile commerce, and enterprise mobility.

Almost everyone told us that security is often the bottleneck in implementing new technologies. It takes real work to assess vulnerabilities in new vendor offerings and to figure out how to engineer a secure solution. For example, the security team has to assess new types of mobile devices to determine what data they store locally and how strong the authentication mechanisms are that prevent unauthorized access. It has to assess new external web-facing functionality to see whether it creates an entry point into customer-facing systems that attackers can exploit. It also has to analyze how an attacker would penetrate a new capability, identify potential vulnerabilities, and engineer controls that are acceptable in terms of cost and convenience.

All these tasks take time, especially for relatively new technologies that have not been extensively pressure tested in the real world, and can significantly delay the introduction of new capabilities. The CISO of a medical devices company explained that it took a year to work out how to integrate the network-connected devices into an operating room environment in a secure way.

For many technologies, the lag time is relatively small—at least so far. IT executives told us that security requirements added less than three months to the implementation of big data analytics, mobile servicing, online servicing, and online payments. Many explained, though, that the business imperatives were such that there was no alternative to rolling out new technologies, even if the security issues were still unclear.

The impact of incorporating security measures is felt most keenly in cloud computing and mobile (Figure 1.4). On average, enterprise mobility capabilities were delayed by more than six months and public cloud capabilities far longer, with many companies saying they wouldn't put sensitive data in the public cloud in the foreseeable future because of security concerns.

Delays in enterprise mobility are driven largely by what many CISOs perceive as a rickety enterprise mobile security model. A financial services CISO told us, "We've started to experiment with mobile devices; however, the delay has been because of the number of potential threats they create." The CISO of a hospital network faces similar challenges. "We've got thousands of physicians who all want access," he said, "but who also want to do their own thing. We have had to make sure everything is going between them securely, so naturally a few of the systems have been delayed."

The result is that most organizations have focused on a relatively narrow set of mobile capabilities such as e-mail and calendar synchronization, that give users only a small fraction of the capabilities they would have on a laptop.

Delays in the use of the public cloud are driven by multiple factors. While some executives highlighted reasons unrelated to security (e.g., compliance considerations or "not invented here" syndrome), a few explicit security considerations came up frequently in interviews, specifically, a perceived lack of transparency into many providers' security models, a sense that multitenant public cloud architectures lack the defense in depth that a well-designed local environment provides, and uncertainty about how contract terms and conditions can be crafted to address cybersecurity concerns.

As a result, 60 percent of executives surveyed said that security concerns were delaying their institution's use of cloud environments by a year or more. As we'll see in the next chapter, such delays, when spread across the global economy, could have major economic implications.

FIGURE 1.4 **Companies Are Most Concerned about Security Implications of Mobile and Cloud Computing**

How many months delay do you think that concern over cyber-attacks will create for the following innovations for your institution? (participants were asked to select at least three innovations)
Delay in months

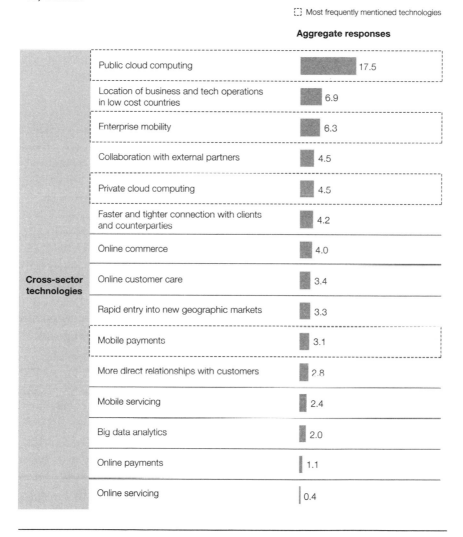

Most frequently mentioned technologies

Aggregate responses

Public cloud computing	17.5
Location of business and tech operations in low cost countries	6.9
Enterprise mobility	6.3
Collaboration with external partners	4.5
Private cloud computing	4.5
Faster and tighter connection with clients and counterparties	4.2
Online commerce	4.0
Cross-sector technologies Online customer care	3.4
Rapid entry into new geographic markets	3.3
Mobile payments	3.1
More direct relationships with customers	2.8
Mobile servicing	2.4
Big data analytics	2.0
Online payments	1.1
Online servicing	0.4

Many CIOs also worry that concerns about cyber-attacks could slow down adoption of the "Internet of Things"—the connection of devices from refrigerators and thermostats to automobiles and heavy machinery to the Internet. It's easy to understand the trepidation in connecting cars to the Internet if attackers could exploit those connections to wreak havoc or even just monitor movement. Cybersecurity researchers in Israel have already proven they can take over a car remotely.[3]

Regulatory scrutiny can add further delay to the rollout of technology innovations. One bank underwent 98 regulatory audits in 2013. When a company has to explain how a new technology can be secured to dozens of different regulators, each with a different agenda and questions, the pace of innovation can slow dramatically.

THE RISKS ARE HIGH FOR EVERYONE, EVERYWHERE

Digitization may be a buzzword in technology circles, but it also represents a real and important dynamic: the pervasive migration of economic value online. Institutions are automating business processes, establishing networked connections with customers and suppliers, and manipulating valuable intellectual property in digital formats. Already today, manufacturers can bid on online platforms for basic materials in fully automated real-time enterprise-scale online auctions. Hospitals increasingly store patients' medical records online so that they can be shared easily, ensuring better collaboration, more comprehensive storage of results, and even enabling remote treatments. Much securities trading never touches a human hand; it is driven entirely by algorithms and happens in milliseconds (or even microseconds in some cases).

Take an example as prosaic as car insurance; every step in the process has become dependent on technology, and often on networks talking to each other (Figure 1.5).

- The customer browses the web for different providers, reading reviews and ratings left by other customers. She may also go to a third-party aggregator site to get the best deal.
- To get a quote, she fills in some basic information online, which carriers can match against a variety of public and proprietary databases to gauge the risk (e.g., public crime statistics for the postcode, and the insurer's own database on the reliability of a particular model of car).

[3] Bigelow, Pete, "Israeli Cyber-security Researchers Remotely Hack a Car," *autoblog*, November 8, 2014. www.autoblog.com/2014/11/08/car-remotedly-hacked-israel-cyber-security.

FIGURE 1.5 **External Connectivity Is Integral to Most Businesses—Auto Insurance Example**

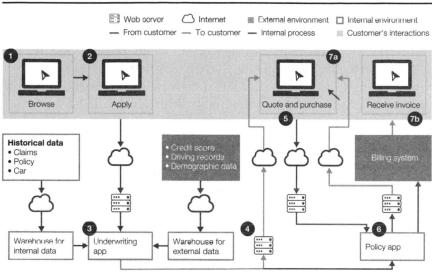

- Next, she fills out a full application—again all done online via secure e-mail and, for the most sophisticated, using a digital signature—and pays via a secure website. The policy and all the details are e-mailed to her.
- When she has to make a claim after a minor accident, the insurer may already be fully aware of what's happened thanks to the car's telematics that are constantly reporting back information to the manufacturer and that are then passed on to the insurer. The company may even have already automatically alerted its preferred body shop to book the car in for repairs.

The value yielded for both insurer and customer is immense, in the form of cost reductions, new customer offerings, more intimate customer relationships, and better customer service. What's true for car insurance is true for almost every industry imaginable.

Companies Must Contend with a Wide Range of Risks and Threats

As digitization continues to increase, companies face a broad range of business risks associated with cyber-attacks.

Fraud   As ever more financial transactions occur online, the opportunity for cyber-fraud is exploding. Cyber-criminals can open up dummy credit accounts to purchase goods and services fraudulently. Or they can take control of legitimate accounts in order to empty them of funds. Any assessment of cyber-crime's impact is necessarily imprecise, but to take one estimate, McAfee's recent report with the Center for Strategic and International Studies calculated cyber-crime to be worth 0.8 percent of world gross domestic product (GDP).[4]

Loss of Customer Information   Customer data such as social security numbers, financial records, and medical records can be used by hackers to commit cyber-fraud or sold on the black market to others with the same aim. The information contained in electronic health records, for example, can be used to bill insurance carriers for care that was never provided. Prescription data can be used to fulfill prescriptions from multiple pharmacies so that the surplus medicines can be resold. In fact, health records often contain enough information to open a new credit card or other financial accounts, leading to more direct theft. Criminals can also sell celebrities' medication information to unscrupulous media outlets or, potentially, use embarrassing medical information to blackmail patients. As a result, the street cost for a stolen medical record can be as high as $500, compared to around $25 for a stolen U.S. identity consisting of a social security number and date of birth, or just a dollar or two for a "stale" credit card number, that is, one that may be out of date.[5]

A large breach of customer data represents customer inconvenience, loss of customer trust, and significant remediation costs. In May 2014, eBay revealed that attackers compromised the user names, passwords, phone numbers, and physical addresses of 233 million accounts, forcing the company to request that all users change their passwords.[6] Since then, polling in the United Kingdom has indicated that nearly half of customers there would be less likely to use eBay in

---

[4] Center for Strategic and International Studies & McAfee, *Net Losses: Estimating the Global Cost of Cybercrime*, June 2014. www.mcafee.com/us/resources/reports/rp-economic-impact-cybercrime2.pdf.

[5] RSA, "Cybercrime and the Healthcare Industry." White paper, September 16, 2013. www.emc.com/auth/collateral/white-papers/h12105-cybercrime-healthcare-industry-rsa-wp.pdf.

[6] McGregor, Jay, "The Top 5 Most Brutal Cyber Attacks of 2014 So Far," *Forbes*, July 28, 2014. www.forbes.com/sites/jaymcgregor/2014/07/28/the-top-5-most-brutal-cyber-attacks-of-2014-so-far.

the future as a result of the attack.[7] In an earnings call later in 2014, eBay CEO John Donahoe said that because the attack had affected commerce volumes, the company had lowered 2014 sales targets by $200 million.[8] In addition to the impact on customers, remediating a breach can be expensive. The Ponemon Institute estimated that the average breach costs $3.5 million,[9] but bills for the largest can easily run into hundreds of millions of dollars. U.S. retailer Target told investors that the costs relating to its 2013 breach of 70 million customer records could include reimbursing fraud, card reissuance, civil litigation, governmental investigation, legal fees, and investigative fees, in addition to the incremental operating and capital expenditures required for remediation.[10]

Loss of Intellectual Property   Much of the value of modern corporations rests in intellectual property (IP) rather than in tangible assets such as machines or buildings. Product designs, manufacturing processes, marketing plans, even film scripts—IP is a tempting target, and with so much of it now kept in digital formats, it is ripe for cyber-attack. The Report of the Commission on the Theft of American Intellectual Property estimates that cyber-enabled IP theft costs the U.S. economy $300 billion annually.[11]

Disadvantaged Negotiation   Executives typically communicate online via e-mail or instant message, even when discussing sensitive negotiations. This might be about a possible merger or joint venture, a new sourcing deal, extraction rights—almost nothing is deemed out of

---

[7] Clearswift, "eBay Cyber Attack Fallout—Consumer Response: Half of UK Adults Have Lost Trust in eBay since Cyber Attack." Press release, May 23, 2014. www.clearswift.com/about-us/pr/press-releases/ebay-cyber-attack-fallout-consumer-response.

[8] Mac, Ryan, "eBay CEO: Sales, Earnings Affected by Cyberattack Body Blow in Challenging Second Quarter," *Forbes*, July 16, 2014. www.forbes.com/sites/ryanmac/2014/07/16/ebay-ceo-sales-earnings-affected-by-cyberattack-body-blow-in-challenging-second-quarter.

[9] Ponemon, "Ponemon Institute Releases 2014 Cost of Data Breach: Global Analysis." Press release, May 5, 2014. www.ponemon.org/blog/ponemon-institute-releases-2014-cost-of-data-breach-global-analysis.

[10] Target, "Target Provides Update on Data Breach and Financial Performance." Press release, January 10, 2014. http://pressroom.target.com/news/target-provides-update-on-data-breach-and-financial-performance.

[11] National Bureau of Asian Research, "The IP Commission Report," Report of the Commission on the Theft of American Intellectual Property, May 2013. www.ipcommission.org/report/IP_Commission_Report_052213.pdf.

scope for e-mail. Yet information about how a company is approaching a deal, for example, the maximum amount it is willing to pay, can be damaging in the wrong hands. A petroleum exploration company calculated that the impact of losing the data on what it was willing to pay a particular government for extraction rights could run into billions of dollars and was therefore one of its most important enterprise risks. Senior managers talked in the boardroom of the "billion-dollar e-mail" with no sense of hyperbole.

Disclosure of Sensitive Management Discussions   Every management team has to have confidential discussions. Naturally, information about how management thinks about future product plans could be extremely harmful if accessed by the wrong competitor. In addition, in the process of formulating and executing strategy, managers often share frank opinions about their customers, their own products, their regulators, and their employees that could harm any number of relationships if they were publicly disclosed. As an example, the U.S. State Department believes that unvarnished opinions about foreign leaders included in the documents Bradley (now Chelsea) Manning downloaded to a USB drive and released via WikiLeaks have jeopardized ties to allies.[12]

Business Disruption   In late 2012 and early 2013, the al-Qassam Cyber Fighters launched a series of distributed denial of service (DDoS) attacks designed to overwhelm U.S. banks' Internet banking presences, rendering them unavailable to customers. In the end, even though disruption was relatively limited, the attacks succeeded in doubling downtime for online banking applications in early 2013.[13]

DDoS attacks are annoying and inconvenient but CISOs tend to worry more about the sort of destructive attacks that go beyond delays and outages and that compromise financial transactions, interfere with electronic medical devices or shut down manufacturing operations. An attack on Saudi Aramco that deleted data from many hard drives significantly hurt business operations for more than two

---

[12] Serrano, Richard S., "Manning's Leaks Jeopardized U.S. Ties to Allies, Diplomat Testifies," *Los Angeles Times*, August 1, 2013. http://articles.latimes.com/2013/aug/01/nation/la-na-manning-trial-20130802.

[13] Schwartz, Mathew J., "Banks Hit Downtime Milestone in DDoS Attacks," *Information Week*, Dark Reading, April 4, 2013. www.darkreading.com/attacks-and-breaches/banks-hit-downtime-milestone-in-ddos-attacks/d/d-id/1109390.

weeks.[14] Aramco said that "the main target in this attack was to stop the flow of oil and gas to local and international markets."[15]

Legal and Regulatory Exposure   In many sectors, losing sensitive customer data has serious legal implications. In health care in the United States, for example, the Health Insurance Portability and Accountability Act (HIPAA) mandates fines of $100 to $50,000 per record up to a total of $1.5 million for a single event. Class action lawsuits have the potential to be even more damaging. The California Attorney General's office has valued lost medical data at $2,000 per record. Sutter Health, a not-for-profit northern California health system with revenues of $10 billion, had one desktop computer stolen via the nontechnical method of throwing a rock through a window. The company had begun rolling out an encryption program but had yet to get to desktop devices. Clinical data for almost 1 million patients and basic data for more than 3 million patients was compromised. The ensuing lawsuit ran to $4.25 billion. Thankfully for Sutter, the case was eventually dismissed three years later because the plaintiffs couldn't demonstrate that criminals had been able to make use of the data, but the suit still consumed management attention for all that time.[16]

These risks stem from a set of attackers whose capabilities have improved dramatically over the past several years.

- Organized crime groups have sought to make a business from cyber-attacks, not only conducting online fraud, but also stealing customers' personal information, which they can integrate into their own data warehouses and use for identity theft.
- There has been much debate and discussion about cyber-warfare, but state-sponsored actors have focused overwhelmingly on espionage either to inform national strategy or to obtain valuable IP that can be passed on to favored domestic companies.
- Hacktivists such as Anonymous and Lulzsec seek to disrupt and embarrass government agencies and companies whose policies and practices they oppose.

[14] Bronk, Christopher, and Eneken Tikk-Ringas, "The Cyber Attack on Saudi Aramco," *Survival: Global Politics and Strategy*, 55(2), April–May 2013, pp. 81–96.
[15] "Aramco Says Cyberattack Was Aimed at Production," *New York Times*, December 9, 2012. www.nytimes.com/2012/12/10/business/global/saudi-aramco-says-hackers-took-aim-at-its-production.html.
[16] Kolbasuk McGee, Marianne, "Sutter Health Breach Suit Dismissed," *Data Breach Today*, July 22, 2014. www.databreachtoday.com/sutter-health-breach-suit-dismissed-a-7095.

In addition, insiders are an increasingly important threat. Technology executives emphasized that the easiest way to get access to sensitive data is to badge into the building in the morning and log in to secure systems using valid credentials. Employees or contractors can be motivated by simple greed or by resentment at having been passed over for a promotion. They may be compromised by an outsider—one criminal organization used threats against a developer's family to coerce him into inserting code that authorized illicit payments into an application. Employees may also convince themselves that they are not even committing a crime, for example, when they download customer lists before leaving to work for a competitor. Perhaps most importantly, employees and contractors have context—they know where to find the most sensitive information and often will have the business insight required to use it effectively.

The Risks Are Strategic

Faced with so many potentially damaging outcomes, technology executives across sectors and regions are highly concerned about the risk of cyber-attacks. Roughly two thirds described it as a significant issue that could have major strategic implications over the next few years. Typically, they explained their perspective in terms of the risks laid out earlier: lost intellectual property, lost customer data, or disruptions to business operations. A relatively small percentage, about 10 percent, described the risk of cyber-attack as existential and believed it could "turn out their lights sometime in the next five years."

Turning out the lights would mean either a devastatingly destructive attack or, more likely, an irreparable breakdown of customer trust. The CISO for one social media company said, "If we lose customer trust, then the product itself goes away." The CISO for a large financial institution said that he was worried about attacks that would compromise transaction data so comprehensively that it would be impossible to unwind.

About a quarter of the people we interviewed believed cyber-attacks are a normal risk of doing business. These executives placed cyber-attacks in the context of other risks facing their institutions, such as liquidity crises for banks or physical disasters for manufacturing companies.

Interestingly, not one person we interviewed agreed with the statement, "The risks of cyber-attacks are overblown. Our institution

FIGURE 1.6 **Cyber-attacks Pose a Greater Risk than Other Technology Risks**

What type of technology risks are most likely to have a strategic and negative impact on your business?
% of respondents who rated response in their top two concerns

☐ Most frequently cited risk

	Aggregate responses	Responses by sector			
		Banking	Health care	High-tech	Insurance
Malicious attack, instigated by someone *outside* your institution	76	69	75	70	75
Malicious attack, instigated by someone *inside* your institution	59	54	75	50	50
Disaster (e.g., fire, flood, earthquake)	22	19	18	10	25
Poorly designed application code	28	28	18	40	33
Inadequate quality in technology operations	33	32	17	50	42

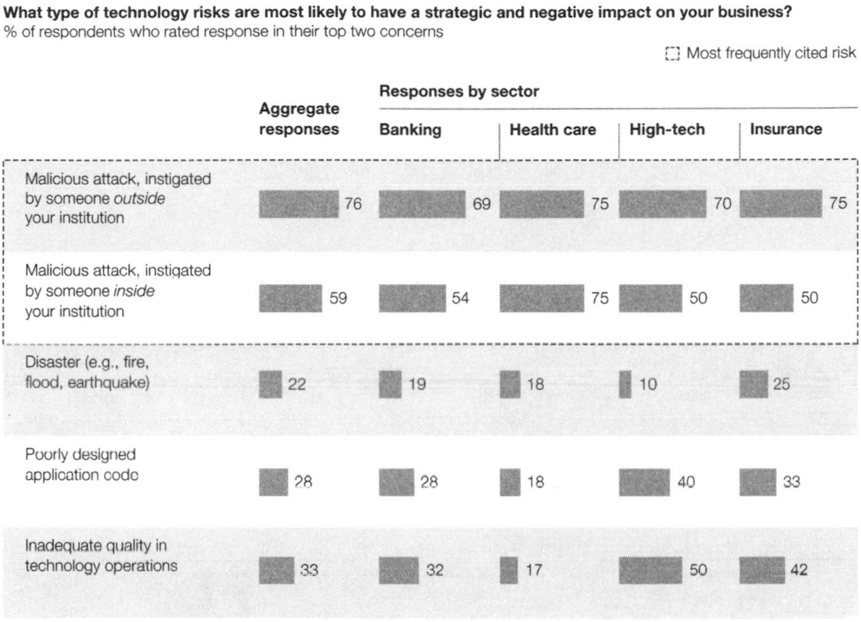

has the issue well in hand." In fact, cyber-attacks were a much greater concern than other types of technology risk. Nearly three quarters of respondents said that external cyber-attacks were one of their top two technology risks. Nearly 60 percent said the same about insider threats. Other technology risks were rated in the top two less than a third of the time. These included disaster, poorly designed application code (which cost Knight Capital $440 million[17]), and inadequate quality in technology operations such as mistakes in server configuration that crash important applications (Figure 1.6).

Although the level of concern varied barely at all across sectors, the types of risks each sector worries about are quite different (Figure 1.7). Broadly speaking, services companies prioritize theft of customer data and interference with business operations, while product companies prioritize industrial espionage. For example, barely any financial institutions cited industrial espionage as a prime concern. Investment

[17] Popper, Nathaniel, "Knight Capital Says Trading Glitch Cost It $440 Million," *New York Times*, August 2, 2012. http://dealbook.nytimes.com/2012/08/02/knight-capital-says-trading-mishap-cost-it-440-million.

FIGURE 1.7   **All Companies Are Worried about Customer Data Theft, but Their Next Priority Varies by Sector**

Which business impact from malicious cyber-attacks are you most concerned about?
% who rated response as 1st or 2nd biggest concern

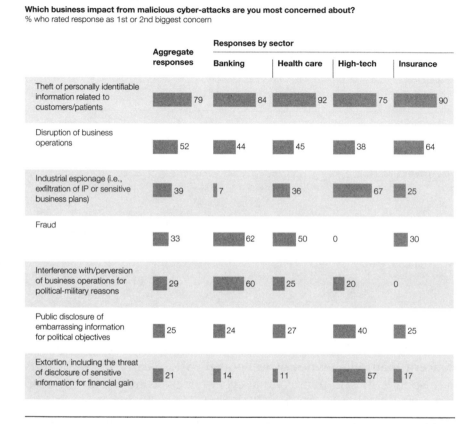

	Aggregate responses	Responses by sector			
		Banking	Health care	High-tech	Insurance
Theft of personally identifiable information related to customers/patients	79	84	92	75	90
Disruption of business operations	52	44	45	38	64
Industrial espionage (i.e., exfiltration of IP or sensitive business plans)	39	7	36	67	25
Fraud	33	62	50	0	30
Interference with/perversion of business operations for political-military reasons	29	60	25	20	0
Public disclosure of embarrassing information for political objectives	25	24	27	40	25
Extortion, including the threat of disclosure of sensitive information for financial gain	21	14	11	57	17

banking CISOs told us that although IP was incredibly important to their business, its structure and format limited the impact of any given breach: trading algorithms were immensely valuable, but the IP was distributed across many algorithms on many product desks (e.g., currencies, interest rate swaps) so the loss of any one algorithm would have only so much financial impact. In addition, many of the algorithms changed rapidly, so any IP stolen would have far less value in just a matter of months. Some retail banking CISOs placed an even lower value on their company's IP; one said, "Checking products aren't all that different from each other and don't change that quickly."

Instead, banks worry about fraud and any breaches that might compromise either corporate or consumer customer data—they considered this to be a core part of their institutions' value proposition. Many also expressed a high degree of concern about politically motivated attacks on the integrity of financial transactions.

High-tech companies, by contrast, are sharply focused on IP loss, especially process-related IP. Detailed insights into a product become widely available the moment it hits the market and competitors apply tear-down techniques to it, but the detailed manufacturing specifications (e.g., what temperature to bake a component at) can stay secret for years.

DEFENDERS ARE FALLING BEHIND ATTACKERS

Technology executives believe almost universally that it is the attackers, irrespective of type, who will not only maintain their lead over the institutions they target but actually increase that lead over the next few years (Figure 1.8). More than three quarters said that the sophistication or pace of attacks would grow faster than their own defensive capabilities, and nearly a fifth believe that the attackers' advantage would increase significantly faster. The stark consensus: the defenders believe they are losing ground.

FIGURE 1.8   **Executives Believe Attackers Will Increase Their Lead**

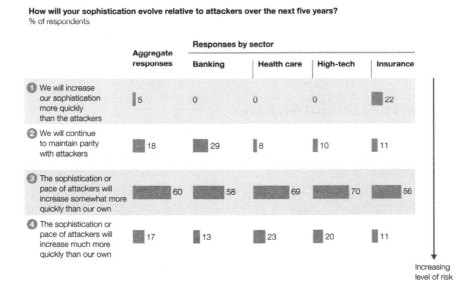

How will your sophistication evolve relative to attackers over the next five years?
% of respondents

	Aggregate responses	Responses by sector			
		Banking	Health care	High-tech	Insurance
① We will increase our sophistication more quickly than the attackers	5	0	0	0	22
② We will continue to maintain parity with attackers	18	29	8	10	11
③ The sophistication or pace of attackers will increase somewhat more quickly than our own	60	58	69	70	56
④ The sophistication or pace of attackers will increase much more quickly than our own	17	13	23	20	11

Increasing level of risk

Insurers were the most confident in their own ability. Slightly more than a fifth of insurance interviewees believed that they would advance more quickly than attackers (although that is, of course, still a minority), while nobody at all outside of insurance had this view about his or her company. This may be partly because cybersecurity is still relatively nascent in insurance—when you're far behind, those first few steps can feel like significant progress.

Interviewees had a range of explanations for their concerns about falling behind attackers.

Technology Changes Favor Attackers

Almost everyone accessing corporate systems used to do so from a desktop computer owned by the corporation and physically located within a company office. Information security professionals focused on defending the perimeter and keeping attackers off the corporate network. Today's world is very different. There are endless ways into networks, vastly expanding each institution's exposure. Customers can access sophisticated applications via the Internet; business partners can connect directly to the corporate network, which enables tighter collaboration but adds to the external interfaces; and users expect to access everything no matter where in the world they happen to be. The idea of an invulnerable "perimeter" is as old-fashioned as a moat. Companies are also littered with older IT systems that may rely on outdated and vulnerable technology and that are retired very slowly. Attackers therefore have a growing array of opportunities to exploit.

Attacker's Jurisdictional Advantage

In the physical world, if a criminal keeps committing crimes, the odds are that he will eventually get caught. All it takes is one slip-up, one caper that puts him in the wrong place at the wrong time. For a cyber-criminal operating from a country not focused on prosecuting cyber-crimes, the story is very different. Rather than increasing his risk, each incremental attack sharpens his capabilities and makes him smarter about the company he's attacking. "The attacker has to be right only once to do a lot of damage but can get away with being wrong time after time," said a CISO. "We have to be right every single time."

The Resources Available to State-Sponsored Attackers

Several CISOs told us that although they have a fighting chance in defending themselves against criminals and hacktivists, they cannot compete with the resources that a nation-state can bring to bear in cyber-espionage. Not only are some states technologically advanced, but they can also afford to devote dozens or even hundreds of people to probing just one company's technology environment for vulnerabilities.

State-Level Capabilities Being More Widely Disseminated

Sophisticated attack strategies developed by states don't necessarily stay exclusively in their hands. Cyber-warfare unit leaders may pass on attack strategies to groups they believe might be politically useful. More junior members meanwhile may seek to augment their salaries by freelancing the skills they've developed. Kristin Lord of the Center for a New American Security said, "We've already seen indications of states using criminal groups as proxies for attacks. We also know that countries like North Korea are aggressively trying to develop their cyber capabilities. The open black market, which already exists in the criminal world, is therefore a big concern. It provides a place for states and criminals to find each other."[18]

The Global Market for Cyber-attacks

Just as the Internet has created a global market for collectable trinkets, it has also begun to excel at connecting buyers and sellers of the tools required to launch sophisticated cyber-attacks—not just the states and criminals Kristin Lord referred to, but a range of players. The Rand Institute reported that researchers who discovered a new "zero-day" vulnerability in a popular piece of software[19] could earn, in some cases, millions of dollars by selling this knowledge to cyber-criminals.[20]

---

[18] Walsh, Eddie, "The Cyber Proliferation Threat," *The Diplomat*, October 6, 2011. http://thediplomat.com/2011/10/the-cyber-proliferation-threat.

[19] A zero-day exploit describes a previously unknown vulnerability that an adversary has discovered for which there is no current threat signature, patch, or countermeasure. All organizations are vulnerable to these. Once an attacker's use of a zero-day exploit is discovered, it can takes weeks or months for a software patch to be developed and deployed to close the vulnerability.

[20] Ablon, Lillian, Martin C. Libicki, and Andrea A. Golay, "Markets for Cybercrime Tools and Stolen Data: Hackers' Bazaar," Rand Corporation, 2014.

Institutions Lack the Insights to Make Intelligent Cybersecurity Decisions

Risk management is at the core of cybersecurity. CISOs seek to put in place a set of controls (e.g., encryption, authentication) that deliver the greatest reduction in the likelihood or impact of important risks (e.g., loss of IP, theft of customer data) at the lowest cost and with the least business disruption. Unfortunately, the overwhelming majority of large institutions simply don't have the required risk management capabilities to make intelligent decisions about cybersecurity investments and policies. They don't understand the assets they need to protect, the attackers they face, the full set of defense mechanisms they could implement, or the implications of each of these mechanisms. As a result, they see too little reduction in risk, coming at too high a cost in terms of both business impact and expenditure.

To get a better understanding of where organizations stand in their cybersecurity capabilities, we asked more than 60 Global 500 institutions to complete our Cyber-Risk Maturity Survey (CRMS). The survey measures an organization's risk management practices across eight domains—specifically, how well it understands:

- Its attackers.
- The assets it needs to protect.
- The vulnerabilities in its environment.
- Its residual risk and risk appetite.
- The range of potential controls it could put in place.
- How effective it is in assessing the cost and impact of controls it might put in place.
- How thoroughly it can implement the decisions it makes.
- The quality of cybersecurity governance and organization.

The CRMS was developed together with CISOs from leading institutions and minimizes subjectivity. Rather than asking companies to rate themselves on how well they fare in a particular area or measuring specific technologies, architectures, or controls, it asks instead whether and how frequently the company performs 28 specific activities and then grades it on a numerical scale to allow for comparisons (Figure 1.9).

FIGURE 1.9 **Cyber Risk Maturity Survey: Fact-Based Questions Lead to Maturity Rating**

Example: Practice C5: Identify vulnerabilities from simulations

C5a How do you run realistic simulations of cybersecurity events? (select all that apply)

☐ We run realistic simulations based on potential scenarios the organization is likely to face

☐ We involve business unit leadership and our executive team (e.g., CEO) in the simulations

☐ Our simulations are focused on the most important assets identified in the at-risk list

☐ Our simulations are focused on potential attacks preferred by our biggest attacker threats

☐ We debrief post simulation to consolidate feedback and potential vulnerabilities identified

☐ We run simulations on replica versions of our current systems

C5a How often do you run realistic simulations of cybersecurity events? (select all that apply)

Never	Less than annually	At least annually	At least quarterly	At least monthly

Level ➊ (Nascent)
- We informally run simulations related to potential attacks

Level ➋ (Developing)
- We sometimes run simulations related to prioritized at-risk business processes and information types using a defined process
- We try to run the simulations at least annually

Level ➌ (Mature)
- We run realistic cross-functional management simulations addressing potential attacks the business is likely to face at least quarterly using a defined process
- We debrief after the simulations to provide feedback and document results

Level ➍ (Robust)
- As 3 (mature) and we have involve the senior leadership team in the simulations that occur on a monthly basis

There are four levels of cyber-risk management maturity:

1. *Nascent.* These are the companies that are doing their best but lack any rigid protocols or centralized security systems in place beyond the bare minimum. They have no defined single point of accountability or a clearly defined escalation path to top management.

2. *Developing.* Companies have a qualitative framework for evaluating and mitigating cyber-risks. The governance model is consistent across the company, with a single point of accountability in each business unit and a defined reporting line to top management.

3. *Mature.* There's a quantitative approach for evaluating and a qualitative approach for mitigating cyber-risks. The cybersecurity

governance model is well defined, with a single point of accountability within a business unit that owns the risks and decision making.

4. *Robust.* A robust quantitative approach for evaluating and mitigating cyber-risks is in place, and clearly identified individuals are accountable for the cybersecurity of each asset.

Companies Have a Long Way to Go to Reach Maturity   The survey results were sobering. More than 9 out of 10 organizations have only nascent or developing maturity, and not one could be described as robust overall (Figure 1.10).

Only one respondent was mature or better in every practice area, and more than two thirds were only "nascent" or "developing" in at least half the areas. Looking at the scores in aggregate, only one area—knowing your systems and people—had an aggregate score of more than 3, indicating it was "robust" in more than half of the companies. Most practices were toward the low end of "developing," with practices around knowing your vulnerabilities being particularly weak (Figure 1.11).

FIGURE 1.10 **Cybersecurity Risk Management Maturity Is Low**

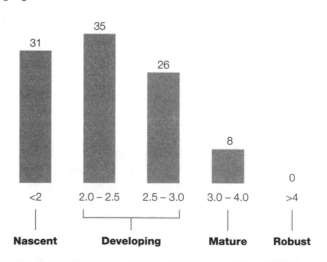

Distribution of overall maturity scores
% of participating organizations

FIGURE 1.11 **Only One Practice Rates as "Mature" on Average across All Companies**

Absolute scores at subpractice level across all companies

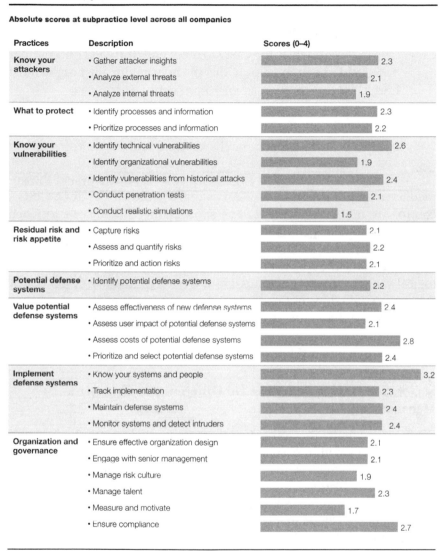

Practices	Description	Scores (0–4)
Know your attackers	• Gather attacker insights	2.3
	• Analyze external threats	2.1
	• Analyze internal threats	1.9
What to protect	• Identify processes and information	2.3
	• Prioritize processes and information	2.2
Know your vulnerabilities	• Identify technical vulnerabilities	2.6
	• Identify organizational vulnerabilities	1.9
	• Identify vulnerabilities from historical attacks	2.4
	• Conduct penetration tests	2.1
	• Conduct realistic simulations	1.5
Residual risk and risk appetite	• Capture risks	2.1
	• Assess and quantify risks	2.2
	• Prioritize and action risks	2.1
Potential defense systems	• Identify potential defense systems	2.2
Value potential defense systems	• Assess effectiveness of new defense systems	2.4
	• Assess user impact of potential defense systems	2.1
	• Assess costs of potential defense systems	2.8
	• Prioritize and select potential defense systems	2.4
Implement defense systems	• Know your systems and people	3.2
	• Track implementation	2.3
	• Maintain defense systems	2.4
	• Monitor systems and detect intruders	2.4
Organization and governance	• Ensure effective organization design	2.1
	• Engage with senior management	2.1
	• Manage risk culture	1.9
	• Manage talent	2.3
	• Measure and motivate	1.7
	• Ensure compliance	2.7

What does this relatively low maturity mean in practice?

- Only one institution in six gives the CISO the authority to stop IT projects that explicitly violate cybersecurity policies or to conduct cybersecurity simulations more than once a year.

- Only one in five ensures that the board has reviewed and approved the cybersecurity strategy in detail or includes the cybersecurity organization's impact on broader IT costs in annual performance evaluations.
- One in three enables the CISO to meet with the CEO on a regular basis, and one in three provides the board with a list of the most important information assets to protect.
- Only about half of institutions even define minimum standards for data protection for sensitive information or update intelligence about attackers more than once a year.

Maturity is weakest where specific practices reach beyond the immediate realm of cybersecurity. Areas that are directly under a CISO's control are more advanced, but as soon as the CISO needs to reach out—even to other people in the broader IT group, let alone the business units themselves—there is a drop-off in maturity level. For example, some of the most advanced areas are the understanding of technological vulnerabilities and assessing the costs of defense systems. For these, the CISO does not need significant cooperation from the rest of the enterprise. By contrast, understanding assets requires significant engagement from business-line executives, and maturity for this practice was much lower (Figure 1.12).

Sector, Size, and Spend Make No Difference to Cyber-risk Management Maturity

Banks scored better than other CRMS participants, but only slightly, and the differences within each sector were far greater than those between sectors. Banks were relatively strong in understanding their attackers (given their investments in intelligence capabilities in that sector), understanding their vulnerabilities, and in governance. By contrast, they were little better than average in understanding potential defense systems and their impact. Insurers were relatively weak across the board, and especially so in understanding the assets they need to protect and the vulnerabilities in their existing environment. However, the more mature insurance companies far outperformed the weaker banks.

Nor were large companies necessarily more mature than smaller ones; in fact, some companies with less than $10 billion in revenues achieved some of the highest maturity ratings. This could be because transparency and coordination are easier to achieve in smaller, simpler organizations.

FIGURE 1.12   **Higher Maturity in Practices that Require Less Collaboration beyond Cybersecurity**

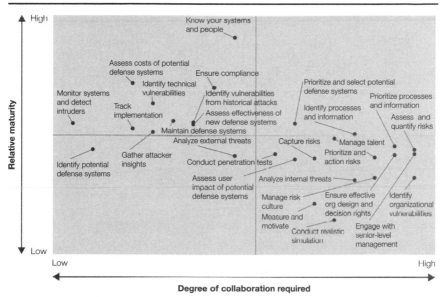

Perhaps most surprisingly, more cybersecurity spending does not lead to greater cyber-risk management maturity. Cybersecurity spend as a percentage of overall IT expenditures is an imperfect metric, but it does give some sense of the resources committed to cybersecurity in relation to the scale of what needs protecting. Plotting a company's risk management maturity against security spend as a percentage of overall IT spend yielded results all over the map, with companies in each of the four quadrants (Figure 1.13).

The unprotected have the lowest level of capability. They have small security teams, invest relatively little in cybersecurity technology, and lack the insights to target their limited expenditures wisely. Senior managers at one financial institution believed that they would not be targeted because they did not operate in the United States. This resulted in a history of underinvestment and an exclusive focus on a very narrow and incomplete set of potential risks.

Institutions *punching above their weight* spend relatively little but are able to get more from their investments than their peers, usually because they have developed a clear idea of what assets are most worth protecting, and therefore are efficient in how they use their

FIGURE 1.13   **Spending Big Doesn't Lead to Risk Management Maturity**

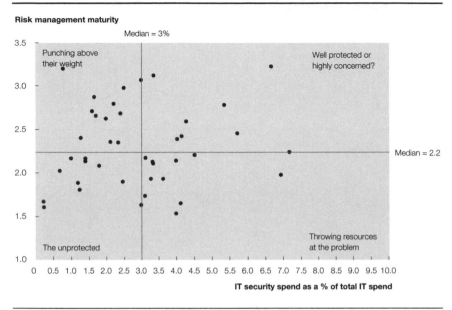

Risk management maturity

limited budget. At one pharmaceutical company, tight budgetary constraints driven by a weakening product pipeline and concern about IP theft forced IT to develop a set of mechanisms to understand risks and focus investments on protecting the company's most important assets.

Highly concerned institutions typically have relatively high levels of both risk management maturity and spend. One sophisticated manufacturing company decided it had no choice but to devote significant resources to cybersecurity and to make smart decisions given the sophistication of its attackers and the expectations of its military and intelligence customers. It put tremendous focus on this issue, starting with very senior executives, and invested the time and effort to develop strong capabilities in understanding its attackers, assessing its own vulnerabilities, and putting in processes to select the highest-impact defense mechanisms. A corporate culture that tended to support and carry out policies once they had been set proved to be invaluable in achieving this.

Finally, there are companies *throwing resources at the problem.* They tend to have large cybersecurity teams who have implemented, or at least purchased, many of the most cutting-edge technologies. However, for all the spending, it's not clear that they are protecting the right things or protecting them in the right way. Some institutions that have great reputations for their technical sophistication in cybersecurity fall into this last bucket. For example, one bank prioritized cybersecurity funding but failed to get the central security team, business unit leaders, and business unit IT to interact effectively. As a result, despite its sizeable budget, the central security team had limited insight into what information assets to prioritize for protection or where the vulnerabilities lay in each of the business units' sprawling application portfolios. The inevitable outcome was a damaging breach despite the heavy investment.

• • •

Institutions face a daunting cybersecurity challenge. Pervasive digitization creates tremendous value but also makes them more reliant on technology, increases the stakes in the event of a breach, and enables capable and determined attackers. Institutions thus face a damaging and expensive array of risks from cyber-attacks, ranging from loss of customer data to disruption of business operations to fraud. Attackers meanwhile can improve the pace and sophistication of their attacks much more quickly than institutions can improve their defenses.

Large institutions are further hampered because they lack the facts and processes to make intelligent decisions about cybersecurity investments and policies, meaning they don't get the maximum protection at the lowest cost and with the least business disruption.

As a result, cybersecurity, as it is practiced today, is hurting large institutions' ability to derive value from technological innovation and investment. In the course of protecting them from real and important threats, organizations' cybersecurity controls are reducing end-user productivity, diverting scarce resources from IT that creates value, and slowing the introduction of important technology capabilities.

2

It Could Get Better— or $3 Trillion Worse

Six years ago nobody accessed e-mail via a tablet. Nobody talked about "big data." Companies didn't have private cloud programs. Most people assumed that security technology companies such as RSA could not be breached. Almost nobody had heard of Anonymous or LulzSec, and didn't think that jihad might be carried out by cyber-fighters. Edward Snowden was an anonymous contractor working on computer security for the CIA. And national newspapers didn't carry front-page stories about governments lobbing charges and counter-charges against each other about the use of cyber-espionage.

The cybersecurity context that companies operate in today is extraordinarily dynamic. The digitization of business processes continues to accelerate, a dizzying array of new technologies is available in the marketplace, and new security products emerge to acclaim but sometimes turn out to be less effective than promised. Attackers proliferate, experiment with new techniques, and become more audacious, while hundreds of government agencies in dozens of jurisdictions shift policies, roll out regulations, and invest in all manner of defensive and offensive cybersecurity capabilities.

Amid this confusing cacophony of activity, companies and other institutions must make decisions that will affect them 5 and even 10 years in the future. They must invest in research and development (R&D) projects so that they can reap benefits later. Technology they implement and applications they develop now will support business processes far beyond. Outsourcing arrangements contracted now will last at least 5 or 6 years, and those frontline technology experts brought on board today need to be able to grapple with problems we have not even though of yet, just as their predecessors are coming to terms with the challenges of today.

The situation is no better for other participants in the cybersecurity ecosystem. Vendors must invest now for the products of 2020 and beyond. Likewise, governments will write legislation that will stay on the books for years or even decades. So how are executives supposed to take the cybersecurity environment into account when making strategic decisions, when it's hard to predict almost anything about how that environment will evolve?

Scenario analysis is one of the most effective techniques for thinking about the implications of highly confusing, dynamic environments such as cybersecurity. Royal Dutch/Shell developed modern scenario planning in the late 1960s. By examining uncertainties, Shell's Group Planning organization, led by Pierre Wack and then Peter Schwartz, first developed scenarios that envisioned the possibility of spiraling oil prices in the 1970s[1] and then their collapse in the 1980s. This enabled Shell to prepare for market conditions it would not previously have considered.[2]

As described in Peter Schwartz's book *The Art of the Long View*, scenario analysis involves creating stories about alternative worlds.[3] These worlds are plausible futures based on a prioritized set of the drivers that could create each future, for example, the technologies that might be developed or how consumer preferences might change.

It is important that the worlds feel real and can be described in detail. What do they look and feel like? Who wins and who loses? What are early indicators that each world might be coming to pass? Business and public policy leaders can then look across all the potential worlds to see how they might steer a course toward the most favorable outcome. For example, are there actions that could increase the chance of a more attractive world coming to pass, and are there early warning signs to look out for that would indicate that managers should adjust their plans as one world or another comes into reality?[4]

---

[1] Wack, Pierre, "Scenarios: Uncharted Waters Ahead," *Harvard Business Review*, September 1985.
[2] Shell, "Sowing the Seeds of Strategic Success," *Impact Online*, Issue 1, 2013, pp. 6–7.
[3] Schwartz, Peter, *The Art of the Long View*. New York: Doubleday, 1996, Chapter 1.
[4] Ibid.

SCENARIO PLANNING AND CYBERSECURITY

We are not the first to apply scenario planning to cybersecurity. For example, Jason Healey of the Atlantic Council's Cyber-statecraft initiative laid out a range of scenarios including Status Quo, Conflict Domain, Balkanization, Paradise, and Cybergeddon in "The Five Futures of Cyber Conflict."[5]

Compared to previous efforts, we focused less on geopolitics and much more on how different cybersecurity scenarios could affect the global economy's ability to derive value from technology innovation. This means looking at issues of commercial, regulatory, and consumer behavior as well as the implications for individual institutions that need to protect themselves. In developing our scenarios, we drew on our interviews to identify more than 20 drivers of the future cybersecurity landscape. They included everything from expansion of the "surface area" of corporate networks to the ability of governments to enforce cyber-crime laws.

Twenty drivers is too unwieldy to be practical for scenario planning, so we prioritized the eight that will have the greatest impact and grouped them into two categories, which became macro-drivers:

Intensity of Threat
- Ease of use of attack technologies
- Level of disaffection among technologically sophisticated young people
- Proliferation of attack tools
- Sophistication of attackers and attack tools

Quality of Response
- Sophistication of institutions in defending themselves
- Pace of defense technology innovation
- International cooperation in fighting cyber-crime
- Quality of information/knowledge sharing across public and private sectors

[5] Healey, Jason, "The Five Futures of Cyber Conflict," *Atlantic Council Issue Brief*, December 14, 2011.

FIGURE 2.1   **The Change in Intensity of Threat and Quality of Response Leads to Different Scenarios**

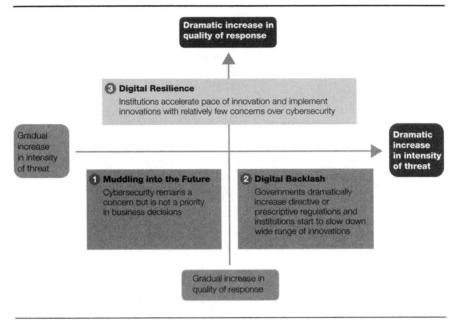

Playing out the possible trajectories of each of these macro-drivers gave us three possible scenarios: muddling into the future, digital backlash, and digital resilience (Figure 2.1).

> *Muddling into the future.* In this scenario the intensity of threat and the quality of response proceed roughly at the same pace. This world has many similarities to the one we live in today. Attackers continue to harass important institutions who, in turn, feel they are engaged in a never-ending game of "whack-a-mole." Cybersecurity is challenging, expensive, and a pain in the neck for most institutions, but, for the most part, cyber-attacks have only a limited impact on the world economy's ability to derive value from technology innovation.

> *Digital backlash.* In this scenario, the intensity of the threat outpaces the quality of institutions and governments to defend against cyber-attacks. There is a series of not only embarrassing but also highly destructive attacks that diminish confidence in the digital economy. As a result, regulators, institutions, and even

consumers apply the brakes to digitization, resulting in dramatically reduced value from technology innovation.

Digital resilience. In this scenario, institutions and governments rally to build resilience against cyber-attacks. Attacks and breaches continue to occur, but it becomes clear that their impact can be limited. Targeted and flexible defense mechanisms reduce the loss associated with protection against cyber-attack. As a result, the adoption of important technologies accelerates noticeably.

Pessimists might ask why there's no scenario that describes societal or economic collapse of the type that Hollywood might portray—indeed has done in low-budget films such as *Dragon Day*, where a cyber-attack destroys American society. In this case, mayhem is triggered by the simultaneous activation of a virus that is installed on every "Made in China" microchip.

The fact is that there is no "kill switch" for the online economy. Planning and executing a series of cyber-attacks sophisticated, wide-ranging, and sustained enough to bring a large, modern, diversified economy to its knees requires the resources of a powerful state. If two superpowers wanted to destroy each other's economies using cyber-weapons, they probably could. However, as Thomas Rid points out in *Cyber War Will Not Take Place*, they could also have destroyed each other at almost any time in the past using other weapons at their disposal.[6]

Cyber-destruction requires actors who have tremendous technological sophistication, available resources, and—most important of all—sufficient motivation. As we write, no state or other actor ticks all three boxes. The interconnectedness of the global economy means that a country that disrupts, for example, a foreign bank's trading operations, may well find that its own economy suffers as a result. The motivation for cyber-destruction is not there when you look beyond film scripts.

What's at Stake?

After identifying and describing the scenarios, we quantified their impact in terms of the world economy's ability to derive value from technology innovation.

[6] Rid, Thomas, *Cyber War Will Not Take Place*. London: C. Hurst & Co, 2013.

McKinsey's independent research body, McKinsey Global Institute (MGI), has been analyzing the value of technological innovations. In its "Disruptive Technologies" report, it focused on 12 technologies that society is counting on to transform life, business, and the global economy with an aggregate annual global economic impact of $14 trillion to 33 trillion by 2025.[7]

However, our interviews with cybersecurity leaders and experts made clear that exploiting many of these technologies successfully hinges on wide-ranging confidence in the confidentiality and integrity of the data on which they depend. It is much harder to convince doctors and patients to accept the use of electronic health records if they believe those records might be stolen or compromised. Many sessions at the World Economic Forum's 2014 annual meeting in Davos echoed this concern with conversations about technology innovations quickly evolving into discussions about whether it would be possible to secure the relevant data.

We argue that 9 of the MGI's 12 technological changes are at meaningful risk of being affected by cybersecurity threats: cloud computing, the Internet of Things, the mobile Internet, rapid entry into new markets, automation of knowledge work, social technologies, e-commerce, autonomous vehicles, and next-generation genomics. Rather than look as far out as 2025, we interpolated the MGI data to determine that in aggregate these 9 could deliver annual value of $8 trillion to 18 trillion between 2013 and 2020, assuming all are implemented aggressively (Figure 2.2).

However, technology executives told us that their company's ability to roll out these capabilities would be heavily affected by its overall position regarding cybersecurity risk. Under the digital resilience scenario, the full $18 trillion could be realized annually, but delays in implementation that would occur under the other two scenarios would have a meaningful impact on that. For example, the adoption of cloud computing could generate up to $2.7 trillion in annual value by 2020—but only under the digital resilience scenario. In the muddling into the future scenario, there would be a delay of slightly more than 11 months in adoption. This would equate to a $470 billion impact on potential value in 2020. In the digital backlash scenario, the delay to the adoption of all the technologies would be

[7] McKinsey Global Institute, "Disruptive Technologies: Advances that Will Transform Life, Business, and the Global Economy." McKinsey & Company, May 2013.

FIGURE 2.2   **Nine Technologies Could Create $8 Trillion to $18 Trillion in Value by 2020**

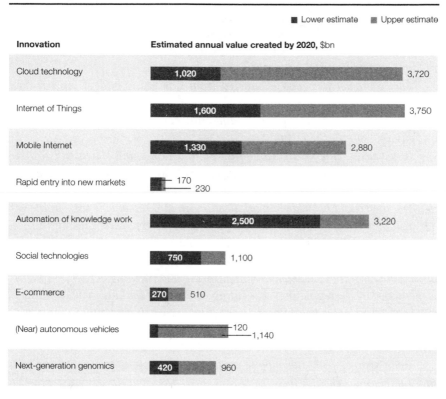

Sources. MGI reports, United Nations Conference on Trade and Development (UNCTAD), International Monetary Fund (IMF), McKinsey Economic Analytics Platform, industry leader interviews

three times worse, so, for the cloud computing example, the delay would be just shy of three years and the economic impact would also be three times as worse: in 2020, $1.4 trillion of lost value in the global economy.

Naturally, these numbers are estimates with margins for error but whatever the precise numbers, the impact is meaningful. If we delve deeper into the three scenarios, we can see what will bring them to pass, what the world would look like in those circumstances, and what their impact will be on realizing the full value of these game-changing technologies. CIOs and other business leaders who already find today's cybersecurity environment challenging may realize that it could get a lot worse.

SCENARIO 1: MUDDLING INTO THE FUTURE

January 15, 2020

It started out just another cruddy day at the office for Jane Schnauggs, chief information officer (CIO) at HyperCare, one of the United States' largest publicly traded hospital networks.

She was frustrated and exhausted from this year's budget process. Her so-called partners in the business expected her to deliver the most recent generation of mobile patient experience and clinical decision support tools, without any increase in the IT budget.

It had taken Jane nearly 18 months to find Frank, but she hadn't realized how expensive and controversial her new CISO would turn out to be. The new tools for detecting malware weren't that expensive, though nobody could show her how they could be made to work together in any reasonable time frame yet. The real budgetary problems were the network and application rearchitectures that Frank insisted were essential. "They just were never designed to be secure." That they didn't show up in the security budget didn't make them any less expensive. What's more, lots of monitoring and patching activity—much of it mandated by the regulator—was eating up many of the hard-won operational efficiencies she had achieved over the past few years. It was only January, and she already feared that she was at risk for this year's budget and the Q4 meeting with the chief financial officer (CFO) would be unpleasant in the extreme.

Even worse, both the mobile and clinical support projects were now months behind schedule because Frank had been able to demonstrate that there were fundamental flaws in the way each application handled sensitive data. And every couple of days she got another e-mail from another senior doctor telling her what a pain in the neck the new password policies were.

Her office door opened, interrupting Jane's silent griping.

"Frank," she said, "Please don't take this the wrong way, but you're not the person I most like to see dropping by my office unexpectedly." Frank gave that apologetic half-smile that typically preceded bad news.

It could have been worse. It could have been a lot worse. Fortunately, these attackers were relatively unsophisticated. They had managed to steal data on roughly 1,500 patients from the electronic health records system.

"If they hadn't been controlling the malware from an IP address range that's pretty well known for cyber-crime," Frank said, "we'd never have caught it this quickly. They were probably planning to use the records for medical fraud. Or resell them to somebody who would. Market price for personal health information is probably getting close to $1,000 per life these days."

The fines would be a couple of million dollars. Probably another two or three million to head off any civil suits. And the medical head of one of their largest hospitals promising a reporter that none of his patients' information had been breached made them all look like idiots.

For a company with $15 billion in annual revenues, it was expensive but definitely manageable. Of course, once Frank came back to her with the costs to actually fix the flaw in the system, Jane knew there was just no way she was going to hit her budget this year.

The realization of the muddling into the future scenario is as much a story of what doesn't happen as what does.

Attackers would continue to improve their skills, but state-level capabilities would remain in the hands of a small number of countries, each of which would be heavily invested in preserving the existing economic order. Countries continue to snoop shamelessly for political/military intelligence and economic advantage, but cyber-weapons remain in their silos. Other cyber-attackers continue expanding their activities, stealing identities, and enabling fraud, but they remain parasitic rather than destructive, diverting only a tiny percentage of the unimaginable sums sloshing through the global online economy into their own pockets. After all, a bank or online retailer they put out of business one day is one they can't steal from the next.

Institutions would continue to protect themselves, devoting more resources to and demanding tighter control from cybersecurity models that are already barely tenable in 2014. Protecting an institution from cyber-attacks continues to be "IT's problem," and even more specifically "the CISO's problem." Senior executives would continue to formulate business strategies and lay out business processes with no consideration of how the underlying data would be protected. Limited engagement from business leaders makes it hard to determine what data needs most protection, so the IT security team tries to protect everything equally, which drives up costs and user inconvenience. Security would continue to be layered on top of application development projects and infrastructure environments rather than being embedded in them, adding to the time and cost of rolling out new technology.

The broader ecosystem offers only limited help to institutions in this scenario. Cybersecurity policy remains disjointed, with little cooperation among states and barely any coordination between different agencies and regulatory authorities within each jurisdiction. Intelligence agencies struggle to find a way to share the massive amounts of cyber-intelligence with private institutions without creating privacy concerns or compromising sensitive sources and methods. CIOs and CISOs, meanwhile, continue to face a bewildering maze of regulations touching on privacy and security. Vendors still bring innovative security technologies to market, but few standards emerge and most products are one-off solutions that don't fit into a broader security platform without lots of labor-intensive system integration.

The Billion-Dollar Implication

For CIOs in this scenario, cybersecurity will feel like stepping back to be a New York City cop in the 1950s or early 1960s. Crime, both petty and organized, never goes away but never truly takes hold or fundamentally threatens the city's society or economy. Nevertheless, CIOs are going to feel that their organization is always a half-step behind the attackers, caught in an endless cycle of applying security patches and trialing the next new security product that promises to identify attacks slightly more quickly. Being compliant with a maze of regulations often diverts resources from more pressing security needs. And reconciling regulations across different countries makes it harder and harder to run anything resembling a global technology environment.

Cybersecurity would continue to be a moderately expensive inconvenience for organizations, and tension would linger between security, business, and broader technology teams over the pace of technology innovation. Most critical innovations would still be implemented in a reasonably timely fashion, but the pace of delivering mobile and public cloud technologies in particular would lag expectation due to the nervousness around mobile security amid the platform's ubiquity, and the lack of transparency into many cloud service providers' security models. If we look at the Internet of Things, for example, the predicted five-month delay in adoption would mean forgoing $210 billion in value in 2020 (about 5 percent of the total annual value lost in this scenario) as regulators and institutions work out how to connect consumer appliances and industrial machinery to the Internet safely. Nobody wants their investment in Internet-enabled home automation to be a mechanism for criminals to know when they're out of town or what valuable goods they own.

The muddling into the future scenario would result in an aggregate loss of just over $1 trillion in value in 2020 due to the deferred adoption of innovation technologies, with most of the impact in cloud computing, the Internet of Things, the mobile Internet, and automation of knowledge work (Figure 2.3).

FIGURE 2.3   **Muddling into the Future Scenario Puts $1 Trillion at Risk**

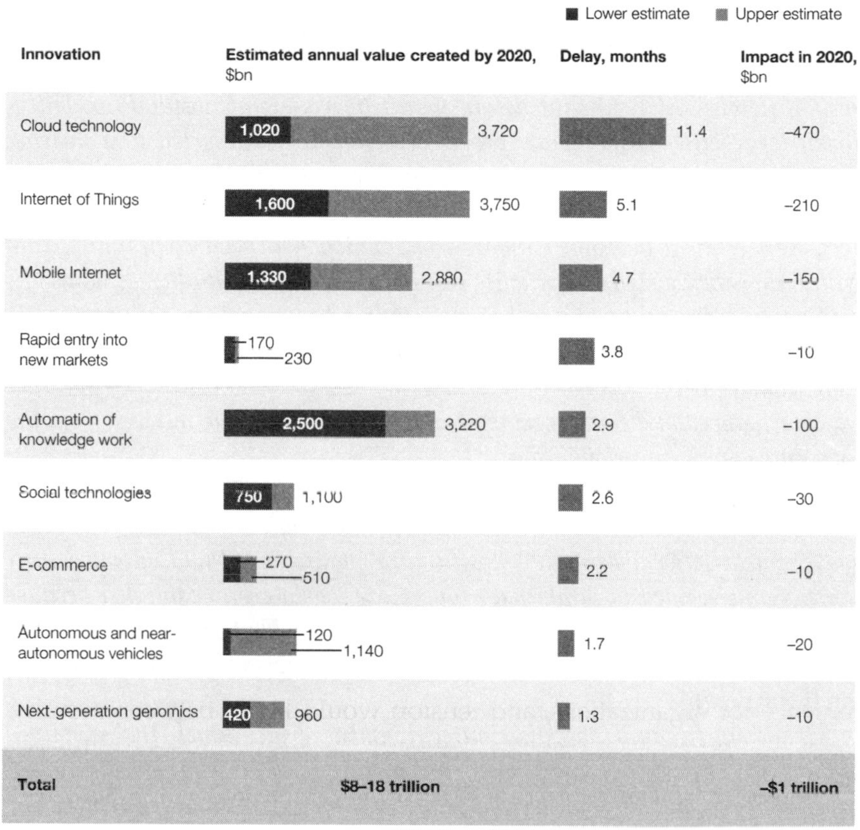

■ Lower estimate   ▨ Upper estimate

Innovation	Estimated annual value created by 2020, $bn	Delay, months	Impact in 2020, $bn
Cloud technology	1,020 — 3,720	11.4	−470
Internet of Things	1,600 — 3,750	5.1	−210
Mobile Internet	1,330 — 2,880	4.7	−150
Rapid entry into new markets	170 — 230	3.8	−10
Automation of knowledge work	2,500 — 3,220	2.9	−100
Social technologies	750 — 1,100	2.6	−30
E-commerce	270 — 510	2.2	−10
Autonomous and near-autonomous vehicles	120 — 1,140	1.7	−20
Next-generation genomics	420 — 960	1.3	−10
Total	**$8–18 trillion**		**−$1 trillion**

Sources: MGI reports, UNCTAD, IMF, McKinsey Economic Analytics Platform, industry leader interviews

SCENARIO 2: DIGITAL BACKLASH

January 15, 2020

"Well, this is certainly isn't just another cruddy day at the office," thought Jane Schnauggs as she sat between HyperCare's CEO and general counsel in the Senate hearing room. Of course, she had tried to push the task of testifying before the Senate's Homeland Security and Government Affairs Committee on Frank, her CISO. But her general counsel had politely but firmly told her that, given the severity of the issues at hand, the Senate committee members would expect to hear from the company's senior-most technology executive.

The senator looked down at his notes, then up at Jane. "I'd like to understand HyperCare's decision making with regard to the security of its Mobile Clinician Experience program—I believe you refer to it as MCE? HyperCare failed to protect itself from a series of attacks that exploited vulnerabilities in MCE to shut down operating rooms at hospitals in half a dozen large cities. Emergency procedures had to be diverted to a nearby, publicly managed hospital, causing significant disruption. I also understand only the refusal of trained nurses to follow the instructions from HyperCare's clinical decision support tool, which had been compromised by attackers, saved dozens of patients from potentially harmful treatments. In particular, Miss Schnauggs, what was your personal role in the process? Is it true that you dismissed concerns about the MCE program raised by your own security team?"

Jane paused and tried to remember all the coaching she received from the corporate communications team.

It had not been a fun couple of years to be the CIO at HyperCare. At some point, any number of hackers with time on their hands and an axe to grind had decided that embarrassing health care companies would advance their cause. Some seemed to think that HyperCare was a crony capitalist because it participated in the implementation of the Affordable Care Act. Others apparently felt that a private hospital chain would sacrifice patient health and safety for profits.

It had started with those distributed denial of service attacks that swamped HyperCare's Internet-facing servers, preventing patients from scheduling appointments or checking lab results. That was mostly an inconvenience. The information that attackers started to release online was more embarrassing: memos and e-mails in which management discussed how to maximize Medicare reimbursements were bad enough; the personal health information of celebrities and politicians was much worse—especially given the fines incurred and doubts it created about the privacy of electronic health records.

Frank's team was sure that cyber-criminals were using the political attacks to distract the security team while they got on with the lucrative work of removing information for the purpose of medical fraud.

Silently, Jane thought about her frustration with the various public bodies. Sometimes it felt like Frank and his team had to deal with an alphabet soup of agencies that represented an overlapping and sometimes contradictory array of regulatory, law enforcement, and national security agendas. Frank told her every request for actionable information got waved aside, either on privacy grounds or because of the need to protect the intelligence community's "sources and methods" in monitoring cyber-attacks.

She had invested a lot in protecting HyperCare's systems and data. She found the budget for every security technology Frank had said the regulators expected, and approved rigorous controls for just about every major IT process. Every phase in the application development process had to be signed off by the security team before the project could advance. This hadn't endeared her to her business partners, who complained that it took forever to get anything done. Yet they were also the same executives who shouted the loudest about IT's incompetence whenever there was a breach.

MCE was supposed to have been the game-changer—the program that would reinvigorate HyperCare's ability to use IT to improve medical productivity by tying enriched medical records with clinical decision support on one mobile screen. Given all the attacks, there had been a lot of skepticism from the board about IT's ability to do big things without putting the business at risk. She had put her own personal credibility on the line in getting support from the senior management team. Ultimately, she had gotten there. The CFO had already baked the operational benefits into next year's budgets. The doctors raved about the user experience.

Frank had told her, "We've spent a lot of time on the security architecture, but, at the end of the day, they required us to push a lot of data to the device for performance reasons. The level of integration from the vendors of the device, the operating system, the container, and the application platform are not what we would have wanted from the vendor. Is it crackable? Anything's crackable. You have to make a call."

Finally, Jane started to speak, so she could try to explain why she had given the approval to move ahead with the project.

The path to the digital backlash scenario is one strewn with inadequate responses, and it is far from being the unrealistic outlier scenario. Art Coviello, vice-chairman at security company RSA and one of the most respected commentators on the security environment, said, "Everyone assumes that we're naturally going to end up muddling into the future. I don't think that's right. Unless something changes, we're going to end up in with a digital backlash."

Attackers would take the lead and the threats would become more worrisome. Network attack specialists realize they can supplement relatively modest corporate or state incomes by reselling malware, scripts, or techniques they have developed to cyber-criminals. Angered by charge and countercharge about cyber-espionage, governments decide not to bother pursuing destructive attacks that originate from within their territory, as long as those attacks are directed outward.

Technologically sophisticated young people, believing that government and business institutions aren't responsive to their needs and concerns, would decide they can best make their voices heard by hacktivism. Some may argue that if large institutions acted ethically, they would have nothing to fear in having their internal deliberations made public.

If this environment crashes against an economy mostly using traditional, compliance-oriented cybersecurity models, those traditional models would buckle. Most application and infrastructure architectures were never designed to be secure. Companies don't know how to focus their security controls on the most important information assets and risks. They can't perform the analysis to identify attacks in real time. They can't respond effectively in the event of a breach. The result would be a series of very public, very destructive attacks on major institutions that would trigger multiple types of backlash.

Many CIOs and CISOs we spoke to said that regulatory overreach was of the biggest cybersecurity risks, that is, that regulatory agencies would seek to establish ever more mandates about what security controls must be put in place, how many organizational lines of defense are needed, and which data must be hosted internally. In Davos, participants raised the specter of a "cyber cold war" in which different countries would use cybersecurity as a pretext to create "splinternets" that had different standards to the global (although increasingly seen as U.S.-run) Internet.

Alongside the regulatory challenges, there could also be an institutional backlash. Security is often the bottleneck in introducing new technologies, and many CIOs and CISOs told us that that it could get tighter and tighter in a more threatening cybersecurity environment: the greater the risk of cyber-attack, the more conservative institutions would become about introducing new technology-enabled capabilities.

Finally, there would be the possibility of a consumer backlash. This may be the least likely but the most destructive reaction. For the most part, consumers have taken publicity about cyber-attacks and breaches in their stride. They still shop at Target and still use Sony's online gaming network. But there are already inklings of concern. For example, CISOs at wealth management and brokerage firms told us that their companies' financial advisers were starting to get asked some pointed questions from mass-affluent customers about the security of their financial data in the wake of recent attacks. A recent survey conducted by the Ponemon Institute confirms that consumers are increasingly aware and concerned about cyber-attacks, even if they are not prepared to do anything about it just yet.[8]

However, if enough data were compromised to wake the sleeping giant of consumer concerns, the impact would be profound. Companies would suddenly find it much harder to convince customers to use mobile payments, service their accounts online, and accept electronic health records, let alone embrace any of the more advanced developments that may come along in the meantime.

Jeopardizing Business Models … and Entire Companies

When we explained the digital backlash scenario to a number of executives at semiconductor companies, their eyes widened. "If this scenario happens," one of them said, "then the Internet of Things doesn't happen or doesn't happen quickly." They went on to explain that their revenue growth projections depended heavily on the volume of chips needed for all these Internet-enabled appliances.

Banking CISOs had a different reaction. They believed their banks were already starting to experience the digital backlash scenario, while their less regulated, nontraditional competitors were still muddling into the future, and the distinction created a competitive disadvantage for the banks.

For CIOs and CISOs, the digital backlash will feel like an endless battle against a particularly creative and persistent insurgency. There's always another potential attack coming from another direction and it will seem impossible to seize the initiative from the attackers. On top of that, many of the restrictions they are forced to put in place to counteract the attacks cause at least as much if not more frustration for their users. For CEOs and other business leaders trying to create value in the digital economy, this scenario would feel like New York in the 1970s, when fear of crime discouraged tourism, depressed investment, and drove residents and businesses to the suburbs and beyond.

As a result, almost every aspect of the digital economy would develop more haltingly. Institutions would invest in the Internet of Things more slowly. Regulators would be more aggressive in limiting which data can be stored in the cloud. Consumers would be more reluctant to adopt mobile commerce.

[8] Bruemmer, Michael, "Evaluating Consumer Sentiment and Business Responses to Data Breaches," *Security InfoWatch*, June 4, 2014. www.securityinfowatch.com/article/11503135/experians-michael-bruemmer-discusses-the-impact-data-breaches-are-having-on-consumer-sentiment-and-how-businesses-should-respond.

FIGURE 2.4 **Digital Backlash Scenario Puts More than $3 Trillion at Risk**

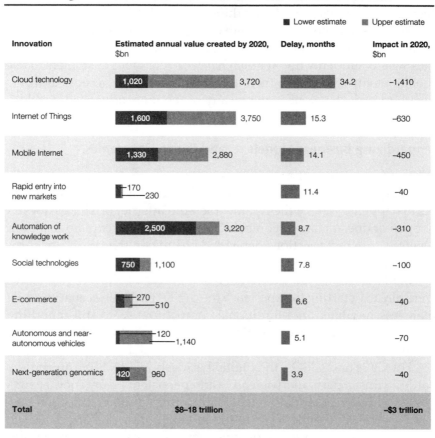

Innovation	Estimated annual value created by 2020, $bn	Delay, months	Impact in 2020, $bn
	■ Lower estimate ■ Upper estimate		
Cloud technology	1,020 — 3,720	34.2	−1,410
Internet of Things	1,600 — 3,750	15.3	−630
Mobile Internet	1,330 — 2,880	14.1	−450
Rapid entry into new markets	170 — 230	11.4	−40
Automation of knowledge work	2,500 — 3,220	8.7	−310
Social technologies	750 — 1,100	7.8	−100
E-commerce	270 — 510	6.6	−40
Autonomous and near-autonomous vehicles	120 — 1,140	5.1	−70
Next-generation genomics	420 — 960	3.9	−40
Total	**$8–18 trillion**		**−$3 trillion**

Sources: MGI reports, UNCTAD, IMF, McKinsey Economic Analytics Platform, industry leader interviews

In this scenario, the value derived from the Internet of Things would be $630 billion less than its full 2020 potential due to a 15-month delay in adoption. In aggregate, the digital backlash would result in a staggering $3 trillion dollars in lost value in 2020 (Figure 2.4).

SCENARIO 3: DIGITAL RESILIENCE

January 15, 2020
It had been a long day at the office for Jane Schnauggs, but it had gone a lot better than it might have.

"We definitely had some data stolen," said her CISO Frank, "but it was mostly general business and operational data. I'm not entirely sure what they'll do with the construction timelines for the new hospital build, but we can't find any evidence that they were able to penetrate beyond our low-security zone. So we have no reason to believe than any personal health information has been affected. It's good that we caught this early."

It never failed to surprise Jane what data attackers would try to take. One country had undertaken a campaign to steal HyperCare's medical practices for treating a range of acute and chronic diseases. The chief medical officer's reaction had been priceless: "Do they know we publish this stuff in medical journals? I know the subscription fees for these journals are on the high side, but this feels extreme!" He also suggested inserting some sort of message into the network telling the hackers that HyperCare would be delighted to host a medical delegation from that country in any of its major hospitals. "Assuming appropriate credentials," he noted dryly, "they would even be welcome to scrub in."

Implementing software-defined networking had been a real battle. Many people in network operations had been highly resistant at first, and getting the initial investment had been excruciating, but it really paid off today. It allowed Jane's team to set up separate zones for more sensitive workloads and data without the operational overhead of old-fashioned network segments. On days like today, it really slowed down attackers' movement toward the most sensitive assets.

Of course, it had been a fight to bring business and medical leaders to the table to talk about cybersecurity. If the CEO hadn't personally chaired that steering committee, it never would have happened. As it turned out, everyone knew personal health information was extremely sensitive and anything related to Medicare and Medicaid reimbursement was very sensitive. But the entire management team had been surprised at how much of their data wasn't actually that confidential: building plans, maintenance schedules, medical practices—the list went on and on.

It had also been a fight to scale the strategic application platform and private cloud environment, but that had proven worthwhile, too. Jane had made the case for the investments based on cost, flexibility, and time to market, but she had an ulterior motive: she wanted to build security into the platform, so that you'd have to work to make a new program insecure. The transparency into their hosting environment provided by their private cloud had helped them identify the compromised system quickly today.

Because of the application platform and the cloud environment (and the lack of security-related holdups before deployment), the team had been able to build the back end for the new Mobile Clinical Experience far quicker than it would have taken even a few years ago. Jane had reinvested some of the savings to hire ergonomic specialists to sit with the doctors, figure out how they would use the new tool, and devise authentication techniques that wouldn't feel intrusive.

"Even though they didn't get any sensitive data," Frank said, interrupting her thoughts, "we still stood up the incident war room. It helped us make sure that no misinformation got out to regulators, customers, or the press."

Jane put her hand on Frank's shoulder and walked him toward the door, gently encouraging him out of her office. She had other things to worry about that afternoon as well.

This is the state we think everyone reading this book should aspire to. It is not a perfect world without cyber-attacks—that is as unrealistic as New York without pickpocketing—but it is a world in which businesses and organizations are able to deliver the maximum benefits of technological advances without becoming entangled in a scrappy fight with hackers or jeopardizing their business models.

The rest of this book is about what it will take to get there—about how we can collectively push for digital resilience to be the scenario that prevails. It will not happen without action. Ultimately, there are two drivers: a fundamental change in cybersecurity operating models that institutions use to protect themselves, and a generally benign broader cybersecurity environment.

Fundamental Change in Cybersecurity Operating Models

In response to more challenging threats, most institutions would put in "control function"–type operating models. Previously, cybersecurity had been underfunded and companies had little insight into technology vulnerabilities. What protections existed focused on the perimeter. There were few consequences for violating policies, and insecure application code and infrastructure configurations were more common than not.

Between 2007 and 2013, especially as companies continued the process of consolidating and professionalizing IT, cybersecurity grew as a control function. Companies strengthened governance authority for the IT security team, especially for anything related to compliance in regulated industries. They locked down the end-user environment and introduced architecture reviews to reduce the risks in application development and infrastructure projects.

CIOs, CISOs, and chief technology officers we spoke to made clear that most institutions still use this model today, even though it is increasingly unsustainable. It places the responsibility for security mostly on the security team without taking the bigger picture into account. It doesn't focus protection on the most important assets. It frustrates end users and creates increasing tension between security and innovation. It is backward looking, protecting against yesterday's attacks, not those of tomorrow. It is also dependent on manual interventions and therefore does not scale well as the threat intensifies.

Our interviews made it equally clear that for the digital resilience scenario to come to fruition, institutions would have to change this model. Cybersecurity would have to be embedded in broader business and IT processes if companies are to protect themselves from escalating threats without destroying their ability to derive value from technology innovation.

There was consensus on the three types of changes that companies need to make in order to get to the required cybersecurity operating model:

1. *Business process changes,* including prioritizing information assets and business risks, enlisting the assistance of frontline personnel, integrating cybersecurity into broader management processes, and integrating incident response across business functions.
2. *Broader IT changes,* including building security into every part of the technology stack as opposed to "layering it on top."
3. *Cybersecurity operational changes,* including providing differential protection for the most important information assets and deploying active defenses to engage attackers.

Technology executives told us that almost all of these changes would be game changers or have significant impact in reducing the risk of cyber-attack to their organization. The only exception was changing frontline personnel behavior, which many told us would be transformative if it *could* happen, but given the challenges in changing user behavior, it was far from clear that it *would* happen.

Worryingly, most technology executives told us that they were not making acceptable progress along any dimension. On average, they gave themselves C and C– scores on progress to date (Figure 2.5).

FIGURE 2.5   **Technology Executives RealizeThey Have Substantial Room for Improvement in Addressing Digital Resilience Levers**

■ Significant impact or game changer

	Critical resilience levers	Impact of lever, % of responses	Average self-assessment grade
Business processes	Prioritize information assets based on related risks	74	C-
	Enlist frontline personnel to protect the information assets they use	49	C-
	Integrate cybersecurity into enterprise-wide risk management and governance processes	55	C-
	Test continuously to improve incident response across business functions	65	C+
Broader technology	Integrate cybersecurity into the technology environment	85	C
Cybersecurity	Provide differentiated protection for the most important assets	73	C
	Deploy active defenses to engage attackers	75	C

Critically, the biggest difference between those institutions that are making relatively fast progress and the others was not funding; rather, it was the level of top management engagement and support.

Benign Broader Cybersecurity Environment

Alongside the active changes that companies must make, many other things would have to *not* happen for the resiliency scenario to come to pass. Regulators would have to avoid providing prescriptive mandates that focus companies on compliance rather than reducing business risks. Countries would have to refrain from imposing restrictive standards on data location and local technology sourcing that could fracture the Internet into a series of "splinternets." Countries would also have to avoid the type of accusations and rhetoric about cyberwarfare that could discourage multinational cooperation.

There is, of course, also a set of positive actions that national and international bodies could take to promote a more benign, broader cybersecurity environment. However, there is much less consensus on which specific levers will have the most impact than there is on how individual institutions can protect themselves. For every CISO who wants more public investment in basic cybersecurity research, another expressed doubt that the public sector could make effective investment choices.

Although the waters may be muddier, we believe that there are actions that, thoughtfully applied, could help bring about digital resilience. Major states could provide more transparency into their national cybersecurity strategies, there could be some harmonization of cybersecurity regulation across major economies, and law enforcement and private enterprise could cooperate more to improve information sharing.

In the area of community action, industry groups such as the Financial Services Information Sharing and Analysis Center (FS-ISAC) could facilitate more joint research, share more intelligence across institutions, and potentially create shared industry utilities for common cybersecurity functions.

Realizing the Full Value

Building digital resilience will enable institutions to break free of the seemingly impossible cybersecurity trade-offs they face today. They will be able to dramatically reduce the risks of losing intellectual property or sensitive data and absorb any disruption to technology-enabled business processes while still capturing the full value from information technology.

Countering cyber-attacks would no longer mean creating an unproductive user experience, nor would it slow down the introduction of innovation technologies.

In the digital resilience scenario, society captures the $8 trillion to $18 trillion in annual value possible from the mobile Internet, the Internet of Things, cloud computing, and other innovation technologies. If we fail to achieve digital resilience, every month's delay caused by cybersecurity issues means leaving money—and tangible benefits for the world's population—on the table.

• • •

The threat of cyber-attack is a daunting issue. The combination of valuable online assets, open and interconnected networks, and sophisticated attackers has propelled cybersecurity up the agenda.

Unfortunately, most companies do not yet have the capabilities in place to protect themselves while continuing to innovate rapidly and expand the value they derive from technology investments.

Over the next several years, the situation could get a lot better—or a lot worse, with as much as $3 trillion at stake between the best and worst scenarios. This divergence in outcomes emphasizes the importance of companies casting aside traditional siloed and reactive cybersecurity models and building the capabilities required for digital resilience. It also emphasizes the need for other participants in the cybersecurity ecosystem—especially regulators, policymakers, and technology vendors—to support companies in these aims.

3

Prioritize Risks and Target Protections

With no natural defenses and fewer troops than his enemies, Frederick the Great admonished his generals, "Little minds try to defend everything at once, but sensible people look at the main point only; they parry the worst blows and stand a little hurt if thereby they avoid a greater one. If you try to hold everything, you hold nothing."

What holds true for Prussian commanders applies no less to business and technology leaders scrambling to protect their companies from cyber-attack. Just as generals must husband scarce divisions for their country's most pressing threats, CISOs must focus their resources on their company's most critical business risks.

Before anything else, achieving digital resilience requires companies to pull two levers successfully. They must prioritize information assets based on business risks and provide differentiated protection for the most important assets.

Too many companies fail to do this. They have limited insight into which information assets are most important and cannot put more stringent protections in place to defend those critical assets. The result: the company gets too little protection for too much money.

The businesses, the risk function, IT, and the cybersecurity group all need a common language and set of mechanisms to assess risks, evaluate potential protections, and make trade-offs.

In prioritizing information assets, cybersecurity teams must balance rigor with practicality and ensure that senior business executives can understand the choices and implications. Once they progress from prioritization to selecting the right mix of protections, it is important to think about the potential set of controls in a holistic way. Companies that get this right find the results extremely powerful. They discover important assets and risks they had not thought about. They find that some assets, such as marketing data, are less critical than they thought. Eventually, they arrive at a combination of controls that reduces their risk, with the minimum impact on the business.

Naturally, input from business executives in identifying information assets, assessing business risks, and making decisions about the right balance between risk, cost, and business impact will be critical to success here.

UNTARGETED SECURITY MEASURES SERVE ONLY ATTACKERS

An information asset is data that has business value for the enterprise. The asset is not a particular application or database or server, but rather the information they store and use, such as customer data, pricing information, underwriting methodologies, or engine designs.

A security control is a measure that mitigates risk. Many controls involve cybersecurity technologies: firewalls keep unauthorized traffic off a corporate network; encryption protects data from those who lack the authority to access it. Some controls are policies that affect the broader IT environment, such as standards developers should use to reduce the likelihood of security flaws in their code. Others are policies about business processes, such as which data should be purged after a period of time.

Figuring out which assets and risks are most important and what controls to put in place is tough.

Companies have to protect themselves against an expansive array of risks that are hard to assess. For machinery accidents, credit card defaults, or worker's compensation claims, there are quantitative data about the historical frequency and impact of these events. This allows companies to make intelligent, fact-based decisions about the relative importance of various risks and how much to spend mitigating them.

Unfortunately, this does not typically hold true for cyber-attacks. The loss of sensitive intellectual property (IP) to a foreign competitor, the release of confidential customer information on the Internet, and the disruption of online customer care for days on end are all extremely worrying prospects for most companies, but which one is most important? Historical data about the impact and likelihood of breaches are sparse and often not available in a format that supports statistical analysis.

Even if companies were less reticent about sharing what information on attacks they do have, attackers are evolving their strategies so rapidly that these experiences may not be relevant. Some risks are catastrophic events so unusual that they would not be addressed by historical data. In other cases, the impact of an event is necessarily contingent and uncertain: a foreign competitor might steal information about proprietary manufacturing techniques, but will it have the requisite expertise to exploit that information? It is impossible to know for sure.

Discussions on what to protect and how to protect it can end up with unhelpful resolutions such as "give us the best protection you can," or "we can't tolerate any loss of data." This puts the decision-making onus onto a CISO, who lacks the power to push back on changing investment priorities and the knowledge about what information assets the company has and how valuable they are to both the business and attackers.

Even banks struggle to get this process right, despite the regulatory pressure they face to implement documented governance processes. In some cases, banks have identified cyber-risks in their enterprise risk register, but the register itself lacks stakeholder buy-in, so it cannot be used to drive cybersecurity policy or investment. In many cases, identifying banking risks has become very compliance oriented—more focused on following a process than on generating actionable insights that can drive cybersecurity decisions.

The result of these challenges is that many CISOs have fallen back on one of three approaches: protect everything to the same level, focus on whatever has generated the most noise from senior management, or determine protection on an ad-hoc basis.

Protecting all information assets equally dates from the era of perimeter protection. As one CIO told us, his environment was "hard on the outside, but soft and chewy on the inside." His organization had invested for years in firewalls, intrusion detection systems, and other controls designed to keep attackers off its network, but had sought to minimize complexity by devoting much less effort to securing individual systems within the corporate data center. Ten years ago this strategy probably made sense, but it is now untenable, with more determined attackers, mobile technology, and pervasive digitization creating more ways into corporate networks. Even if the perimeter is not as dead as some have claimed,[1] it can no longer be the sole line of defense protecting the enterprise.

In any event, a homogeneous level of protection can be expensive and unnecessary. A heavy manufacturing company spent years debating whether to disconnect or "air gap" all of its plants from the corporate network. The cybersecurity team argued that an air gap would be best practice given the production control systems in each plant. The IT infrastructure team countered that the complexity created by disconnecting the plants from the corporate network would require hundreds of millions of dollars in additional expenditure. Senior management struggled to adjudicate between the competing, technically arcane arguments. Finally, the company started to tease apart the different risks in different plants. It found that a cyber-attack on a production control system could theoretically cause a catastrophic event at only a small fraction of the company's plants. A line stoppage was the worst that could happen at the remainder. Based on this analysis, the company air gapped only about 10 percent of its plants from the corporate network, dramatically reducing the expenditure required without jeopardizing the company's operations.

Controls are not always inadequate; they can also be excessive. An aerospace company applied the same document control policies and technical restrictions on sales and marketing materials as it did for confidential engineering documents. As a result, multiple approvals were needed just to share marketing content with external parties, enforced by the file-level access rules in its collaboration platform. This process could take weeks, which led to missed opportunities to share materials that had already been designed for external distribution, for example, for trade shows, sales meetings, and press conferences. In one often-discussed case, the marketing team showed up to a conference completely empty-handed. Once the materials were properly classified as intended for public consumption, the access control restrictions were lifted, and the marketing team could respond to requests much more promptly.

Rather than try and protect everything equally, some companies focus protection on a small subset of assets and risks based not on

---

[1] EnergySec, "Network Perimeter Defense: 'The Perimeter is Dead' Should Be Laid to Rest," September 2014.

rigorous analysis but on incomplete and sometimes emotional input from senior management. This usually results in major risks being left unaddressed. For example, a bank had suffered major operational outages driven by distributed denial of service attacks. Therefore, the lion's share of additional cybersecurity investments was directed at preventing attacks of the same nature. However, this led to the bank underinvesting in protecting itself from other types of attacks (e.g., fraud and insider threats). This problem is particularly acute where customer data are deemed disproportionately important—institutions become so focused on protecting customer information that they all but ignore other types of important data such as corporate strategy information or business process data.

The final common but flawed approach is for companies to try and focus their controls on the most important information assets but in an unsystematic way with limited or ineffective input from the business. An insurer left cybersecurity investments almost entirely to the discretion of the CISO. The result was that the level of security controls bore no relationship to what the business thought were the most important assets to protect or to its tolerance for the impact the controls had on user experience. The security team felt isolated from the rest of the business, and whenever it asked for more money to cover a specific need, the business leaders had no way to judge whether the additional spend was justified.

PRIORITIZE INFORMATION ASSETS AND RISKS IN A WAY THAT ENGAGES BUSINESS LEADERS

Only a few companies have cracked the code of bringing together the business, risk, IT, and cybersecurity to identify and prioritize risks using a common frame of reference.

Business executives in the organizations that get cybersecurity right understand the value-at-risk from cyber-attacks and the value of selected, high-impact cybersecurity initiatives. They understand which information assets are most important and that the risk of those assets being exposed should drive the level of protection and therefore the investment allotted. In these organizations, cybersecurity executives have meaningful and fruitful discussions with the business on the benefits of various mitigating options and on the implications of accepting the risks rather than investing in mitigation. Cybersecurity leaders help the business take tough trade-off decisions, and have the authority to supervise the implementation of the initiatives with IT and with the business, and escalate where there are roadblocks and delays. The CIO is comfortable justifying the security spend in terms of its contribution to the organization's security and can defend it as part of the overall portfolio of IT initiatives.

There are three specific aspects of a successful information asset prioritization program: defining the assets and risks in business terms, engaging senior business leaders, and diving deep into the long-tail risks.

Define Assets and Risks in Business Terms

It is easy for CISOs and their teams to think about risks in technical terms given cybersecurity's history as a technical discipline. However, to make sure they surface the full set of risks and engage business leaders effectively, cybersecurity teams need to build their prioritization efforts around business concepts, rather than technology.

Focus on Information Assets Rather than Data Elements   When asked about prioritizing information assets, many CISOs will say they have a data classification program. That means they have a team going through every field in every database and categorizing each one as "restricted," "confidential," "internal," or "public"—typically over the course of two to three years. This type of approach is great in theory, but in practice it often excludes important unstructured data that live outside databases; and attackers are unlikely to wait politely for three years while a company finishes its classification program. To address the full set of data and derive a set of insights they can act on, cybersecurity teams need to start at a higher level of abstraction and look at information assets rather than fields or tables in databases.

An information asset is a coherent body of information that has recognizable and manageable business value and that is defined by business needs and objectives rather than the specifics of how and where it is stored. As noted earlier, it is not a system, a database, or an application. It could be customer information for a consumer auto business, business plans for upcoming mobile products, or manufacturing specifications for paint application. The assets will vary by business, and the importance of different types of assets will also vary.

There is no hard-and-fast rule about the right level of granularity for an information asset—for example, should manufacturing specifications for 10 different products in a given business unit be treated as 1 information asset or 10? That said, there are two heuristics for answering such questions: materiality and distinction. Which of the products are big enough to matter? Are there enough business differences among the products so their manufacturing specifications will have different levels of sensitivity?

Typically, a business will have between 25 and about 80 information assets, depending on its size and complexity. Table 3.1 shows a typical list of assets for an insurance company.

TABLE 3.1 **Information Assets Span All Functions—Insurance Example**

Function	Assets
Finance	Account data Securities Payment data Tax records
Investment management	Strategic asset allocation Tactical asset allocation
Human resources	Employee data records Applicant data records
Audit	Audit reports
Legal	Compliance data Specific lawsuit data Legally mandated data
CEO function	Board/management documents (decisions, business plans, strategies)
Market management	Customer segmentation Customer value Marketing plans
Products, actuarial, reinsurance	Product and risk model (including historic database) Product road maps Customer name/address data
Sales/distribution	Customer financial data (including credit card data) Private customer personal data Business customer inside data
Policy management/underwriting	Contract information and risk assessment Contract appendices (e.g., power plant plans)
Claims management	Claims Expert reports (legal, medical)
IT	System access logs Identity/access/authorization data IT architecture blueprints and source code
Operations support	Facility access logs Provider/vendor costs

Assess Business Risks, Not Technology Risks   When we ask a CISO what risks he is worried about at the moment, he is likely to say, "Ten percent of our servers are running on an operating system that's about to go off support. Our network is almost entirely flat, so I can't slow down attackers once they get in. And did I mention our developers' buggy insecure code?" These are all incredibly important vulnerabilities that almost certainly need to be addressed, but in what order? And which applications with buggy, insecure code should be tackled first? It is impossible to answer this without having a sense of what information assets the application might use, who the attackers might be, and what business harm could result.

A business risk is the combination of:

- A valuable information asset (e.g., personal health information, a manufacturing process for a new product)
- An attacker (e.g., organized cyber-criminals, state-sponsored actor)
- A business impact (e.g., regulatory or legal exposure, industrial espionage)

A business risk for a health care provider therefore might be regulatory and legal exposure as a result of cyber-criminals stealing patient medical data. For a technology provider, it might be the loss of competitive advantage after a state-sponsored attacker steals a manufacturing process and sells it to a competitor.

Companies find it much easier to think about impact and likelihood in terms of business risks than for technology risks or vulnerabilities. Perhaps more importantly, senior executives find business risks to be a tangible way to engage on cybersecurity.

Proactively Engage Senior Leaders

Prioritizing business risks and information assets means answering some strategic questions: How would customers react if a company allowed attackers to steal their personal data? How much would a foreign competitor benefit from access to a product's underlying IP (and how would that affect the product's growth and margin expectations)? How would regulators react to a public breach? Addressing questions such as these requires a fact-based, detailed discussion between the cybersecurity team and senior business managers with each group seeing the other as equals.

Start with a Hypothesis   When CISOs ask senior business leaders what cybersecurity risks worry them, they seldom receive deep, thoughtful answers based on underlying business drivers. More commonly, the answers are along the lines of "I hadn't really thought about that" or "Customer information is most important, I guess." Answers like these highlight why the cybersecurity team cannot just listen and record the business perspective—it must develop its own hypotheses and engage business leaders as peers.

Use Value Chain and Risk Classification   A business value chain identifies each step in important processes. In insurance, for example, these would be origination, underwriting, servicing, and claims. For each step, a classification of business risks reveals important questions to ask:

- Are there data associated with this step in the value chain that would cause reputational damage if publically exposed?
- What IP does this step use that might be valuable to competitors?
- What sensitive business information could be disclosed about this step?
- What are the opportunities for cyber-fraud?
- What is the potential for business disruption or data corruption?
- What regulatory actions could occur?

This exercise helps the cybersecurity team develop a first view on what business risks and information assets it needs to raise with business leaders. It also helps ensure that important issues are not missed in the process. Figure 3.1 shows how this mapping clearly flags the priority risks.

Ground Discussions in Underlying Business Drivers   The question of which risks to which information assets matter most has to be based on underlying business drivers such as scale, share, growth, and competitive position.

For example, one manufacturing company struggled to differentiate the risk of IP being compromised for different products until it started to look at these products' revenues, margin, and growth. For the first cut, business managers suggested taking a product life-cycle view. Some of the potentially most valuable IP was for new products

FIGURE 3.1 **Rank Types of Risk across the Value Chain to Help Engage Business Leaders**

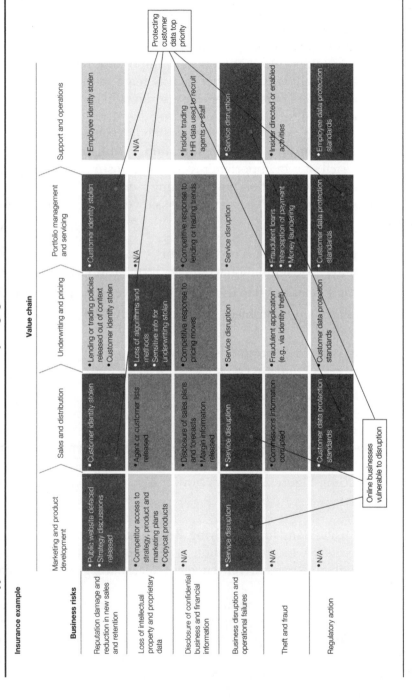

Insurance example

Value chain

Business risks	Marketing and product development	Sales and distribution	Underwriting and pricing	Portfolio management and servicing	Support and operations
Reputation damage and reduction in new sales and retention	• Public website defaced • Strategy discussions released	• Customer identity stolen	• Lending or trading policies released out of context • Customer identity stolen	• Customer identity stolen	• Employee identity stolen
Loss of intellectual property and proprietary data	• Competitor access to strategy, product and marketing plans • Copycat products	• Agent or customer lists released	• Loss of algorithms and methods • Sensitive info for underwriting stolen	• N/A	• N/A
Disclosure of confidential business and financial information	• N/A	• Disclosure of sales plans and forecasts • Margin information released	• Competitive response to pricing moves	• Competitive response to lending or trading trends	• Insider trading • HR data used to recruit agents or staff
Business disruption and operational failures	• Service disruption	• Service disruption	• Service disruption	• Service disruption	• Service disruption
Theft and fraud	• N/A	• Commissions information corrupted	• Fraudulent application (e.g., via identity theft)	• Fraudulent loans • Interception of payment • Money laundering	• Insider directed or enabled activities
Regulatory action	• N/A	• Customer data protection standards	• Customer data protection standards	• Customer data protection standards	• Employee data protection standards

Protecting customer data top priority

Online businesses vulnerable to disruption

that had yet to catch on in the market. This led to a discussion about which product value propositions most depended on IP. Ultimately, the cybersecurity team developed a perspective on which IP was most valuable to the company in terms of growth and margins over the coming years.

Taking a similar business perspective also helped a financial institution clarify the value of its pricing information. Many of its businesses said that their pricing information and databases were highly proprietary and that they worried about employees taking copies when they left to work for competitors. However, the markets for some financial products are very liquid, with highly transparent market prices. Other markets are less liquid and prices vary quite a lot. The less liquid the market, the more valuable the pricing data is as an information asset and the greater priority it needs.

Remember that the Enemy Gets a Vote   Any discussion of business risks has to include a perspective on whether there is a credible attacker with the capabilities and motivation to compromise and exploit an information asset. If a company has a valuable piece of IP that it has invested hundreds of millions of dollars developing, then this is clearly a valuable information asset, but that does not necessarily mean that there is a large business risk associated with it. The cybersecurity team has to talk to business managers to find out whether executives at traditional competitors would be willing to commission a cyber-attack to steal the IP and risk exposure and prosecution to pick up a few points of market share. A competitor from another country might be more aggressive if it were less likely to be prosecuted, but cybersecurity teams and business managers must then consider whether it would have the expertise to take advantage of the IP within a reasonable time frame?

Use Pragmatic and Transparent Decision-Making Criteria   Nobody has yet developed a robust, usable, generally applicable model for the expected economic impact of different types of cyber-attacks. However, that does not mean companies should make cybersecurity investment and policy decisions based purely on subjective inputs.

A scorecard-based approach provides a workable mix of feasibility and rigor. For any given business risk, the *impact* can be scored in terms of the company's reputation, competitive position, economic losses, and regulatory impact. For example, a financial impact of less than $100 million might be considered low impact; between $100 million and $1 billion medium impact, and anything more than $1 billion high impact. From a reputational standpoint, a breach likely to be reported only in trade publications would be low impact, but one that might reach the front page of regional or national newspapers would be high impact. In terms of regulation, a low-impact event might result in regulatory inquiries but no findings, a medium impact event may have findings but a clear path to remediation, while a high-impact event would be one with a substantial negative impact on a company's relationship with the regulator.

Alongside impact, cybersecurity teams can score the *likelihood* of an attack as low, medium, or high in terms of:

- User exposure: Number and type of users who have access to the system (e.g., internal users only, suppliers, customers, semi-public, public).
- System exposure: Number and type of systems on which an information asset sits or passes through.
- Vulnerability: Quality and extent of existing controls.
- Attacker: Value to potential attackers and the capabilities of likely attackers.

Using these criteria, companies can stratify risks according to expected impact (Figure 3.2). Done well, this can have a transformational impact. Broad alignment on the most important business risks can shape every cybersecurity decision, from how to structure the organization to where to deploy resources and which technologies to invest in. Even more directly, more stringent controls can be put in place to protect the most important information assets where the business risk is considered critical.

Perform Deep Dives for "Long-Tail" Risks

Stratifying business risks by impact and likelihood is hugely beneficial and allows companies to make practical decisions about policies and controls. However, some business risks are so severe that they require special consideration, in part because there may be little to no historical data or any experience at all from which to evaluate the impact of such an event.

FIGURE 3.2 **Plotting Risk Likelihood against Impact Helps Drive Decisions about Cybersecurity Investments**

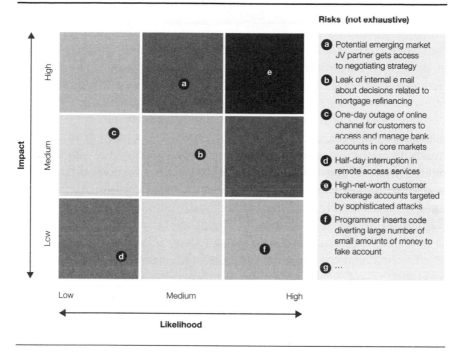

Risks (not exhaustive)

a Potential emerging market JV partner gets access to negotiating strategy

b Leak of internal e mail about decisions related to mortgage refinancing

c One-day outage of online channel for customers to access and manage bank accounts in core markets

d Half-day interruption in remote access services

e High-net-worth customer brokerage accounts targeted by sophisticated attacks

f Programmer inserts code diverting large number of small amounts of money to fake account

g ...

In these cases, full event scenario analysis can help companies understand the investments required to prevent or mitigate such an attack. It may even be a regulatory requirement, for example, to determine the necessary capital reserve levels for a bank.

Event scenario analysis is the process of identifying, understanding, and evaluating a company's exposure to and ability to respond to extremely large or serious events that could plausibly occur given the nature of the organization's activities. These events are typically low in frequency or probability but high in severity.

The company must first define the high-level story it is investigating. For a bank, the story might be that a political hacktivist group, perhaps with ties to an unfriendly foreign government, is trying to disrupt and corrupt trading operations in order to inflict economic damage to the broader economy.

The bank must then define types of impact. The simple direct impact of the proprietary trading desk being out of the market can be measured in dollars per minute multiplied by the number of minutes the system is down. However, the longer the bank is out, the more the market becomes aware of the situation and starts to trade against the bank and its positions. So the relationship between direct cost and time is not linear. Then there are potential legal implications for corporate client trading, and possibly goodwill compensation to pay as well as direct compensation to manage reputational impact. If the attacker manages to alter data about who made what trade, additional forms of exposure appear.

Next, the bank must put some numbers against these effects. The team needs to decide the extent to which losses grow over time, how much its trading positions move against the bank, what other channels customers have for their assets, how long the breach will be open, and what level of fines they can expect (fines vary enormously but tend to be driven by the number of customers affected and the expected impact on each customer). The output is a consensus estimate of the potential impact of the risk scenario in dollars.

The final stage is to launch a process that creates specific business, technology, and security recommendations that can mitigate the potential economic loss.

PROVIDE DIFFERENTIATED PROTECTION FOR THE MOST IMPORTANT ASSETS

Knowing which business risks are most pressing and which information assets are most important is good but yields only conceptual benefits. Real protective power comes from moving beyond a one-size-fits-all cybersecurity model and systematically applying a more rigorous combination of controls to protect a company's most important information assets. This represents a significant change in capabilities for most cybersecurity organizations, and introducing multifactor authentication or encryption at rest for some assets but not all increases complexity. Even organizations that have already applied some more rigorous controls rarely do so in a consistent, systematic way that is aligned with a company's most critical business risks. Getting this right requires a new level of coordination across business, IT, and cybersecurity.

There are four elements to effective differentiated protection: layering more rigorous controls on top of basic security measures, mapping the priority assets to systems, using the full range of controls and grouping them into tiers, and evaluating how different controls work together to minimize the impact on users.

Selectively Layer Enhanced Controls on Top of a Baseline Level of Security

Differentiated protection for a company's most important information assets supplements, rather than replaces, an effective baseline of protection that spans the entire environment. Firewalls, web filtering tools, and intrusion detection systems have to keep out inappropriate traffic and protect all information assets. Identity and access management (I&AM) capabilities have to prevent unauthorized users from accessing the corporate network. The security operations center must monitor the environment for anomalous events that could indicate an attack. All these capabilities have to be in place before a company thinks about differentiated protection.

While many aspects of cybersecurity are highly dependent on an individual company's mix of businesses, information assets, and technology strategies, baseline levels of protection are more standardized. Benchmarking basic controls against peers can therefore give a company a rough sense of whether it has the right level of protection.

For example, when a pharmaceutical company compared its basic level of security to its peers, it found troubling gaps. Dozens of sites lacked appropriate firewall protection; hundreds of applications ran outdated, insecure hardware; and many businesses lacked even the most rudimentary password discipline. As a foundation for putting differentiated protections in place, the company had to do the hard work of going site-by-site, business-by-business to close these gaps in its basic protection.

Map Information Assets to Technology Systems

No CISO, no matter how innovative, can apply technology controls directly to an information asset. Differentiated controls such as more stringent password requirements and encryption are applied to systems like applications and databases.

Cybersecurity teams therefore must work with application development teams and other IT stakeholders to identify all the systems that touch each priority information asset. This need not be complicated. The IT group in one bank (in particular, the head of infrastructure, the lead architect, the chief data officer, and the main application owners), filled in a simple matrix that had the bank's systems and applications on one axis and the assets on the other. This low-tech solution was both faster and more reliable than turning to the bank's official asset inventory, which was already out of date. Rather than try to update the inventory as part of this project, the CIO realized that 100 percent accuracy was likely to remain elusive and 95 percent would be good enough for the purposes of this exercise and to maintain the momentum of the whole project.

Life in IT would be simpler if each information asset could be associated with a single application or system. In reality, most companies find that some assets are distributed widely across IT systems—some managed internally and some owned by vendors. In particular, customer data are often stored in several systems, including a central customer database, a customer relationship management system, billing system, trouble ticketing system, and several data warehouses. They are also managed in smaller sets within a number of satellite systems and user devices that are difficult to map and even harder to keep track of.

As a result, cybersecurity teams need to focus on the systems that have the most significant concentrations of information assets. One bank found that 20 percent of its applications held more than 80 percent of the occurrences of its high-priority information assets. It therefore decided to focus its implementation of differentiated protections on that 20 percent of applications.

USE FULL RANGE OF CONTROLS BUT ORGANIZE INTO TIERS

Even savvy technology executives may instinctively believe that differentiated protection means tighter password controls and more extensive encryption. Naturally, it does, but there is a much broader set of options available. Cybersecurity teams should consider the full gamut of options (Table 3.2), which will help them defend priority information assets against a wider range of sophisticated attacks.

At another institution, the senior IT leadership team proudly pointed out that it had a "fit for purpose" control strategy; it had figured out the appropriate mix of controls based on the sensitivity of the data associated with the application. When prodded, the team acknowledged that, for the most part, individual application owners made decisions about what "fit for purpose" meant and that the approach had introduced a fair bit of complexity into the environment. It

TABLE 3.2 **Differentiated Controls Span Business Processes, IT, and Cybersecurity**

Type of Control	Area	Examples of Differentiated Controls
Business process	Access management	More stringent requirements for authentication and authorization More frequent access rights reviews
	Data management	Accelerated purging
	Vendor management	More thorough vendor assessments More stringent requirements built into contracts Limitations on data that can be shared with vendors More frequent audits of vendor compliance
	People management	Secure paths through core processes Targeted surveillance of insiders Targeted training
	Human resources	Enhanced background checks and monitoring
Broader IT	Document management	Mandatory use of document management systems Digital rights management (DRM) for files containing priority information assets
	Application security	More extensive security reviews for application development projects More frequent vulnerability scanning and penetration testing
	Client security	Expanded use of desktop virtualization
	System security	More frequent security patching
	Network security	Use of higher-security network segments
Cybersecurity	Identity management	Multifactor authentication More rigorous password policies
	Data protection	Encryption in motion Encryption at rest
	Data loss protection (DLP)	DLP rules and file tagging targeted at priority information assets
	Perimeter security	More restrictive firewall rules
	Incident response	More rapid escalations
	End-point security	Transition from blacklist to whitelist model

also meant developers and system administrators had to do considerable research into any application before updating it to make sure they would not break something in the security model.

Assuming they are not using the same types of controls everywhere, companies often find a fair degree of randomness when they look at the controls deployed across applications. One industrial company found almost no correlation in its applications between stringency of controls and sensitivity of data housed.

Most controls can be applied at varying degrees for a tighter or more relaxed security level. Authentication controls at their most basic, for example, are simple user name and password forms. At the next level, multifactor authentication introduces the "something you know" (password) and "something you have" (e.g., a token) concept. At the most complex level, they use "out-of-band authentication," where passwords might be valid for only one session and users need to authenticate using an additional entirely separate channel, such as sending a text message (Figure 3.3). The tighter the controls, the greater the impact on the user experience, as well as on the setup and operating cost and maintenance. Cybersecurity teams can help business leaders understand gradated controls in a simple framework that lays out three or four levels of rigor for each type of control.

Evaluate Different Combinations of Controls

CISOs and their teams should create combinations of controls that mutually reinforce each other. Combining controls also allows cybersecurity teams to analyze the aggregate security and convenience impact for each application or class of applications. Different mixes of controls can provide the same level of end protection but the impact on user experience, cost, and maintenance can vary widely.

Tighter, more restrictive controls can definitely reduce risk but there are trade-offs. Stringent I&AM controls can limit insiders'

FIGURE 3.3 **The Same Controls Can Be Retuned for Optimal Protection**

	Level 1 (Strict)	Level 2 (Stricter)	Level 3 (Strictest)
Authentication	• Single-factor authentication - Username & password - Challenge questions	• Multifactor authentication ("something you know and something you have")	• Out-of-band authentication (e.g., text messages) • One-time session passwords
Identity management	• Role-based permissions for user access and admin rights	• Access logging • Object-level access policies on data	• Auto deprovisioning linked to HR systems
End-user protection	• No DLP or DRM	• DLP in place and enforced based on standard libraries	• DRM tagging of files/data and DLP custom tags and signatures
Data protection	• No encryption for data	• Data encrypted when in motion (both within the network and to external systems) and at endpoints	• Data always encrypted
...			

(including contractors) access to priority assets but also absorb significant administrative and user time; data loss protection (DLP) tools can reduce the ease of stealing valuable data, even after penetration, but every additional layer of protection adds friction to everyday logins. More thorough logging and detailed network inspections make it easier to spot a breach, but real-time monitoring can absorb system resources and slow applications. Even more thorough background checks before hiring can meaningfully reduce the risk, yet are costly and slow down the recruitment process. It is therefore imperative to get the right set of controls that deliver protection where needed without damaging the user experience too greatly.

One manufacturing company needed to increase protection for applications that held valuable IP. The security team held a series of workshops with business leaders and application owners about which types of controls they thought would be ideal for their underlying assets and how they might work together at different layers. The group agreed that given the highly sophisticated attacks they faced, simply installing better firewalls was unlikely to be sufficient.

Instead, it looked at a range of controls that would work together and help the company understand and prevent certain types of losses with relatively minimal impact on employees. It increased the use of multifactor authentication and the level of log retention and analysis, and introduced new digital loss prevention software. Employees already had access cards, so using them for digital authentication meant it did not need to distribute and manage a new set of security devices. Most visitors were on-site more than once, so the effort spent registering their computers would pay off over time. The team even addressed the patching regime (the process of fixing known vulnerabilities), which had essentially been arbitrary but now moved to a risk-based approach that was welcomed by the business. Evaluating these trade-offs early and paying particular attention to the end-user experience made it much easier for users to accept the new protection model.

DELIVERING TARGETED PROTECTION OF PRIORITY ASSETS IN PRACTICE

Aligning on the prioritized information assets and business risks and using them to put in place a differentiated set of protections may sound conceptually simple, but it requires real effort and discipline.

Imagine that in light of a minor breach, a medium-sized auto parts supplier realized that it had to understand its cybersecurity risks better and started to orient its protections around them. Based on the levers we have described, it could use a three-phase process: preparation and data collection, asset and risk assessment, and defining and implementing differentiated protection.

Phase 1: Prepare and Collect Data

The CIO and CISO would use this preparatory phase to get all the preconditions for success in place. The CIO would make sure she had senior management's backing for the effort and would then spend time with the executives responsible for each of the major business units and enabling functions, explaining the effort, getting input on whom to interview, and asking for points of contact in each area.

In a larger company, the CIO and CISO would probably start with one or two pilot businesses so they could show progress and refine their approach before moving on to the next one. In this case, however, the CIO and CISO agree that the company's moderate size and straightforward business model allow them to cover the entire business in one wave.

The CIO would also convene a working group of herself, the CISO, and representatives from each of the business product lines and functions to ensure access to data, check progress and review analyses, and deliver recommendations. Meanwhile, the CISO would work with each of the business unit CIOs and their teams to assemble all the data required, especially catalogs of applications in each business, along with any available information on supported processes, risk classifications, and technical configurations.

Phase 2: Assess Risks and Assets

The CISO and his team would use this phase to capture and prioritize the full set of information assets and business risks.

Step 1: Identify Assets across the Value Chain   The group's first task would be to discover what the critical information assets were. The team would look at the business processes that occurred along the value chain—product development, marketing, sales, and after-sales service—and develop a set of hypotheses about the important information assets at each step. At that point, the CISO would sit down with senior executives from each business area and rather than just ask what keeps them awake at night, he would test the hypotheses his team developed and use them to get a better understanding of which information assets might be most important.

For example, the head of sales might explain that the company gets incredibly sensitive forecasts and specifications from its auto manufacturer customers as part of the process of bidding to supply a subsystem for a new vehicle under development. If the manufacturer believed that such information could be compromised, the impact on the supplier would be devastating from a business standpoint. By contrast, sales forecasts related to models already in production might be much less sensitive because competitors could already estimate this from existing publicly available projections.

Step 2: Analyze the Risk and Prioritize the Assets   The company would now have a good list of important information assets but would not yet understand the risks. Based on their discussions with business leaders, the CISO and his team would ask themselves about the impact on the confidentiality, integrity, and availability of each information asset should it be compromised. They would score each combination of compromise and asset in terms of competitive disadvantage, customer impact, reputation impact, fraud loss, regulatory exposure, and legal exposure. This would take into account issues such as the underlying product economics and competitive pressures (e.g., the impact of losing IP underpinning a marginal product might be quite low).

They would now take the attackers' perspective and try to understand who would benefit from compromising important information assets and whether those who would benefit have both the incentives and the capabilities to act on any information they extract. A traditional competitor would benefit from understanding a company's manufacturing processes, but executives might not be willing to risk destroying their careers and forfeiting their freedom to take advantage of that information now. A new market entrant might be less worried about prosecution but might lack the expertise to take advantage of sophisticated manufacturing techniques. The CISO and his team would also know that not all attackers are external and that insiders often take sensitive product and pricing information with them when they start jobs at competitors, which they also need to factor into their decisions. The team would complement this attackers' view with high-level perspectives on the current level of exposure. For each asset, they would ask how many people have access to it and whether it has already been targeted for more restrictive controls.

Based on this analysis and a structured set of criteria, the team would now have a prioritized list of information assets. These would likely be stratified into a few categories, for example, crown jewels, restricted data, baseline data, and public data. It could also synthesize a prioritized list of business risks stratified by business impact and likelihood. Both would be invaluable in communicating its findings with business leaders. The team would conduct one or more workshops with its partners in the business to test its findings and reprioritize the risks and information assets as required.

Phase 3: Define and Implement Differentiated Protections

Step 1: Evaluate Current Level of Protection   The team cannot apply protections directly to information assets, so they would need to determine which systems house priority information assets and what protections were already in place on those systems.

First, it would define three or four levels of rigor for each major type of control—I&AM, data protection, DLP and digital rights management (DRM), application security, infrastructure security, network security, vendor management, and others. Then it could launch a survey of application development managers asking them to map the priority information assets to systems and to score each system in terms of the rigor of each type of control applied.

This would enable the CISO to answer several important questions, such as:

- How rigorous is each type of control (e.g., do most applications use single-factor or dual-factor authentication?)
- Are the most important information assets protected by more rigorous controls?
- What drives choices about controls—do some parts of IT use more rigorous controls, regardless of whether the system houses the most sensitive information assets?

Step 2: Define Future Protection Levels   Four levels of rigor, even for only six control areas, would result in more than 4,000 distinct control combinations. Therefore, the CISO and his team would need to create bundles of controls.

If they wanted to be very simple, they would define one bundle of controls for the crown jewels—the company's most important information assets—one for restricted information, one that would be for the baseline, and one for public or less important data. However, they might decide to have variations of each bundle for structured data (e.g., customer order history and other information found in databases) and unstructured data (e.g., proposals and other data stored in documents). In defining the bundles, the CISO would use existing technologies and capabilities as much as possible but might conclude that some new capabilities are required (e.g., out-of-band authentication). In all cases, the team would assess the effect of each bundle of controls to ensure that any additional impact on user experience made sense in the context of reducing the risk, and then validate this using focus groups, demos, and other techniques.

Finally, the team would use the classification of information assets and the mapping of information assets to systems to define which bundle of controls needs to be applied to which system.

Step 3: Transition to Implementation   Once the CISO has identified the optimum levels of protection, his team needs to assess what they and others have to do to put these controls in place. In some cases, the change will be a simple policy or process change—vendors that handle a certain type of information asset will need a more thorough assessment; passwords for applications that house a certain type of information asset will need to be changed more frequently.

In many cases, the company will already have the underlying security capability, but a system might need to be adjusted to adopt it. The company might have tools that support multifactor authentication, for example, but many systems may need enhancing so they can use the company's latest I&AM platform.

There may be cases where the CISO needs to launch or accelerate the introduction of a new technology or capability. For example, the company might need to implement DRM in order to control who can access documents with data such as product road maps and manufacturing specifications. Therefore, the team would build all the implementation activities into its work plan for the coming year and those of many of its partner organizations.

Finally, the CISO and his team would make sure that they had a documented methodology for prioritizing information assets and putting differentiated controls in place so they could easily repeat the process, reflecting changing business conditions, an evolving attacker environment, and new innovations in defense mechanisms.

• • •

Any company, no matter its size or complexity, will have many different types of information assets and face a bewildering array of business risks. No company can protect everything effectively, especially not at a reasonable cost and with acceptable levels of impact to the business.

Therefore, companies have to prioritize. They need to understand their most important information assets and the business risks they face, and they need to use this insight to put more rigorous business process, broader IT, and cybersecurity controls in place to protect these critical information assets.

This cannot be a one-time event. Business models change, creating new types of information assets. Attackers improve, creating new risks and heightening old ones, while state-of-the-art cybersecurity also evolves, creating new options for differentiated controls.

Companies therefore need to put in place repeatable, structured processes that allow the cybersecurity team to engage with the business leaders to discover important information assets, prioritize business risks, and align on differentiated protection. Moreover, these processes should be a critical input to the development of annual cybersecurity budgets and plans.

Input and validation from senior business leaders will be essential. The CEO must set overall expectations about risk appetite, while business unit executives must provide input on identifying information assets, assessing business risks, and validating trade-offs between the risk, cost, and business impact of the different protection options.

4

Do Business in a
Digitally Resilient Way

Most organizations think of cybersecurity as a technology responsibility, and it is—at least to an extent. Cybersecurity addresses the risks of information in digital form, and many of the ways companies can protect their information assets are indeed technological, in the form of either security controls or improvements to the broader IT environment.

However, achieving digital resilience requires far more than technology change. As noted in Chapter 3, changes in business processes can have an enormous impact in protecting important information assets. Two levers in particular point the way in driving change far outside the IT organization: integrate cybersecurity into enterprise-wide risk management and governance processes, and enlist frontline personnel to protect the information assets they use.

The first lever requires getting managers in almost every business function to take protecting information assets into account as they make an endless set of decisions that affect their company's exposure to cyber-attackers.

Most, if not all, of these decisions involve trade-offs between accepting some form of business risk and furthering a business objective. Companies cannot force executives to take cybersecurity into consideration with rules and mandates; they have to help them both understand the risk implications of the actions they take and also accept their responsibilities as stewards of the company's information assets—just as they are of the company's financial assets.

The second lever pushes the change in mind-set from executives down to frontline users. Every day, every employee who has access to a desktop, laptop, or mobile device has the potential to increase the company's risk by clicking on the wrong link or e-mailing a file to the wrong place. Companies need to help frontline users understand the value of the information assets they touch every day and put in place a set of mechanisms that encourage and enable them to interact with the company's technology environment in a responsible way.

To do business in a digitally resilient way, executives across a range of functions will have to provide ongoing support for some fairly extensive behavioral changes among managers and frontline employees.

BUILD DIGITAL RESILIENCE INTO ALL BUSINESS PROCESSES

Cybersecurity is intertwined with almost all of an institution's major business processes. As we saw when we looked at prioritizing information assets, every step in most business processes uses sensitive data, and every cybersecurity policy places some constraint on how functions such as marketing, operations, and product development undertake core business processes.

Unfortunately, collaboration between the cybersecurity team and many business functions is weaker than it could be. Business managers see cybersecurity as the CISO's or chief information officer's (CIO's) responsibility, and cybersecurity managers have been developed and promoted on the basis of their technical expertise rather than for their ability to understand and connect with business leaders. As a result, business decisions involving product design, customer interactions, and vendor contracts can expose important information assets to unnecessary risks, and cybersecurity policies can diminish customer experiences or hurt a company's negotiating position with vendors.

To achieve digital resilience, companies must create much tighter connections between the cybersecurity team and each critical business function—product development, marketing and sales, supply chain, corporate affairs, HR, and risk management—in order to make the appropriate trade-offs between protecting information assets and operating key business processes efficiently and effectively.

Product Development and Management

Bank customers and hospital patients quite reasonably expect that their personal data will be protected from theft. They also expect to be able to access their information online with relative ease and without cumbersome security controls. Hospitals themselves expect to be able to integrate connected medical devices into their operating rooms without creating new security vulnerabilities or forcing medical staff to learn complex protocols. However, these tensions will increase as ever more companies create richer digital connections with customers and the Internet of Things builds an even wider variety of network-connected products.

No wonder, then, that cybersecurity issues increasingly feature in products' value propositions. Both retail and commercial buyers think about security when making purchasing decisions, especially in sensitive industries, and negative press coverage of a breach can hurt the reputation of not just the producer but also the vendor, re-seller, or adviser. The customer experience, of course, also features highly in buying decisions, and cybersecurity has enormous implications for that experience. The ability to incorporate both security and a positive user experience at the product development stage will increasingly give companies a competitive advantage, but it requires a change in mind-set from both the product development and cyber-security teams.

Understand Customers' Preferences and the Impact on Customer Experience   Companies must understand how customers value data privacy, convenience, and the trade-offs between them. They are likely to react badly if their data are at risk because there is no protection against cyber-attacks, but if all the controls that companies install to manage that risk make their experience too painful, then they are also likely to turn their backs on the product. Standard customer research methods such as polling and focus groups can help companies understand the pain thresholds, and the business can observe customer behavior and reactions to different pilot approaches and combinations of controls, in the same way they would test the options of other non-security features.

An online brokerage measures how long it takes, on average, for customers to complete a variety of tasks on its sites and then assesses new security controls on the basis of the additional time, in seconds, that they will add to important customer activities. These additional delays become part of the design and launch decision, with the business actively engaged in making trade-offs between customer experience and the security risk. If a particular control significantly hurts the customer experience, then the business can either decide to spend more to optimize the control and improve the experience, delay or cancel the feature that requires the new control, or sign off and accept the additional residual risk. Banks have learned that customers can view additional authentication layers as a positive. One institution tried to improve the customer experience by replacing its personal identification number (PIN) requirement with device recognition, so that the PIN was not necessary if a customer logged in from his or her own laptop or smartphone. Rather than appreciating the convenience, customers in fact contacted the bank because they were concerned that the security was broken. The bank reinstituted the PIN process.

In business-to-business (B2B) markets, less formal methods can be effective—it can often be enough to talk to customers on a regular basis. In some companies, informal connections with customers' IT security teams can provide invaluable insight into those customers' rising expectations that data will be protected and how those expectations will be translated into terms and conditions or decision criteria in upcoming requests for proposals (RFPs).

Incorporate Cybersecurity Costs and Considerations into Commercial Business Cases New products often create new types of data or new ways of interacting with customers, which in turn create new vulnerabilities. The cybersecurity team therefore needs to make sure it has input before a new product is launched—and ideally even earlier in the product development cycle to avoid wasted or misdirected resources. The head of cybersecurity at a financial information services provider simply refuses to approve the business case for a new product until he fully understands the costs of securing the information assets associated with that product. He is fortunate to have that much power—not every CISO has an effective veto—but senior managers at the company understand the importance of security for their service offerings, and so they strongly support this requirement. They do not want to encounter unpleasant and costly surprises down the road, and they want to make sure their customers have full confidence in their security.

Build Security into the Product Development Process   The overlap between IT and product has steadily increased, even in many more traditional industries. Medical diagnostic tools are, in essence, network-connected computing devices that bear a health care logo rather than a technology provider's logo on the box. New cars can have as many as 100 million lines of code.[1] Even thermostats now connect to the Internet. Unfortunately, organizational structures have not moved as quickly as product characteristics. In many companies, there are organizational silos that divide information technologists working on new business products from their counterparts in the core IT organization. As a result, it is much harder to get an end-to-end view on risks and vulnerabilities across network-connected products and the IT applications used to manage and support them. This increases the risk that attackers could steal customers' sensitive information or sabotage their business processes.

Companies need to increase their level of focus on the cybersecurity aspects of business products and build links between product engineering and corporate cybersecurity teams. One industrial company named a group-wide head of product security, ensured that each business had a head of product security, and created forums for the product and corporate cybersecurity teams to collaborate on assessing risks and prioritizing remediation actions.

Align Product Development Processes with IP Risks   Product development and R&D teams typically handle some of a company's most sensitive intellectual property—information that could be devastatingly damaging if it fell into the wrong hands. However, imposing too many restrictions on the flow of information can slow innovations and add months to development efforts, which can also be damaging if a competitor is able to launch first. In some sectors, such as outsourced contract electronics manufacturing, we have seen companies adjust their business processes and risk appetite based on a better understanding of their exposure. A company with short product life cycles accepted the risk associated with a freer flow of information in order to maintain its rapid time to market, while another company, whose product life cycles were measured in years rather than months, decided to tighten its security controls to reduce the risk of sensitive plans

---

[1] Zax, David, "Many Cars Have a Hundred Million Lines of Code," *MIT Technology Review*, December 3, 2012. www.technologyreview.com/view/508231/many-cars-have-a-hundred-million-lines-of-code.

leaking to competitors. The end results are different, but what the two have in common is a cross-functional approach to balancing the competing demands for speed, collaboration, and security.

Sales and Marketing

The relationship between cybersecurity and the sales and marketing function can be simpler for consumer industries than for B2B. Companies are reluctant to be too vocal about privacy and security issues in consumer-facing marketing campaigns, partly because it raises customers' awareness of a risk that most companies would prefer they forget. Moreover, it can be a risk in itself to have too high a public profile on this topic because hackers may see it as throwing down the gauntlet and make an extra effort to break in. However, since customers are increasingly concerned, collaboration between cybersecurity and consumer marketing is essential. For example, we have seen mass affluent customers begin asking their wealth management providers about the security of their financial data, which means the CISO has to be able to give the financial advisers the right messages that explain and emphasize the precautions in place without making unrealistic promises.

By contrast, suppliers and customers in B2B markets are having increasingly frank discussions about data security as part of the sales and contracting processes. Customers want to know how their data will be protected, what risks they bear, and what guarantees their suppliers will provide. As a result, companies are starting to act both to protect themselves and to prevent cybersecurity issues from becoming a competitive disadvantage. Of course, this works both ways: business customers are focusing on security as a key buying factor when selecting suppliers, and suppliers are responding by increasing both their investments in security and their emphasis on what measures they can provide.

Support the Sales Force in Explaining Security Capabilities   Typically, only the CISO's team can effectively explain the diligence with which a company will protect its customers' data. The topic and language are too arcane for nonexperts to readily grasp, but this means companies must ensure that the cybersecurity team has the time to offer this support to the sales force. The team is also likely to need coaching in order to be effective in front of demanding customers—cybersecurity experts are not hired for their sales skills after all. We know of one health insurance CISO who spends a third of his time on just such sales activities, and naturally this has had a positive effect on the overall relationship between security and the business. The CISO was helping the sales force win business, not standing in the way. Companies must also ensure that the sales teams understand the importance of turning to the CISO's team when they need to address customer demands and concerns.

Create Explicit Guidelines for What Guarantees Can Be Included in Contracts   As concerns about cybersecurity grow, business customers are making ever more forceful demands of their suppliers in terms of liability, inspection rights, or procedures for handling sensitive data. One insurer received a request from one of its largest customers to purge almost all of its data after underwriting. This was an impossible request to fulfill as regulators in some jurisdictions required the insurer to retain the data for many years. Suppliers need to understand therefore exactly what they are willing (and able) to promise in contracts before negotiations begin.

Many commercial contract negotiations get bogged down in discussions over unlimited liability. Customers want suppliers to accept unlimited financial responsibility for the economic implications of any breach it causes. Suppliers are naturally loath to agree. As the cybersecurity market matures, some suppliers are considering buying insurance to cover this risk—up to whatever amount the customer requires—and then explicitly incorporating the premium into the deal structure, passing the cost on to their customer (we discuss the nascent cyber-risk insurance market later in the book). This simplifies the responsibility for any breach, and clarifies the direct economic impact for both the supplier and customer.

Companies must invest in educating the sales teams, procurement groups, and legal staff on all these security and compliance requirements, and determine when they should reach out for more specialized support.

Operations

From order capture to customer servicing and billing, operational processes necessarily touch some of the most sensitive customer information a company has. In addition, as more network-connected devices make their way into the core service delivery process, they create the possibility for disruption and sabotage via cyber-attack. Digital resilience will require companies to design core business processes with cybersecurity considerations in mind and make sure mechanisms are in place to manage the risks of network-connected devices.

Redesign Core Processes to Minimize Business Risks   One of the most powerful business process changes for reducing cybersecurity risk is purging sensitive but nonessential information, and then segmenting interactions based on a thorough "need-to-know" analysis. A property and casualty insurer has adopted this mind-set and is splitting off those claims related to high-visibility litigation, so only the best-trained and most trusted claims agents will handle them. Although this means fewer agents are able to handle any claim that comes in, this reduced flexibility is balanced by the reduction in risk that comes from fewer people handling the most sensitive claims. In a similar vein, an aerospace manufacturer segments its design teams based on the sensitivity of the engineering work so that collaboration is uninhibited within the team, but any valuable intellectual property (IP) is prevented from spreading across the whole department. Some of the "flattening" that organizations have been pursuing for operational efficiencies may have inadvertently introduced greater exposure, in a similar way that creating single, flat network environments may increase risk compared to a network that is segmented based on the sensitivity of information.

In short, an organization needs to ensure that its IT systems provide users (internal or external) with only the minimum information necessary for them to perform their work. Any more access puts the organization and its information assets at unnecessary risk. For example, a vendor that provides a specific IT service should be able to accomplish its duties with virtual private network access to a segmented part of the network, or a virtual desktop interface, rather than being given the considerably riskier system-level administrative credentials and controls. The vendor management team will not typically manage the detail of vendor access controls directly, but they should actively be involved in this discussion with the IT security team.

Give Cybersecurity Team the Mandate to Set Network-Connected Device Policies   Many sectors are seeing a dramatic increase in operational devices that are connected to corporate networks but are managed outside the IT organization (e.g., medical instruments, production line control equipment, sensors). These devices are computers in all but name, but security has not always been a priority for their developers, as they are often devices that have evolved in technological sophistication over time and therefore are not viewed as computing devices. For example, x-ray and other imaging machines have moved from analog devices using physical film to digital devices based on image files. Nor do the people managing them in the business always have the necessary experience or expertise to secure them without more specialized support. As a result, companies have to rely on the cybersecurity team, which means the team needs both the insight to understand and the authority to assess these devices and put the required defense mechanisms in place. This can go beyond just setting requirements and includes incorporating security specialists into the design and engineering teams for products, just as they would be incorporated into a secure development process for new software.

Procurement

Products and services from third-party suppliers can contain a broad range of cybersecurity vulnerabilities: vendors could treat a customer's sensitive information with less care than required by regulations, new connected devices can create pathways for attackers to infiltrate a corporate network, and so on. Leading companies adopt several tactics to improve the cybersecurity team's relationship with operational and procurement functions in order to address these issues. Although, as we mentioned earlier, buyers increasingly include security as a buying consideration, it is still rare for companies to incorporate cyber-risk fully into the sourcing process. Achieving digital resilience means taking cybersecurity into consideration in vendor strategy, RFP construction, vendor/bid diligence, final negotiations, and ongoing performance management, including (where necessary) termination.

Apply a Risk-Based Approach to Vendor Assessments   Institutions still have tens of thousands of vendors (one hospital network we know has almost 30,000!). Without effective vendor governance, it is all but impossible to understand which vendors have what type of sensitive information. Risks to information assets should therefore join more traditional objectives, such as cost, quality, and operational control, as important drivers for vendor rationalization—it cannot be an afterthought.

However, even after introducing effective vendor management, large organizations will still have thousands of vendors: there are simply too many different types of specialized services, too many locations that require local providers, and too many different types of software for the number to be much lower. A thorough cybersecurity assessment of each vendor would grind contracting to a halt, so sophisticated companies are determining the depth of analysis needed based on the types of information transmitted, the size of the relationship, and the nature of the connection with the company's technology environment. Just as companies need to prioritize controls and apply different levels of protection to different information assets, they also need to create appropriate vendor management processes that match the level of exposure. One way to create efficiency for smaller vendors with lower risk is for security and procurement teams to collaborate across companies to standardize assessment questionnaires so that vendors will not have to respond to a slightly different set of questions from each new customer. Major partners such as outsourced manufacturing or infrastructure providers can start from standardized reviews and audits, but the value of the relationship and the extent of exposure would require a more hands-on and customized approach.

The organization should outline which function is ultimately responsible for managing vendors (e.g., a central risk function vs. the contracting function), the amount of access and risk that is acceptable to expose through third-party vendors, and the governance processes in place to review and manage this vendor. Critically, these policies should also outline steps to terminate noncompliant vendor contracts; one CISO deplored his company's vendor management function, complaining that he had never seen a vendor contract terminated despite poor information security risk management.

Keep Some Negotiation Power When Defining Vendor Security Requirements There is an intrinsic tension between the security requirements a company imposes on vendors and the negotiating power it has over them. The more stringent the requirements, the fewer vendors will qualify and the less room to maneuver the company has. One manufacturing company had nine vendors respond to an RFP, only to see that set winnowed down to just two qualifying candidates based on compliance with security requirements. To avoid situations like this, procurement and security teams will have to assess RFP security requirements in the context of common market practice, aggregate business risks, and overall contract economics. Expecting vendors to comply with a customized set of standards will tend to narrow the participation pool, while grounding requirements in industry or international standards enables more vendors to participate without needing to meet bespoke requirements.

At the same time, vendor contracts, service-level agreements (SLAs), master service agreements, and any other documentation should be consistent with established vendor management policies. Ideally, these would lay out acceptable and required behavior for vendors' management of information security risks, including regular security reviews and tests, employee background checks, data encryption and storage, and disclosure of breaches. SLAs should outline minimum performance levels for services that could be affected by security issues, for example, network availability for online Software as a Service applications.

Reduce the Number of Vendors   One large company, because of historic governance challenges, had nearly 2,000 IT vendors (of whom 700 had truly sensitive data) and about 25,000 vendors overall. Even the most disciplined organization cannot exercise oversight fully across that many vendors. Cost and service quality will typically be the primary driver for vendor consolidation, but the CISO must add his or her voice to the discussion, pointing out that a proliferation of vendors vastly complicates the task of tracking who touches what data and ensuring that vendors comply with company security policies.

Human Resources

Cybersecurity and HR managers need to collaborate to strike the right balance between protecting the employee and protecting the corporation's information assets. In today's increasingly digitized world, frontline employees handle sensitive IP and customer data that could hurt the company to the tune of hundreds of millions of dollars in terms of competitive position or legal liability.

Ensure Transparency for Employee Responsibilities   As more companies allow employees to bring their own devices to work, the line between corporate and personal technology can blur, and employee responsibilities about how they can use smartphones and even laptops can become ambiguous: What software may they install on their own device? Which devices can they connect to corporate networks? To make sure employees see security policies as fair, both cybersecurity and HR teams need to make sure that employees understand what is expected of them and the potential consequences for failing to meet those expectations. We address communication and other mechanisms to create and reinforce this culture in greater depth later in the chapter.

Align Insider Analytics with Corporate Culture   Increasingly, cybersecurity teams use sophisticated analytics to identify employees who may be exfiltrating sensitive information. These analytics can go far beyond IT-usage information. Precursors of insider risk such as financial difficulties, performance reviews, and plans to leave one's job are often visible to the HR team but invisible to the cybersecurity team. Balancing employee privacy with protecting information assets will depend on corporate risk tolerance and culture and the regulatory environment of the relevant jurisdiction. Already, some defense contractors and hedge funds ask new employees to sign their life away in terms of the level of surveillance they agree to. In other sectors, this level of intrusiveness would be hard to imagine or even illegal. Regulatory requirements need serious consideration and appropriate legal review. The availability of extensive online employee surveillance is uncertain in some U.S. states and many parts of Europe. As a result, it will be up to senior management to determine how deeply these analytics should delve, and cybersecurity and HR will both need to help them strike the right balance, as informed by legal and compliance professionals.

Risk Management and Compliance

Cybersecurity naturally overlaps with risk management and compliance. Cyber-attacks are, after all, just another form of operational risk, and cybersecurity can be viewed as a risk management function, with the enterprise risk management team as the natural partner of the cybersecurity team. Moreover, in a growing number of sectors, regulators exercise some degree of oversight over cybersecurity decision making. This means cybersecurity teams must work with risk management and compliance managers to emphasize the risk management aspects of cybersecurity and make sure compliance does not dominate cybersecurity policies and investments. This may seem basic, but the fact is that few organizations treat cybersecurity as an operational risk domain and manage it accordingly.

The relationship between risk management and cybersecurity can vary by industry. In the financial sector or in industries that depend heavily on intellectual property (e.g., pharmaceuticals, defense), risk management programs are usually well established. These are generally effective at managing traditional market and liquidity risks but rarely systematically address information and cybersecurity risks; the solution is usually to apply classic risk management approaches to a new domain.

In the middle of the pack, critical infrastructure sectors and regulated industries such as energy and health care are beginning to improve their risk management capabilities beyond business continuity planning and disaster recovery. They very rarely cover cybersecurity risks, but the cybersecurity risk program can plug in to what is typically an increasingly mature enterprise risk function. Finally, less mature industries, such as retail, may not have a formalized risk management group at all. For these industries, the cybersecurity group may be the pioneering risk function and will need to drive the establishment of core risk processes and methods.

Collaborate with Compliance Functions to Understand Regulators' True Bottom Line   In our interviews, we heard again and again that compliance is not security, that regulators tend to apply a checklist mentality, and that regulatory standards may be years out of date compared with the latest defense mechanisms. Managing the regulatory environment will always be challenging, but there are ways cybersecurity and compliance teams can cooperate to mitigate the impact. Given regulators' affinity for process, providing them with transparency into mechanisms for assessing risks, prioritizing investments, and setting policies can increase their comfort level; avoiding margins placed on top of regulatory guidance may be even more important. One financial institution accepted significant inefficiencies in some of its core IT processes in order to comply with— its managers believed—regulatory mandates. The compliance team helped determine that in fact many of the most inefficient constraints stemmed from perceptions of what the regulators wanted, rather than actual regulatory guidance.

Integrate Cybersecurity into Enterprise-wide Risk Management Processes   After the challenges companies have faced since the economic crisis, boards and senior management teams focus on enterprise risks today in a way that would have been hard to imagine even 10 years ago. They depend on risk management functions to drive risk assessment, mitigation, and reporting across many different types of risks: liquidity, credit, regulatory, legal, and operational. But if cybersecurity is seen as the responsibility of IT and separate from other types of enterprise risk, then boards and senior management will not give it the required attention, support, and funding. Some of the companies that have most effectively engaged boards and senior management teams on cybersecurity have integrated the language and frameworks they use to assess, prioritize, and report on cybersecurity risks into the way they talk about their types of operational risk. For example, some banks view information security risk as a top-level risk event category, even though it is not one of the seven top-level categories defined by the international banking recommendations set out in the Basel II Capital Accord. For a life insurer, information security risk was moved from the purview of the board's IT committee to the enterprise risk committee, where it shared the agenda with market and other business risks.

ENLIST FRONTLINE PERSONNEL TO PROTECT THE ASSETS THEY USE

A few years ago, a senior database administrator (DBA) at a financial institution received an e-mail about his upcoming college reunion. It addressed him by name, made reference to specific reunion events, and included a link to a site with more information.

Naturally, given his warm feelings for his alma mater, the DBA clicked on the link. Unfortunately, the e-mail was a spear-phishing attack.[2] By studying the DBA's posts on social media, cyber-criminals had been able to craft a credible message that sounded like it came from his former classmates.

When he clicked on the link, it took him to a site that installed malware on his computer. The malware was a keystroke logger that captured his passwords for several databases that contained sensitive customer information. The company avoided the acute embarrassment of having customer data disclosed only by agreeing to pay a substantial ransom to the cyber-criminals.

---

[2] A phishing attack is an e-mail sent to a user with the intention of getting him or her to click on a link that will install malware on the user's device. A spear-phishing attack is an e-mail targeted at a very specific user who has access to especially sensitive information.

At a financial institution, an account manager made a simple mistake. She was sending a customer a summary of his account over the past year, but in her haste to reply she attached the wrong file, which had personal information for tens of thousands of customers. Fortunately for her, the customer alerted her to the mistake, and the ramifications were limited to a few awkward phone calls.

Such unintentional behavior that puts companies at risk is common to the point of pervasiveness. Who hasn't attached the wrong file to an e-mail, or sent the right file to the wrong recipient? Third-party researchers can unthinkingly put sensitive IP on untrusted, external cloud storage services. Call center agents might jot their multiple passwords down on notes stuck on the side of their monitor. IT managers might let access rights to important computer systems grow obsolete. The list of unintended security breaches employees can trigger is endless.

As a result, companies that need to protect their information assets in ever more challenging environments have two choices. They can place more and more stringent controls on the technologies that employees need to do their job—reducing productivity and sometimes encouraging extravagantly insecure workarounds—and keep turning up the volume on security communications and trainings. Or they can move beyond security awareness and rules-upon-rules to put in place programs that will change frontline behavior. In the quest for digital resilience, organizations need to bring employees on board with cybersecurity's requirements and make them allies rather than vulnerabilities.

Many CIOs, CISOs, and chief technology officers are skeptical of the potential value of trying to change people's behavior. We asked them what the impact would be of helping frontline personnel understand the value of information assets. Less than half believed it would have a significant impact or be a game changer. In fact, technology executives rated this the least important of the seven levers we asked them about. However, their skepticism did not come from a belief that user behavior was unimportant but from a concern that it could not be changed: they took it as a constraint and not an opportunity.

Again and again, we heard technology executives talk about how hard it was to change frontline behavior. As one CISO said, "Cybersecurity awareness training doesn't work. You've got sexual harassment training, regulatory compliance training, and a host of other things. We're just one more thing that people don't really pay attention to."

Fortunately, there are a few institutions that have made more progress in this area than others by doing four things differently. They segment users according to the type of information they use; they draw on existing safety and quality efforts; they use design thinking to create tools and services that make it easy for users to do the right thing; and they bring all this together by applying a broad set of mutually reinforcing actions.

Segment Users Based on the Information They Need

Different types of users see vastly different types of information with varying levels of sensitivity. Manufacturing R&D teams handle incredibly sensitive proprietary IP but never touch customer data. Insurance call center agents may see health or financial information for high-profile customers but see little other data of interest to outsiders. Senior managers in all sectors have access to the company's most critical business strategies, and sometimes it seems that administrative assistants have access to everything.

Different groups also have different attitudes toward handling sensitive information and toward risk in general. Attorneys in the general counsel's office will (or at least should) have an inclination toward protecting confidential information that dates back to their time at law school. Traders, however, may be so focused on keeping up with the market that they never think about protecting valuable information. Researchers, especially those from an academic background, may believe that "information wants to be free," which can terrify their bosses when multimillion-dollar IP is at stake.

Given such disparities in the types of information different users see and in their attitude to protecting that information, it should be clear that generic approaches that treat all users in the same way will have only minimal impact on digital resilience. They struggle to cut through the noise and to avoid becoming one more thing the head office has to ask everyone to worry about on top of their "real" jobs. Standard approaches are not effective in motivating people to take action.

Companies that have made progress in this area start by understanding how users in different groups and locations think about protecting information. For example, bosses at one bank learned that employees in the capital markets business were often unaware of cybersecurity risks at all, while managers in the bank's retail business felt that they had the issue well in hand. Knowing each group's concerns, inclinations, and blind spots enabled the bank to craft a far more challenging and ultimately effective set of messages. The group that lacked basic awareness received communications that focused on explaining that cybersecurity was a material risk, shared examples of damages other companies had suffered, and introduced initial measures they could take to address the risk. The communications to the more advanced group touched on the business case only briefly, and instead focused on next-level mitigation measures and how to interpret information security reporting. Each group got the training and support appropriate to their place along the journey to maturity.

Leading companies also draw a direct line between those assets that they have identified as critical in the prioritization process and the users that have access to them. Again, this allows for a far more targeted and effective set of interventions. If managers and employees understand what information is particularly sensitive and needs to be kept within a smaller group of people, then they can manage it so that access rights are a backup technology control measure and not the first line of defense against excessive distribution.

An oil exploration company identified its negotiation strategy for extraction rights as its most sensitive information asset. Executives joked that a note instructing an executive to "Bid $1.5 billion for a property, but don't go above $2.5 billion," could be a "billion dollar e-mail" if it wound up in the wrong hands. After some investigation, the company determined that only 500 people out of tens of thousands of employees had any reason to access this information (of whom, interestingly, nearly half were assistants and other support personnel). Based on this insight, it developed a "top 500" program focused on helping this tiny fraction of their employees understand how to better protect information about negotiations. This better-trained group was then given greater access rights to sensitive information within corporate applications and collaboration platforms. Given that this assessment provided only a snapshot, the company also created a regular process to review membership in the group and a mechanism to move people in or out based on their changing need to know.

Draw on Existing Safety and Quality Efforts

Organizational change is undoubtedly hard, yet many companies have proven that it can be done in a systematic and sustained way. We have seen some companies, particularly in natural resources, manufacturing, and life sciences industries, make dramatic improvements in safety and quality.[3] Not only are cybersecurity teams learning from their peers in manufacturing safety, they are also building on quality and safety programs themselves to create change. This has multiple benefits. It emphasizes to employees that cybersecurity is a core business practice rather than a separate "IT issue." The approach underscores the importance of changing behavior, given the level of senior management backing provided to quality and safety programs. It is also more efficient, using organizational infrastructure such as reporting, governance, and incentive systems that already exist.

At many natural resources, petroleum, and process manufacturing companies, every meeting starts with a "safety share" in which participants offer a suggestion on how to avoid accidents. At one petroleum company, managers at headquarters increasingly include a cybersecurity-related safety share, because they believe that just as it is important to protect people and physical assets, it is also important to protect information assets. This process draws a connection to something that is already a core value and part of the culture, rather than setting up information security as a new or separate issue. Each time someone talks about how they found a sensitive document lying on a conference table and disposed of it appropriately and followed up with the document owner, it reinforces behavior just as it would if they shared a story about cleaning up spilled liquid that could have led to someone falling down the stairs, or about ending a conference call when a participant mentions they are driving a car.

Employ "Design Thinking" to Make It Easy to Do the Right Thing

Employees at many, probably most, companies will tell you that information security is a pain in the neck. It forces them and often their customers to remember complicated passwords. It prevents them from using many of the online tools that they use on their personal devices. It even causes laptops to take forever to boot up, forcing them to arrive for work five minutes earlier. No wonder so many technology executives told us that cybersecurity had a material, negative impact on frontline productivity at their companies.

---

[3] Centers for Disease Control and Prevention, "Achievements in Public Health, 1900–1999: Improvements in Workplace Safety—United States, 1900–1999," *Morbidity and Mortality Weekly Report* 48(22), June 11, 1999, pp. 461–469.

Some of this inconvenience is unavoidable. Not every device, service, or application is secure enough for enterprise environments; and there is simply no way to protect sensitive information without robust authentication—the company can't protect your data unless it knows that it's you trying to access it.

Much of the inconvenience, however, stems from poor design. While Apple, Google, Amazon, and others make a virtue of creating delightful user experiences for their external customers, many other companies have deprioritized the user experience for both staff and customers alike. This is true of security measures perhaps more than anything else. One company started requiring employees to use more complex passwords, but didn't explain specifically what types of passwords would pass muster (What length? Mixed case? Special characters?), leaving users to sort it out by tiresome trial and error. Naturally, this increases the chance that employees view security as an obstacle to getting things done rather than as an ally in protecting the business, and in turn it reduces the chance that employees view themselves as allies.

A bank started requiring customers to answer one of a set of "challenge questions" before accessing its online payment service. A customer would typically know that her first car had been a Camaro, but would she remember whether she had entered "Chevrolet Camaro," "Chevy Camaro," "Camaro," or some other variant of the car's name years before when she set up the account? Needless to say, this change resulted in a flood of angry calls into the customer service center. Although employees access systems on a much more regular basis and build "muscle memory" around the challenge questions, the lesson still applies: the way real users interact with the system has to be taken into account.

Design thinking requires technologists (and others) to reframe their work in order to give the end user a positive experience, even if delighting them remains a tall order when it comes to multifactor authentication protocols. Tim Brown, CEO of design firm IDEO, said that design thinking means "innovation is powered by a thorough understanding, through direct observation, of what people want and need in their lives and what they like or dislike about the way particular products are made, packaged, marketed, sold, and supported."[4]

[4]Brown, Tim, "Design Thinking," *Harvard Business Review*, June 2008. http://hbr.org/2008/06/design-thinking/.

Cybersecurity tools must, first and foremost, ensure that the company's assets are protected. However, it is possible to achieve this while also creating a positive user experience—assuming there are direct trade-offs between the two ideas leads to missed opportunities for improving both security and the experience simultaneously. One nonprofit organization found that employees were using a wide variety of public file-sharing services to store sensitive deal-related documents even though these services' security capabilities had never been validated. To counteract this, the organization introduced its own secure application. Employees felt that IT was responding to their needs to collaborate, while the organization was able to increase compliance rates substantially.

A narrow focus on compliance can, of course, mean the organization is blinkered to some of the real risks. A bank was in full compliance with device security standards and passed every audit, yet all these controls were slowing boot-up time so much that staff were using unsecured personal laptops and relying on web-based e-mail when traveling. These real risks were not being captured on any security audit but still needed addressing. The bank therefore launched a concerted effort to reduce laptop boot time when it upgraded staff laptop operating systems, and startup time is now tracked as a top-level performance metric for cybersecurity. The onus was on the IT department to make compliance as easy as possible, even if the compliance standard is slightly lower.

Apply a Broad Set of Mutually Reinforcing Actions

Experience, backed up by our interviews, suggests that getting people to change their behavior to make a company more secure is hard. Indeed, McKinsey research shows that organizational change is difficult in almost any context and that even when there is a burst of attention given to a topic, it is easy for an organization to slip back into old habits over time.[5]

We often see institutions opt for a cybersecurity awareness program when what they need is a full-blown change management program. They put up posters urging employees to "think before you

---

[5] Keller, Scott and Price, Colin Price, "Organizational health: The ultimate competitive advantage," *McKinsey Quarterly*, June 2011. www.mckinsey.com/insights/organization/organizational_health_the_ultimate_competitive_advantage.

FIGURE 4.1 **Hardwire the Mind-Set and Behavior Changes into the Organization**

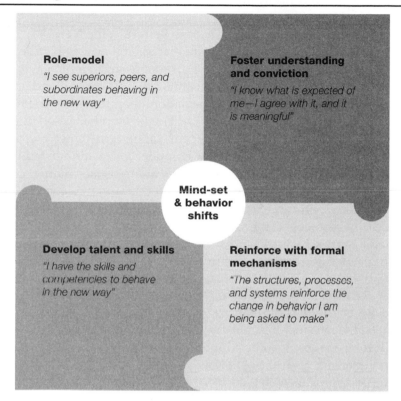

click" and conduct simulated phishing campaigns to determine which employees will follow a link included in a clearly fraudulent e-mail. This is not enough given the dramatic impact that user behavior has on overall security. Awareness programs are, at best, only one element in changing user behavior. Communication is just one element of creating a shift in mind-sets and behaviors.

Instead, companies need to sustain change, which requires four mutually reinforcing conditions to be in place (Figure 4.1).

People Need Both Understanding and Conviction   People need to know what is expected of them and, crucially, agree that it is meaningful and worthwhile. This means engaging them on why cybersecurity matters and on the critical role each of them plays in protecting the organization's assets. This is often where organizations are relatively strong—the other three mechanisms typically need the most improvement

People Need the Skills to Enable Them to Behave in the New Way   For example, businesses need to integrate material on how to handle documents securely into broader training sessions and employee induction days. Part of this can be basic technology controls—if encryption is required for certain kinds of information, then that software needs to be provided (or, better, automated). The other pillar is moving beyond "what and why" types of communication into "how" conversations that use concrete examples to help employees understand and incorporate new behaviors. For example, an aerospace manufacturer added a security management module so that an engineer joining a team working with an external manufacturing partner would learn the security protocols at the same time she learned about collaboration methods, team schedules, and so forth: security was part of the core training, not a secondary measure.

Senior Leaders Need to Role-Model the New Behaviors   Role-modeling is essential to reinforce any requirements or behaviors and to embed the idea that this matters and is taken seriously by the leadership. If someone sees their boss (and their boss's boss) treating customer information with respect, not talking about sensitive data in public, and voicing disapproval when security protocols are not followed, then they know to take the rules seriously. On the flip side, if their boss mocks the rules or shows active resentment and a "game the system" mentality, then the official and implicit messages come into conflict and many employees will align with their supervisor's viewpoint.

Leaders Need to Reinforce the New Behaviors through More Formal Mechanisms Such as Incentives   There are usually clear penalties for egregious misuse of corporate technology resources, but incentives that reward good cybersecurity behavior are scarce. Many companies test to see how many employees respond to a phishing attack. Very few, however, track phishing hit rates over time and build them into senior management scorecards and incentives. At the most basic level, security performance can be incorporated into performance indicators and dialogues. For greater effect, security behaviors can be included as part of compensation and performance reviews, together with other types of risk. People tend to prioritize what is measured and what is rewarded (and punished), so if cyber-security is not included, then that sends an implicit message about the priority of security needs.

• • •

Policies and processes in every part of the business—product de-velopment, marketing, sales, operations, procurement, HR, risk, and compliance—affect a company's ability to protect its information assets. Decisions and actions on the part of frontline users in every part of the business matter just as much.

Making the right changes to policies, processes, and user behav-ior requires a high degree of collaboration between the cybersecurity team and the rest of the business. Too passive a posture on the part of the cybersecurity team would mean forgoing important levers in protecting information assets, but a series of mandates formulated without business input could have a dramatically negative impact on productivity.

Naturally, cybersecurity teams will have to develop a nuanced understanding of business practices and processes to develop realis-tic options for changes that will protect information assets. However, they cannot do this alone. They require active support from a range of senior managers: business unit executives have to help synchro-nize customer offerings, product designs, and end-to-end processes with security requirements; procurement managers have to help strike the right balance between vendor security requirements and contract economics; compliance managers have to help align regulatory man-dates with the company's risk reduction priorities; and managers in every function need to communicate and reinforce the expectation that frontline users will understand the value of and protect the infor-mation assets they use every day.

5

Modernize IT
to Secure IT

As a leading CISO in the health care industry points out, "Everybody likes to pretend that security is this extra, expensive thing you need to do. Much of what's important for good security is just good IT."

Unfortunately, as companies established cybersecurity as a control function, they layered security on top of existing technology environments along a number of dimensions. They installed not only antivirus software but also a range of security tools on the client device. They surrounded the network with not only firewalls, but also technologies such as intrusion detection and web filtering in order to repel attackers. They even created governance to encourage new applications to be developed in accordance with secure architecture standards.

Much of this activity was utterly necessary and dramatically improved companies' levels of security. It did not, however, address two critical underlying problems: first, companies were designing their technology environment around everything *but* security, making them intrinsically insecure, and second, a set of trends was making technology environments themselves less rather than more secure (Figure 5.1).

Just as manufacturers have found that it's impossible to "inspect quality in," IT organizations increasingly find it hard to "layer security on top." This approach does not address gaping vulnerabilities in the environment, and at least some of the bandages applied to compensate for an intrinsically insecure environment have downgraded user experiences and reduced the ability of IT organizations to innovate.

FIGURE 5.1   **Broad Set of Components in Technology Environment Contribute to Vulnerabilities**

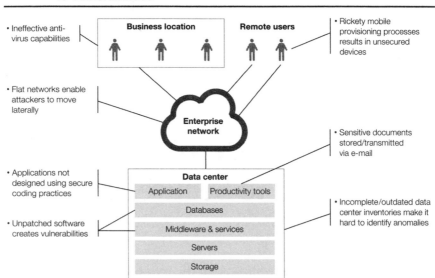

Many high-impact mechanisms for protecting critical information assets involve changes in the broader application, data center, network, or end-user client environments—areas that cybersecurity teams can influence even if they are controlled by application development and infrastructure managers.

SIX WAYS TO EMBED CYBERSECURITY INTO THE IT ENVIRONMENT

The most forward-thinking companies have recognized the challenge of trying to add security in a piecemeal fashion and are starting to act aggressively to put security at the very heart of their technology environments. Specifically, they are accelerating their adoption of private clouds, using public cloud services selectively, building security into applications from day one, virtualizing end-user devices, implementing software-defined networking, and reducing the use of e-mail as a substitute for document management.

Naturally, many of these improvements depend on the success of major initiatives led from outside the security team and implemented for a combination of reasons, including efficiency and flexibility even more than for their security benefits.

1. Accelerate Migration to the Private Cloud

Motivated by lower costs and vastly improved flexibility, most large companies are putting in place standardized, shared, virtualized, and highly automated environments to host their business applications. These are—with all their various permutations—known in practice as the "private cloud."[1] As early as 2011, nearly 85 percent of large companies we interviewed said that cloud computing was one of their top innovation priorities, and 70 percent said that they were either planning or had launched a private cloud program.[2] Those that are further along have often found that they could migrate 60 percent of their workload[3] to these much more capable and cheaper private cloud environments (Figure 5.2).

FIGURE 5.2 **Private Cloud Hosting Will Become Dominant Model by 2019**

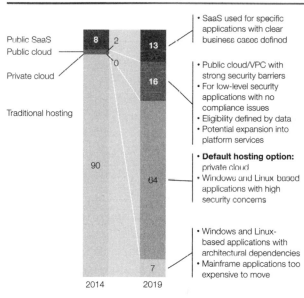

[1] A private cloud is a highly standardized, highly automated, highly virtualized hosting environment, with dynamic provisioning and capacity management that is dedicated to a particular enterprise without cotenancy or shared network access.

[2] Andersson, Henrik, James Kaplan, and Brent Smolinski, "Capturing Value from IT Infrastructure Innovation," *McKinsey & Company Insights & Publications*, October 2012. www.mckinsey.com/insights/business_technology/capturing_value_from_it_infrastructure_innovation.

[3] For the purposes of this book, a *workload* is an application or a component of an application running on either a physical or virtual server.

However, despite the uptake, there remains a debate over the benefits of hosting applications in a private cloud environment. Some cybersecurity professionals argue that the drivers of the improvements in efficiency and flexibility can also make it easier for attackers to exploit the corporate network. Virtualization—the co-locating of multiple images of operating systems on a single physical server—allows malware to spread from workload to workload. Standardization simplifies a data center environment, which makes life easier for IT teams but also creates a security monoculture that is easier for attackers to understand. Similarly, while automation helps system administrators enormously in managing the data center environment, it can be tremendously destructive if an attacker gains access to a system administrator's login credentials.

Some of the most sophisticated IT organizations have exactly the reverse point of view. They have concluded that traditional data center environments are entirely unsustainable and that well-designed private cloud programs provide the opportunity to improve cost, flexibility, and security simultaneously.

Data Center Complexity Breeds Insecurity   Senior (or at least long-tenured) technology executives will still remember the days when data center environments were pretty simple. As recently as the early 1990s, even a top-tier investment bank might have run all of its business applications on a few mainframes, a few dozen minicomputers, and perhaps a hundred or so Unix servers. The pace and extent of change since then has been dizzying.

Now that same investment bank might still have only a few mainframes (each with orders of magnitude more processing capacity), but it would also have more than 100,000 operating system (OS) images running on tens of thousands of physical servers. More importantly, the bank's IT team would have to support a dozen or more OS versions (some of which could be years out of date) and thousands of configurations that require heavy manual activity to maintain. This complexity makes it harder and harder for large enterprises to protect their data center environments.

Two issues are especially vexing. First, keeping track of complex, rapidly changing data center environments makes it hard for security teams to identify the anomalies that would indicate a server has been compromised. When a company adds hundreds of server images and performs thousands of configuration changes per month, it is virtually impossible to maintain an up-to-date view of what the data center environment should look like. Without this overview, it is much harder for the security operations team to notice that a server is transmitting data externally when it shouldn't be, for example.

The second issue is that data center environments make it hard to install security patches for commercial software in a timely fashion, which exposes servers to new types of attacks. Developers constantly find new vulnerabilities in the software tools (operating systems, databases, middleware, utilities, and business applications) that run in corporate data centers and issue software updates known as patches that are designed to address these vulnerabilities.

Security expert Bruce Schneier described 2014's Heartbleed bug as "catastrophic" because it enabled hackers to coax sensitive information such as passwords from OpenSSL, an open source tool designed to enable encrypted communications between users and Internet applications.[4] OpenSSL made a patch available at almost exactly the same time that it announced the vulnerability.[5] This is normal; vendors usually make patches available to fix 80 percent of vulnerabilities the same day they disclose them,[6] but there can be a (sometimes lengthy) delay between the patch being released and a company applying it to protect itself. Nor do all patches solve the problem. For example, many initial patches for the Shellshock Bash vulnerability in 2014 proved ineffective, leaving many companies exposed.[7]

Patching is a constant responsibility for data center teams. For example, Microsoft releases security patches for its products on the second Tuesday of the month, every month, although for more urgent security situations, it releases patches as needed.[8] Staying on top of this is incredibly hard. In one organization, there were weekly patching meetings to determine what needed doing next. It was impossible to automate this process, as there was no complete software inventory, which is not unusual. OS patches tend to be applied and distributed very quickly,

---

[4] Schneier, Bruce, "Heartbleed," *Schneier on Security*, April 9th, 2014. https://www.schneier .com/blog/archives/2014/04/heartbleed.html.

[5] Grubb, Ben, "Heartbleed Disclosure Timeline: Who Knew What and When," *Sydney Morning Herald*, April 15, 2014. www.smh.com.au/it-pro/security-it/heartbleed-disclosure-timeline-who-knew-what-and-when-20140415-zqurk.html.

[6] Secunia, *"The Secunia Vulnerability Review, 2014."* http://secunia.com/vulnerability-review/time_to_patch.html.

[7] Bell, Lee, "Ineffective Shellshock Fix Means Hackers Are Still Exploiting Vulnerability," *The Inquirer*, September 29, 2014. www.theinquirer.net/inquirer/news/2372788/ineffective-bash-shellshock-bug-fix-means-hackers-are-still-exploiting-the-vulnerability.

[8] Microsoft, "Windows Update FAQ." www.microsoft.com/security/pc-security/updates-faq.aspx.

while those for less business-critical software might be addressed only quarterly. Of course, these are the very applications through which hackers can gain access. Some extremely vulnerable applications had dozens of variant versions sitting on end-users' devices and servers, either because they were deemed noncritical or simply because the previous version had not been uninstalled after an update.

IT executives tell us that staffing limitations mean teams have neither the time nor resources to test patches to see whether they can be applied safely. Fragile architectures make developers reluctant to install any patches to some applications except in the most extreme circumstances. One bank had issues with the stability of some of its systems, so it started including the servers in a list of "do not touch" assets, which were not to be patched until they could be made stable. Within two years, this do-not-touch list included hundreds of server images, with thousands of patches not applied. An internal audit uncovered this, and a special one-off remediation program had to be instigated to make everything secure.

Distributing patches across the company is both time consuming and labor intensive, and some patches get constantly pushed down the priority list. The number of changes required mean there may not be enough maintenance windows—typically, time slots in the early morning hours or weekends—to install all the patches. Vendors can also stop supporting outdated technologies, meaning security patches may no longer be available for software that companies use. In 2014, Microsoft stopped support for Windows XP (first released in 2001), yet more than 90 percent of ATMs were still running on the outdated operating system.[9]

Faced with all these challenges, it is easy to see how organizations fall behind when it comes to patching. One insurance company found that more than half of its servers were at least three generations behind in terms of security patches, making it vulnerable to any attacks that capitalized on a more recently discovered vulnerability. It is not alone—the large majority of breaches can be traced to failure to patch a relatively small number of software packages.[10]

Private Cloud May Make It Possible to Secure the Data Center   Can private cloud be a mechanism for reducing vulnerabilities and

[9] Bass, Dina, "Six Things You Need to Know About ATMs and the Windows XP-ocalypse," *Bloomberg*, April 4, 2014. www.bloomberg.com/news/2014-04-03/six-things-you-need-to-know-about-atms-and-the-windows-xp-ocalypse.html.
[10] Grimes, Roger A., "Stop 80 Percent of Malicious Attacks Now," *InfoWorld*, July 23, 2013. www.infoworld.com/article/2611443/security/stop-80-percent-of-malicious-attacks-now.html.

improving security? If companies design and manage their private cloud program appropriately, they can substantially reduce exposures in their data center environment. The highly standardized hardware and software associated with the cloud should drive down the use of outdated technology over time, while patching becomes part of the standard offering and does not require manual effort for every server. Automated provisioning[11] reduces the risk of configuration mistakes that create vulnerabilities and also makes it much easier to enforce policies on which applications can run on the same server or on a certain part of the network. The combination of automated provisioning and standardization creates far more transparency into the environment, which makes it easier to spot the anomalies that can signify a breach.

Some companies are even using private cloud technologies to facilitate sophisticated security analytics. One health care company is using the virtualization tool[12] in its private cloud environment to inspect network traffic in real time and flag workloads when they act in unexpected ways that may be indicative of a malware infection.

However, concerns that moving to private cloud could introduce new types of vulnerabilities are not spurious. Private cloud programs require careful planning to build security in. For example, cutting-edge companies are configuring their environment to minimize the risk of an attacker jumping from one system to another once inside by requiring the virtualization tool to be run from read-only memory and placing limitations on how programs can give instructions to the virtualization tool. They are also separating some operational roles to limit the damage that a single malicious insider could do if he had access to management tools. Not only must the security team help design in security measures from the outset, security considerations must also play a much more important role in the business case for private cloud programs.

Obviously, migrating to a private cloud requires both a sizeable investment, and organizational change. As a result, many companies' private cloud programs stall, and executives are left underwhelmed by the speed and level of migration.

---

[11] Provisioning includes all the activities required to deploy a new or updated application, including the installation of the underlying physical server (if required), the creation of a virtual server (if required), and the connection to the enterprise network, as well as installation and configuration of all required software.

[12] Server virtualization divides a physical server into multiple logical servers, each with its own operating system, so that it can run multiple applications reliably at the same time.

The companies that have succeeded so far have distinguished themselves in four ways.

1. They *focus on alignment among executives* on the business case for private cloud, including the extent to which their company's security will improve by migrating workloads from outdated data center environments. One investment bank decided to implement the next version of its private cloud environment not because of the potential efficiencies that also came along but because of the additional security.

2. They *roll out functionality in stages*, so they can learn and build capabilities over time; in particular, they focus on creating an increasingly attractive developer experience with each release, so they create demand for the new platform.

3. They *build and automate new operations and support processes* for the cloud platform so that it does not replicate the inefficiencies of the legacy platform and can scale efficiently.

4. They *create a focused team* with top management support to specify, design, roll out, and operate the new platform so that it does not become an afterthought compared to existing environments.

2. Use the Public Cloud Selectively and Intentionally

A few years ago, account executives from a major public cloud provider called on the head of infrastructure at one of the world's largest banks. They made a compelling presentation about how much they had invested in their cloud platform and the richness of its capabilities. As the pitch concluded, the head of infrastructure complimented the account team but had just one question: "I have data that can't leave the United States. I have data that can't enter the United States. I have data that can't leave the European Union. I have data that can't leave Taiwan. If I used your service, how would I know all those things would be true?"

One of the account team replied, "That doesn't make any sense. Why would you want to run your business that way?"

To which the head of infrastructure said, "You seem like nice boys. Why don't you come back in a few years when you have this figured out."

It is for just these reasons that large enterprises have been reluctant to turn to public cloud services (especially infrastructure). They remain unconvinced that providers have figured out how to provide enterprise-grade compliance, resiliency, and security. Our survey results back this up. On average, companies are delaying the use of cloud computing by almost 18 months because of security concerns. In many interviews, we heard chief information officers (CIOs) and CISOs express concerns that malware could move laterally from another company's public cloud-hosted virtual servers to their own because they would both be running on the same underlying infrastructure.

Nevertheless, if companies put in place the mechanisms to channel the right workloads to the appropriate cloud services, then it is perfectly possible to make exciting capabilities available while continuing to protect important information assets.

Therefore, IT organizations cannot take an absolutist position against public cloud services. Given the resources that providers are investing in new capabilities and the attractive costs—especially during the price war that is being waged as we write—there will continue to be strong demand for these services. As a result, IT organizations that try to prevent their use may find themselves in a challenging position. From one direction, business partners will see them as being obstructive—grist to the mill for those who constantly perceive cybersecurity as blocking value creation. From the other direction, end users and even application developers will simply work around or ignore corporate policies given how easy public cloud services are to procure. If your users have credit cards, they have access to the public cloud, but without guidance they may select services with weaker security capabilities and use these services without the additional security controls that enterprises can apply.

An approach that protects an institution's important information assets while supporting innovation by providing access to public cloud services must take into account four factors:

1. *The sensitivity of information assets.* There are huge variations in the sensitivity of corporate data, as we discussed earlier in the book. Some workloads process incredibly sensitive customer information or intellectual property (IP). Others process important information, but disclosure would not have grave business consequences.[13] Ensuring that only those less

---

[13] Kaplan, James, Chris Rezek, and Kara Sprague, "Protecting Information in the Cloud," *McKinsey & Company Insights & Publications*, January 2013. www.mckinsey.com/insights/business_technology/protecting_information_in_the_cloud.

sensitive workloads are directed to the public cloud would ease the concerns of cybersecurity managers.

2. *The security capabilities of specific public cloud offerings.* There are also huge variations in the security models for public cloud offerings. At one end of the spectrum there are security practices that might be politely described as "consumer grade," while at the other end we see providers employing robust perimeter protection, encrypting data at rest, and placing strict controls on how and when operators can access their customers' data. Choosing the right vendor is therefore paramount.

3. *The security of comparable internal capabilities.* When the business asks cybersecurity teams about the security of public cloud offerings, the response has to be "compared to what?" There are many situations where a public cloud offering might be riskier than a service from the company's strategic data center but far more secure than a comparable service hosted by an internal regional IT organization that has been starved of investment for years.

4. *The possible enhancements of public cloud offerings.* Many start-ups are racing to develop the technology that will allow enterprises to use public cloud offerings securely by encrypting data transmitted to cloud providers or entire cloud sessions and allowing enterprises to retain the keys required for decryption.

A transportation company seeking to develop a cloud strategy identified all the workloads required to run its business and assessed each one in terms of critical requirements, including the sensitivity of data processed. It was then able to map each workload to a hosting model: traditional hosting, private cloud, Software as a Service (SaaS), or public cloud infrastructure (Figure 5.3). For workloads that could be hosted on SaaS or public cloud infrastructure, the company identified specific vendors that could at least match its own internal capabilities in terms of security and then examined ways to put additional software around these public offerings to enhance security further.

3. Build Security into Applications

Application security mattered less when employees accessed corporate applications from desks inside the company's buildings. Today, companies cannot control such a clear bricks-and-mortar perimeter,

FIGURE 5.3   **How to Assess Public Cloud Services versus Other Options**

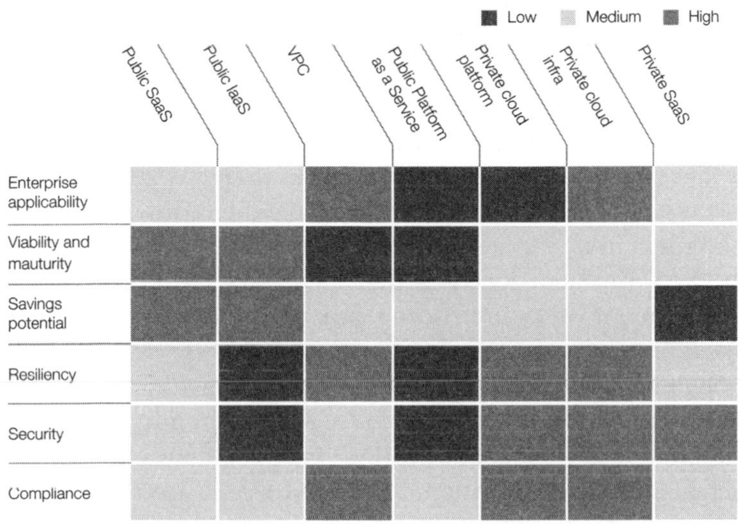

Legend: ■ Low   ▨ Medium   ■ High

	Public SaaS	Public IaaS	VPC	Public Platform as a Service	Private cloud platform	Private cloud infra	Private cloud	Private SaaS
Enterprise applicability	Medium	Medium	Low	High	High	Medium	Medium	Medium
Viability and maturity	Low	Medium	Low	Low	Medium	Medium	Medium	Medium
Savings potential	Low	Medium	Medium	Medium	Medium	Medium	Medium	Low
Resiliency	Medium	Low	Medium	Low	Low	Medium	Medium	Medium
Security	Medium	Low	Medium	Low	Low	Medium	Medium	Medium
Compliance	Medium	Medium	Low	Medium	Medium	Low	Medium	Medium

and highly functional applications are available to both customers and employees who expect to access such applications anytime, anywhere. The result is that hackers can use application-level attacks, gaining entry through the web browsers that provide a gateway into the application. For example, hackers were able to lift customer data from one bank because developers exposed sensitive information via the browser bar in the company's online banking applications.

To the layman—or the board member with no IT background—this sounds like a rudimentary error from the developer. The reality is that application developers do not understand how to write or test for secure code; most computer science courses do not require much information security training and what does exist tends to be a checkbox set of practices, rather than an immersive course that teaches the problem solving required for secure application development. Many development teams, for example, do not follow best practice and include libraries to scan for known code vulnerabilities or run them as part of their nightly build. Instead, security functionality tends to slip down the agenda as understaffed teams rush to deliver business functionality. Even intelligence agencies have asked for rigorous password capabilities to be deprioritized so that time could be spent improving an application's user interface.

On top of all this, many companies have weak identity and access management (I&AM) capabilities for validating which users can access which application. Applications may use home-brewed or out-of-date I&AM and a wide variety of different capabilities. This makes it even harder to enforce common password policies and requires users to remember a variety of passwords. One industrial company found that senior executives had to use as many as 20 different passwords; no surprise that some of them wrote them down in a notebook or saved them in files stored on their desktop.

The final problem for IT is that legacy applications can predate the development of secure coding practices. An insurance company reviewed its cybersecurity setup and found that it was doing a pretty good job of securing new applications, but the backlog of applications that could not be made secure cost-effectively ran into the thousands.

Although enhancing application-level security can be an even more challenging organizational change than addressing other technology issues such as networks or end-user devices, some companies have found effective practices that can help them improve their position:

- Incorporate instruction on secure coding practice and security problem solving into development training from day one; one financial institution devotes nearly 25 percent of developer training hours to security topics.
- Build a rich set of security tools and application program interfaces (APIs) (for code scanning, security monitoring, and I&AM) into the development environment. This helps minimize the extra time developers need to secure applications.
- Constantly challenge the application portfolio using penetration testing. One bank has a team of 50 security specialists who do nothing but try to break into its applications.
- Use the creation of agile teams as a forcing device for change, and make sure that security requirements are incorporated into agile methodologies.
- Perhaps most importantly, get serious about lean application development. Applying lean operations techniques to application development and maintenance can improve productivity by 20 to 35 percent, but it also reduces security vulnerabilities in application code by bringing all the stakeholders on board early,

stabilizing requirements, and putting quality first throughout the development and maintenance processes.[14]

4. Move to Near Pervasive End-User Virtualization

For all the creativity and resourcefulness of cyber-attackers, one common situation remains the starting point for many attacks. The attacker sends an employee a phishing e-mail and the employee clicks the link, which takes him to a website that installs malware on his device. The attacker is in.

Cybersecurity teams used to rely on antivirus software to protect desktops and laptops from malware, but two developments have reduced the effectiveness of that model. Advances in malware technology have meant more and more of it can slip past antivirus software, and as employees expect to work anywhere, companies have to manage new types of client devices with new types of security vulnerabilities, specifically mobiles and tablets. As a result, sophisticated institutions are finding they have to move to virtual end-user environments, where both traditional and mobile end-user devices simply display information and collect user input but store very little.

For some time, leading CISOs have said they continue to use antivirus software mostly for cosmetic purposes. Antivirus packages used to compare a piece of the software's executable file against a database of known malware to determine whether the software was safe. Now that cyber-attackers have developed malware that changes form over time, it is no longer effective to compare it against a blacklist. As a result, many CISOs say they continue to pay for antivirus tools mostly to appease regulators or just in case they happen to foil a simplistic attack that would not have been prevented otherwise. The debate over antivirus effectiveness came to an end when executives at Symantec, a leading developer of antivirus tools, announced the death of the antivirus model in the *Wall Street Journal*.[15]

[14] Kinder, Noah B., Vasantha Krishnakanthan, and Ranjit Tinaikar, "Applying Lean to Application Development and Maintenance," *McKinsey Quarterly*, May 2007. www.executiveson-demand.net/managementsourcing/images/stories/artigos_pdf/produtividade/Applying_lean_to_application_development_and_maintenance.pdf.

[15] Yadron, Danny, "Symantec Develops New Attack on Cyberhacking," *Wall Street Journal*, May 4, 2014. www.wsj.com/news/articles/SB10001424052702303417104579542140235850578.

Just as antivirus tools became less effective for desktops and laptops, the rise of enterprise mobility presented a whole new challenge. Back in 2009, nobody knew what a tablet was. Today, they are pervasive in executive suites and among mobile professionals. By 2017, enterprises will account for nearly 20 percent of the global tablet market of nearly 400 million units.[16]

Again and again, CISOs have expressed their nervousness about the immaturity and fragility of the software that connects smartphones and tablets to their corporate networks. Integrating mobile device management, virtual private networks (VPNs), and other software from multiple vendors creates seams and crevices that attackers can exploit. In addition, the complex manual processes required to use mobile devices in an enterprise environment increases the likelihood that security policies will not be implemented correctly on any given device, creating additional footholds for attackers. Bring-your-own-device schemes (in which employees use their own tablets and smartphones for work purposes) and the bewildering proliferation of devices and client OS versions (especially within the Android ecosystem) make secure operations even more difficult.

These challenges exacerbate tensions between embracing mobility and enabling innovation on the one hand and securing the devices and the network on the other. One insurance company CISO had to field calls from board members on successive days, first asking him to promise that a breach couldn't happen and then protesting that he hadn't approved the use of tablets for board documents.

Virtualize the Client   In a virtualized model, the user's device (desktop, laptop, tablet, or smartphone) performs no processing—it just captures input and displays output (e.g., video, sound). The underlying OS is run on a server in a corporate data center, which can be effectively protected and means that the end-user's device is functioning inside the network perimeter at all times, irrespective of where the user is physically located. It can be protected by web filtering, intrusion detection, and antimalware controls, so sensitive data can remain secure. Even if the device does become compromised with malware, it is easy to flush the OS. Nor is there any need for the device to connect to the enterprise via a VPN, with all the complexity and absence of

---

[16] Donovan, Fred, "Forrester: Enterprises Will Make 18% of Tablet Purchases in 2017," *FierceMobileIT*, August 6, 2013. www.fiercemobileit.com/story/forrester-enterprises-will-make-18-tablet-purchases-2017/2013-08-06.

transparency than VPNs imply. In addition, no data sits on the client device so there is almost no risk if a device is lost or stolen.

The overwhelming majority of enterprises still use mobile device management to provide basic e-mail, contact, and calendar synchronization for tablets and smartphones. As users demand more sophisticated services on their mobile devices (e.g., access to enterprise applications and shared document repositories), companies may have no choices but to bring virtualization to the smartphone and tablet.

Virtualization does not just apply to mobile devices, however. Increasingly, companies are applying the same principles to desktop clients. This brings additional benefits, not least to the user experience. Getting started on a new device becomes nearly instantaneous. A user's complete desktop environment—applications, settings, data—can follow her from location to location, removing the need to travel with a laptop. Power users, such as traders, engineers, and data analysts, also find they can enjoy much faster processing performance as demanding applications run on powerful servers rather than their own desktop hard drives.

Financial institutions are ahead of the curve, and many are in the process of moving 70 to 80 percent of their end-user environments to virtual desktops, largely to improve control and reduce risk. In most cases, these banks are starting with high-risk users, such as financial advisers in wealth management (who may be independent agents rather than employees). A relatively small percentage of users who travel frequently will continue to have traditional laptops, though some IT executives believe even this will become less necessary over time as wireless becomes pervasive.

Pushed by their financial services clients, some of the largest law firms have also made aggressive moves to virtualize their desktop infrastructure, again for reasons of risk and control. One large New York law firm has moved entirely to virtual desktops: when a lawyer works from home or a client site, she simply logs into a virtual desktop via a web browser. The law firm shut down its VPN a couple of years ago.

Most infrastructure leaders we spoke to report good experiences with early virtual desktop deployments, and enterprise-grade levels of performance and stability are readily achievable. There is far less consensus, however, around the economics. Some companies believe virtual desktops cost about the same as, or a little more than, traditional ones because of back-end hosting costs. This has led them to limit their rollout to specific segments. Others, however, say they have achieved savings of 30 percent over traditional environments because of lower installation and support costs and therefore plan to migrate much of their user base to virtual desktop services over time. The difference between these two views on costs seems to stem from variations in virtual desktop solutions (i.e., whether users get a "thin" device or a full-fledged laptop, how much storage each user gets allocated) and the efficiency of back-end hosting environments.

Forcing users to access enterprise services via a virtual device would create a very different user experience with a hard separation between their work and personal information, but it would enable enterprises to provide extremely rich mobile services and feel confident in their security.

5. Use Software-Defined Networking to Compartmentalize the Network

In a world where nobody can eliminate breaches, it becomes especially important to contain the attacker's ability to move from one infected node of a technology network to the next. This "lateral movement," as it has become known, is getting harder to prevent as the corporate network environment has evolved, leaving IT organizations with a tough choice between preventing attackers from expanding their reach and introducing too much operational complexity.

Historically, as companies consolidated their IT organizations, they stitched enterprise networks together from departmental networks and networks picked up in various acquisitions. Different networks used different architectures, different technology standards, and, in some cases, different protocols—and they were walled off from one another by gateways and firewalls. This created complexity and inefficiency and hurt network performance. Network managers had to make manual configuration changes to install new applications and perform detailed analyses to identify the root causes of slow traffic between sites managed by different business units.

Over the past 10 years, most large enterprises have simplified their networks. One global financial institution went from 25 networks to just 2, saving more than $50 million a year. A pharmaceutical company created a global flat network because it wanted to allow seamless videoconferencing between any two offices globally, from Peru to Madagascar (without in fact assessing how many executives in Peru needed to videoconference with their counterparts in Madagascar).

Simplification had a downside, though: it created more entry points into its networks.

As companies integrated their supply chains with vendors and exposed more of their technology capabilities to customers, they created more direct network connections between themselves and their business partners. This allowed investment banks to give prime brokerage customers the performance they required and allowed pharmaceutical companies to collaborate closely with research partners. However, it also created more opportunities for attackers to jump from one company's network to another's and created more network entry points that network or security operations teams had to monitor. Once an attacker gains entry to the environment, he or she can see all the other systems, which makes them easier to analyze and compromise. The high-profile breach of Target occurred partly because one of its vendors, which needed access only to the billing system, also had access—unwittingly—to the point-of-sale system. Once an attacker had breached the vendor's security systems, it suddenly had access to data inside Target that never should have been visible.

A particularly important potential vulnerability is having the security controls themselves sit on the same network they protect. This is one of the easiest things to segment, and it is essential to do so; otherwise, the first thing a sophisticated hacker will do once inside the network is disable the organization's ability to track where he or she is.

Find a Middle Ground between Security and Simplification   The traditional approach to containing lateral movement is network segmentation, but this can seem like a reverse step, removing some of the hard-won benefits of network simplification. Separating two business units' servers into two separate network segments does dramatically reduce the risk of an attacker moving from one server to another, but it also means that the security team will have to make firewall changes (with all the time and effort that implies) before those two business applications can share data.

Many companies have sought to strike a middle ground and put in place approaches that provide some degree of segregation for their most important information assets without adding too much operational complexity. Some have really focused on protecting a small class of the most important assets. An industrial company decided to divide its networks into a "higher-security" network for its most sensitive IP and a lower security network for everything else. Other companies use less onerous techniques that rely on firewalls and gateways to demarcate networks. One bank used network segmentation in a targeted way to provide differential protection to some of its most important information assets. It created a separate network zone just to host systems supporting its payments processes, which it deemed suitably sensitive, while its far less sensitive ATMs remained outside the zone.

Ultimately, all these tactics are half measures, neither meeting the objectives of operational simplicity nor sufficiently reducing lateral movement. The answer is for companies to adopt software-defined networking (SDN). SDN separates the decisions about where network traffic is sent from the underlying system that transmits the traffic (i.e., the control plane from the data plane). Practically speaking, SDN allows an organization to set up a network in software rather than in the configuration of the underlying hardware. This means that networks can be managed via a set of APIs, and a library of different network configurations can be stored for reuse.

No one should be under any illusion—implementing SDN is a dramatic change that will require investment in new hardware, new operational processes, and new management capabilities. But it also brings huge efficiencies, saving as much as 60 to 80 percent of data center network costs thanks to vastly improved productivity and the use of commoditized hardware. It also helps enormously in the fight against lateral movement by making it much easier to set up network zones and segments in a rapid, automated way, thereby eliminating the tough choice between efficiency and compartmentalization.

6. Use Dedicated Document Management and Workflow Tools Instead of E-mail

Some CISOs say that they are quietly confident about how their company protects the structured data it stores in databases, but have sleepless nights about the extremely sensitive information that executives pass back and forth to each other via e-mail attachments. Documents make up a growing share of their company's data, and many of the controls they use to protect structured data just do not apply. A few companies have started to get control of this type of data by creating and mandating the use of sophisticated capabilities for managing sensitive documents. More need to catch up with them.

Stories about the theft of millions of customer records often reach the front pages of the broadsheet press. These are embarrassing for the companies concerned; however, some of a company's most sensitive and valuable corporate strategic information sits around in documents or just in plain text. Senior executives communicate with each other about acquisition targets, markets to enter, business strategies, layoffs, negotiations, divestitures, and so on, using presentations they create on their desktops and share via e-mail. Managers and analysts collaborate on business plans, valuation models, financial forecasts, and pricing strategies using spreadsheets they, again, create on their desktops and share via e-mail. Often, once all these incredibly sensitive documents have been created, they languish either in e-mail inboxes or in file shares.

Documents like this can be extremely complicated to secure because companies have little control and no visibility into who opens, alters, and transmits them. In many cases, entire departments have access to shared folders that hold sensitive documents. Any executive or manager can access an important strategy document and, perhaps without thinking about how sensitive it is, forward it to dozens of people. The more places a document exists in a company's environment, the more likely an attacker will be able to find it. The insider threat is even more pronounced—the more people have access to a document, the greater the chance that one of them uses it inappropriately.

The companies that are making progress in addressing this issue have fundamentally changed the way their staff work with documents. Law firms may have a reputation for being technology laggards, but in this area they have made the most progress. Spurred by the demands of their clients, most of the largest law firms now use document management tools extensively. If a lawyer works on a client matter, she has no choice but to create all the relevant documents within the document management platform. That means that only a small number of her fellow lawyers can access any set of documents, reducing the impact if attackers compromise any one lawyer's credentials. Perhaps more importantly, this rigor in document management provides the firm with visibility into who is accessing, transmitting, and altering client materials, which makes it much harder for insiders to exploit client information undetected. Document management systems can also insert tags about the sensitive information any given document contains into its metadata. This makes it exponentially easier for data loss protection (DLP) tools to stop users from e-mailing or printing a document that they should not.

Other companies go even further in protecting their most sensitive information. An oil and gas company moved discussions about negotiation strategies for extraction rights out of clear text in e-mail and into documents secured with digital rights management (DRM), reducing the risk that an unauthorized party could see the maximum amount it bid for a property. A manufacturing company is implementing DRM for the materials containing technical specifications it sends to its suppliers. This makes it much harder to forward this information inappropriately because DRM prevents users from opening, printing, or copying a file unless they have authorization from the document's creator.

As with the other security improvements discussed in this chapter, protecting unstructured data requires dramatic changes far beyond the cybersecurity function. That said, it does not have to mean a worse user experience. In a world where everyone complains about e-mail overload, how much frustration results from version upon version of a single document clogging up inboxes? How much time do executives, managers, and other professions spend trying to find the latest version of a document or extracting comments from complicated e-mail threads? The browsing, tagging, and search features of a well-designed document management capability make it much easier to find the right document, and collaboration tools make it much easier to aggregate and act on feedback. It is a change of mind-set, but one that can prove popular once adopted.

ENGAGE WITH IT LEADERS TO IMPLEMENT REQUIRED CHANGES

For obvious reasons, relatively few novels focus on enterprise IT or have a head of IT infrastructure as the protagonist. *The Phoenix Project*,[17] a business book masquerading as a novel, clearly harks back to 1980s management classic *The Goal*.[18] Just as *The Goal* describes how a beleaguered operations executive learned how to remove constraints

---

[17] Kim, Gene, Kevin Behr, and George Spafford, *The Phoenix Project: A Novel about IT, DevOps, and Helping Your Business Win*. Portland, OR: IT Revolution Press, 2013.
[18] Goldratt, Eliyahu M. and Jeff Cox, *The Goal: A Process of Ongoing Improvement*. Great Barrington, MA: North River Press, 1992.

in order to deliver finished goods efficiently and effectively enough to meet customer demands, *The Phoenix Project* describes how a beleaguered IT executive learned how to remove constraints in order to deploy and scale a critical e-commerce platform quickly enough to save the business. As the story begins, the CISO himself is one of the biggest roadblocks, constantly raising issues just before a release or demanding additional controls that had not been contemplated in the original architecture. His outdated attire serves as a metaphor for his outdated mind-sets. By the end of the book, just as all the other IT executives and their business partners have learned to operate in new ways, the CISO has both upgraded his wardrobe and started to engage with the rest of the team as a valued peer.

The book's authors are probably still smarting from a few run-ins with security teams over the years, but the CISO's evolution over the course of the story is a good road map for how cybersecurity teams broadly, and CISOs in particular, should engage with their colleagues on the IT management team. None of the improvements described in this chapter can be sponsored or orchestrated by the CISO; executives responsible for application hosting, application development, enterprise networking and end-user services will have to be the driving force behind any changes. That said, the security team has both the right and responsibility to initiate discussions about how structural issues across IT introduce vulnerabilities, to weigh in on the business case for major initiatives, to shape new architectures from the outset to make sure they can be protected, and to serve as a thought partner to fellow executives in discovering ways to make IT faster and more efficient. CISOs also need to encourage more of a resiliency culture across IT by sponsoring technical security training for IT personnel, by integrating security managers into application and infrastructure decision making, and by investing in reporting to track progress in addressing technical vulnerabilities.

• • •

Insecure application code, servers with unpatched operating systems, flat network architectures—the typical enterprise technology environment is rife with security vulnerabilities. However, there is an emerging technology model characterized by lean application development processes, cloud-based hosting models, virtual clients, and software-defined networking. It has the potential to improve efficiency, agility, and security compared to what exists in most companies today.

Along with risk management and delivery, cybersecurity also has influencing responsibilities. A company's overall technology architecture can have a profound impact on its ability to protect itself while continuing to drive technology innovations; therefore, applying these responsibilities to the rest of the IT organization purposefully and ambitiously will be a major factor in achieving digital resilience. Naturally, this will require CISOs and the cybersecurity team to work closely and effectively with the rest of the IT team. It will also require CIOs, Chief Technology Officers, and other senior technology executives to prioritize investments in more robust architectures—sometimes at the expense of tactical business requests—and create a culture of risk management and resilience throughout the IT organization.

6

Engage Attackers with Active Defense

Companies can protect their important assets and make sure that enterprise-wide policies and structures are in place to minimize risk, but attackers are still out there. They are increasingly well funded and sophisticated, supported by a well-developed marketplace for malware and other tools for infiltrating networks, and using innovative tactics such as multistep attacks, misdirection, and stealthier malware, all designed to defeat corporate defenses.[1] As a result, companies' cybersecurity approach has to move from passive to active defense.

Passive defense means putting in place protections to keep attackers away from sensitive information assets. In a passive defense model, companies use security operations centers (SOCs) to monitor and manage their defense mechanisms. In military terms, the Maginot Line—the Second World War fortifications along the French/German border—was a passive defense strategy.

Active defense means engaging attackers long before they might succeed in causing a breach. The Royal Air Force embraced active defense when it used the new technology of radar to identify Luftwaffe raids while the German planes were still over the English Channel. The alerts enabled the RAF to dispatch aircraft to disrupt these attacks before they reached British cities.

---

[1] Ablon, Lillian, Martin C. Libicki, and Andrea A. Golay, "Markets for Cybercrime Tools and Stolen Data: Hackers' Bazaar," Rand Corporation, 2014.

The basic passive defense capabilities that a traditional SOC offers are utterly essential, but companies also have to turn on their radar; they have to create active defenses to engage attackers, gather intelligence, divert attention from the valuable assets, and tune defenses in real time. Attackers will not wait, so companies need to simultaneously establish basic SOC capabilities and learn how to engage in active defense.

THE LIMITATIONS OF PASSIVE DEFENSE

Companies started creating SOCs to deal with the deluge of security data generated by disparate systems, platforms, and applications—from business applications and identity and access management (I&AM) platforms to antivirus tools, intrusion detection system (IDS) devices, and firewalls.[2] They integrated all this information, at least to an extent, into security incident and event management (SIEM) tools that provide aggregation, correlation, alerting, and reporting capabilities.[3]

SOC activity is triggered when a sensor detects the signature of an action that is known to be bad; this might be an access request from an Internet Protocol (IP) address associated with cyber-criminals or a piece of code that has a known malware signature embedded within. When the alert sounds, an analyst determines whether it signifies a legitimate threat or a false alarm. This triage function can account for up to 70 percent of an analyst's time. If they believe the threat to be a genuine risk, then it is escalated and addressed by SOC analysts with the appropriate level of expertise.

In short, SOC analysts review alerts, filter out false positives, determine the level of severity, and request action to remediate the issue—reimaging a server that has been infected with malware, for example. In some cases, the SOC team may recommend that the company launch its incident response process in order to address a significant breach in the environment that is compromising sensitive data.[4]

---

[2] Rothke, Ben, "Building a Security Operations Center (SOC)," RSA Conference 2012, February 29, 2012.
[3] Stephenson, Peter, "SIEM," SC Magazine, April 1, 2014. www.scmagazine.com/siem/grouptest/316.
[4] Pyorre, Josh, and Chris McKenney, "Build Your Own Security Operations Center for Little or No Money," Def Con 18, July 29, 2010.

SOCs have provided tremendous value for companies that have implemented them. The very process of building an SOC often reveals gaps in a company's perimeter defenses and highlights where it needs to enhance its antimalware, web filtering, intrusion detection, and firewall infrastructure.[5] Once up and running, SOCs bring together security data and expertise in one place, which means companies miss fewer security events and catch them earlier. The basic concept has now reached a stage where a robust market for managed SOC services exists, and many companies choose to outsource the capability rather than build it themselves.

This SOC approach certainly helps reduce risk, but it is severely limited, especially in the face of determined and creative attackers. Analysts engage only when prompted by an alert from the network sensors and then respond with the same level of energy to every alert, which means wasting considerable time filtering out those false alarms when they could be addressing real issues. Organizations do not have enough staff for that luxury. Most do not even have enough analysts to review all of the incidents that occur, which means the network sensors end up being tuned to generate only the number of alerts that analysts can manage. This means that a host of potential incidents are never scrutinized at all. Even with today's advanced analytic approaches, it is not possible to act in real-time to block all the potentially serious threats that are detected.

SOC operations rely on tools but if the tools are poorly configured they will not see everything they should. Add in the fact that the most sophisticated attackers already know how to circumvent the most popular security applications, and it is clear that companies' safety nets have some big holes.

Perhaps the most important limitation however, is that that SOCs work on the principle of looking for fingerprints of malware that is already known. This signature-based approach provides no protection against zero-day exploits, for which no known signature exists. Even if a firm consistently has up-to-date virus definitions and good cyber-hygiene practices across its networks, adversaries can use new zero-day exploits and techniques such as spear-phishing to defeat or circumvent such signature-based defenses. Some criminal hackers

---

[5] "Do You Need a Security Operations Center?" *Information Week*, Dark Reading, January 28, 2012. www.darkreading.com/analytics/security-monitoring/do-you-need-a-security-operations-center/d/d-id/1137004.

already have advanced tradecraft, and the black market for advanced tool kits means that companies have to defend themselves against an ever wider range of adversaries. In 2013, for example, security firm Secunia reported that the 25 most popular software programs contained 9 zero days.[6] Assuming a monthly vendor patch release schedule, companies relying on a signature-based approach are exposed to previously unknown threats on 270 days out of 365.

The final limitation of the signature-based approach is that it cannot tackle the growing threat from insiders. Insider threats range from operator error (e.g., failure to update virus definitions and sustain firewalls) to user error (e.g., being spear-phished by clicking on the wrong link in an e-mail), to malevolent actions spurred by a range of motivations. CISOs must adopt an active approach to mitigating such insider threats, just as they must do for many external threats. In short, SOCs are woefully inadequate at coping with the multitude of cybersecurity threats faced by companies today, and companies need to deploy active defenses to engage attackers.

KNOW THE ENEMY AND ACT ACCORDINGLY

Active defense uses both manual and automated processes to not only detect but also deceive, deter, and manage attackers. In some cases this means stopping and expelling them when they are discovered in the network; in others, it means actively engaging them on the network to monitor their actions, developing additional intelligence on their methods and keeping them occupied so they cannot inflict harm. It also means having the ability to tune defenses in real-time to thwart emerging attacks.

As tempting as it might be, active defense should not include hacking back against adversaries. Cyber-vigilantism may seem an appealing way to retaliate, but it is illegal in most jurisdictions. In addition, given the challenges in attributing attacks (driven in part by attackers using others' infrastructure), a reverse hack could easily damage an unwitting third party, with all the legal and reputation exposure that entails.

Adopting an active approach to defense has three appreciable benefits. First, it makes better use of existing people. Second, it allows organizations to focus on the specific hackers who present the greatest

---

[6] Secunia, *The Secunia Vulnerability Review, 2014.* http://secunia.com/vulnerability-review/ time_to_patch.htm.l.

threat. Finally, it allows a hypothesis-based approach that allows the security team to come to a better answer faster than the signature-based approach. It is a more sophisticated defense strategy at a time when any company with valuable data or with accounting or financial systems linked to the web must assume that it will be targeted and, in many cases, will be penetrated.

Taking an active defense stance means taking four actions:

1. Maintain up-to-date intelligence.
2. Mitigate insider threats.
3. Engage the adversary on the organization's own networks.
4. Partner to mitigate external threats.

Each element requires investments in both technology and capabilities, and the four must be pursued aggressively and integrated into a comprehensive active defense program even as companies work on improving their basic cyber-hygiene and incident response capabilities.

Maintain Up-to-Date Intelligence

The only thing proliferating faster than cybersecurity threats is the number of companies providing information about those threats. There is a trend for companies to turn to third parties—both state bodies and commercial operators—for more information on cybersecurity threats. However, most companies lack the internal resources to then separate the wheat from the chaff or, more importantly, to use this data to make effective operational decisions.

Companies that have a strong active defense program need to develop an internal intelligence function that is integrated with the cybersecurity operations team (Figure 6.1). The intelligence function has five elements (commonly referred to as the intelligence cycle).

The first step in the intelligence cycle is to define requirements. In the cybersecurity world, this means developing educated hypotheses about what threats your organization is most likely to face, who the attackers are that have the capability and intent to target your organization, and what techniques they typically employ. These questions help the threat intelligence function identify its intelligence gaps—the specific information it needs but does not yet have in order to identify and counter adversaries effectively.

FIGURE 6.1 **Integrate a Proactive Cyber-Intelligence Function with the Security Operations Team**

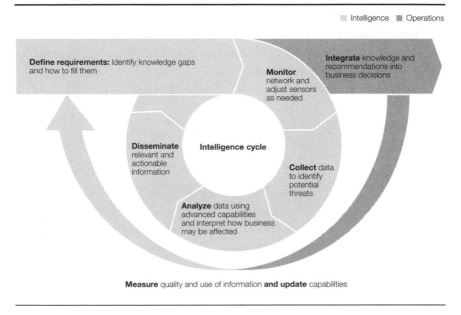

■ Intelligence   ■ Operations

Define requirements: Identify knowledge gaps and how to fill them

Monitor network and adjust sensors as needed

Integrate knowledge and recommendations into business decisions

Disseminate relevant and actionable information

Intelligence cycle

Collect data to identify potential threats

Analyze data using advanced capabilities and interpret how business may be affected

Measure quality and use of information **and update** capabilities

Once it knows what information it needs, the threat intelligence team needs to find the right internal and external sources for that information. Internally, this requires installing network sensors to detect the specific indicators of potential suspicious activity. This may involve actions such as setting an IDS to look for indicators that are specific to a known adversary's typical tactics, techniques, and procedures (TTPs—the cybersecurity term for what would be known as an "MO" or *modus operandi* for other criminals), and monitoring internal user behavior to identify potential patterns of compromise. Priority should be given to alerts that most closely resemble the TTPs of the groups the organization is most concerned about in order to focus on the most valuable data from what can be a multitude of network sensors. Advanced organizations also employ hunting teams and create internal deceptive sandboxes (more on these later) to identify attackers and lure them into using additional tools, thereby increasing the information about their TTPs.

The quantity of external cybersecurity intelligence is rapidly expanding with maturing third-party vendors, government agencies, and industry associations such as the FS-ISAC in financial services that are starting to serve as clearing houses and centralized repositories for threat information. The information all these bodies can provide may include specific threat profiles, attack "vectors" (specific paths hackers take to get inside a network) or contextual information on threats. Broader, real-world information also helps organizations make sense of the threat, and understand attackers, their motivations and the political/legal environment in which they operate. Intelligence teams should make sure they collect both technical and this contextual information. Forward-looking organizations are even collecting threat information directly from the hacker "dark net"—those underground networks that sell the attack tools, share vulnerability information and attacker tool kits, and seek to profit from compromised information. Getting inside these hacker forums allows sophisticated organizations to collect threat intelligence directly from some of their most determined adversaries.

The information is only one part of the intelligence; analyzing it is the critical step. Dedicated analysts must pore over the data in order to draw out insights, context, and actions. This type of analytic activity attempts to correlate actions and produce perspectives on real and anticipated threats. It provides internal decision makers with perspectives on the risks facing the organization; it provides defenders with queuing information that allows them to tackle threats in real time; and finally, it allows the organization to prioritize its actions in order to position its defenses most effectively and make informed business decisions. In short, intelligence drives operations.

The final arc in the intelligence cycle is the dissemination of the intelligence. This may include strategic threat bulletins to help business leaders make effective business or investment decisions, alerts to help the cybersecurity team orient its decisions or tactical critical notifications that result in direct actions on the network (e.g., closing a port, blocking an IP address, or taking direct action against an entity on the network).

A cyber-intelligence function should not only aggregate threat information and develop strategic threat assessments; it also needs to develop hypotheses about the most likely intrusion tools and targets. These hypotheses, updated over time, guide cybersecurity specialists to where they need to focus their attention. As the cyber-intelligence function matures, organizations can refine their hypotheses into much more detailed definitions of the threats targeting their network. The intelligence gleaned may not be sufficient to attribute malevolent activities to a specific actor, but the TTPs of different adversaries will increasingly differentiate them and allow cybersecurity operators to tailor their defenses to each identified attacker.

The most sophisticated organizations gather enough information to devise playbooks for each adversary that can become an entire defensive campaign. Sustained success depends on consistently updating intelligence and tweaking the playbook accordingly. Analysts review the outcomes of each playbook action to refine the campaign still further, incorporating new insights to develop actions that are particularly effective against each adversary.

Making threat intelligence actionable in this way requires a different way of doing business. The traditional approach of feeding intelligence into a managed SOC will not get the job done because it overwhelms the organization and triggers alerts based on every piece of intelligence regardless of its applicability to the organization. More importantly, it does not focus the actions of the cybersecurity operators and there is no feedback loop to determine the quality of the intelligence and supplement it with additional findings. Instead, organizations need to embed the intelligence analysts with the cybersecurity team, accelerating the deployment of knowledge and enabling faster decision making.

The increase of internal sensors and external sources of threat intelligence means organizations have to dramatically increase their use of automation and advanced analytics to avoid being swamped by this tidal wave of information. Given the scarcity of human talent to separate the signals from the noise, many organizations are turning to complex algorithms to correlate known and unknown events, search for anomalies and filter out false alarms. Following the Target breach, for example, there was a rash of reports describing how the initial indications of the compromise were identified but dismissed by the security operations team because they were buried by reams of similar alerts that posed no real threat.[7]

Mitigate Insider Threats

Most companies have been focused on the external threat and, and as a result, most defenses are oriented toward external actors. By default, outsiders are not trusted. Conversely, insiders are trusted and must be

[7] Ragan, Steve, "Information Overload: Finding Signals in the Noise," CSO, May 29, 2014. www.csoonline.com/article/2243744/business-continuity/information-overload-finding-signals-in-the-noise.html and 60 Minutes, "What happens when you swipe your card," CBS, aired November 30, 2014.

trusted. From system administrators who can access raw databases, to cybersecurity personnel who have access to usage logs and credentials, to customer services staff with access to client files, insiders need access to sensitive information to do their jobs properly. Insiders not only have access, but also have the contextual information to locate and exploit especially sensitive and valuable information. As we said earlier, the easiest way to get hold of valuable information assets is to badge into the building in the morning and use valid credentials to log in to a secure system.

Many companies are realizing that they have underinvested in addressing insider threats for a number of reasons. The media has often focused on external, overseas attackers; addressing insider threats is harder and requires more insight into processes and collaboration with business partners; and addressing insider threats raises uncomfortable HR issues, especially in companies that emphasize a trust culture.

Organizations need to worry about three types of insiders, all of whom have access to critical data or systems. The *errant insider* is unaware of security protocols, ignores cybersecurity policies, or simply commits errors resulting in sensitive data being compromised or networks becoming vulnerable. The *hijacked insider* has their credentials compromised by someone externally, giving the outsider the same level of access as the insider. Finally, the *malevolent insider* is willing to steal or compromise data for personal gain. Companies must use active defense strategies to address each type of insider.

Errant Insiders   Users can easily (surprisingly easily) accidentally send files with privileged information to customers, vendors, and other third parties. They can forward sensitive e-mails to dozens or hundreds of people who have no need to read them. They download files to USB drives and upload documents to consumer-grade web services that have—at best—vague security policies.

Naturally, all the mechanisms for changing the mind-sets and behaviors described in Chapter 4 are important, but they must be backed up by an operational model that can identify an errant act or errant behavior.

Data loss protection (DLP) tools can stop sensitive data from being e-mailed externally, uploaded to websites, downloaded to external drives, or even printed. This all helps stop careless employees from sharing information inappropriately. For highly structured information, this is relatively straightforward—it is not difficult to set rules that tell a DLP tool to look for customer account data, for example.

Stopping unstructured data from being lost is much more complicated and can require sophisticated cybersecurity analytics. Business plans, pricing strategies, and many types of intellectual property cannot be identified by their structure in the way a social security number can. For example, when a developer uploads Java code to a website, how can a tool determine whether he is contributing to an important open-source project or putting a highly proprietary algorithm on an insecure site so he can work on it at home?

For these reasons, 90 percent of alerts from newly installed DLP tools can be false positives. Obviously, that is unsustainable. Cybersecurity analysts need to engage in a constant process of understanding business processes, analyzing alerts, and tuning business rules, so they can identify truly errant behavior and support management teams as they put consequences in place for employees who consistently choose to ignore their responsibilities in helping protect corporate information.

Hijacked Insiders   External attackers will often use an employee's credentials without the person even realizing it. In fact, about 80 percent of breaches involve stolen credentials at some point in the attack. As the database administrator mentioned in Chapter 4 found out, clicking on the wrong link can install a keystroke logger that captures an employee's account information and passwords for any number of important systems.

Changing employee mind-sets and behaviors is again critical, but not sufficient, in addressing the risk of hijacked credentials. More than 30 percent of employees commonly fail spear-phishing tests, so companies have to accept that users will sometimes create opportunities for malware to install itself on their devices. Companies cannot count on even the latest antimalware tool to keep creative and innovative attackers off the corporate network. They must use active defense techniques to identify, investigate, and respond to anomalous activity that may indicate hijacked credentials.

Close analysis of identity and access management (I&AM) data can be especially powerful here. For example, a key employee's account may begin accessing sensitive information from a new IP range, suggesting a potential hijack of her credentials. However, that could also mean she is traveling on business or has gone on vacation. If the employee's credentials are used hundreds of miles apart or if her account stays active for 10 hours on a day that HR systems say she is on vacation, that may all but confirm that attackers have hijacked her credentials.

Malevolent Insiders   An employee might be compromised by external attackers through either bribery or coercion. He might decide he finds his employer's business practices to be repugnant and believes they should be exposed. Most commonly, he might be contemplating an offer from a competitor and want to bring customer lists or pricing information with him to get off to a fast start in the new job.

Traditional mechanisms that influence mind-sets and behaviors will be less effective with a malevolent insider, making active defense especially important. Companies need to develop the analytics to identify current and even future malevolent insider behavior. For example, if an employee has been accessing documents that are "out of profile" for him and has generated two hits from the DLP tool in the previous month, that could be an indication of a potential cybersecurity risk. Depending on the precise nature of the analysis, the cybersecurity team could recommend increased surveillance, a friendly visit from his manager about the importance of protecting sensitive information, reduced access rights, or, in extreme circumstances, revoking all privileges and considering his position.

Deep insight into the employee base is important here. Cybersecurity analysts' task will be more manageable if they can identify segments of employees who have access to sensitive information (e.g., researchers working on critical R&D projects) and focus their analysis on those groups. Likewise, if cybersecurity analysts can partner with HR to identify which employees with access to sensitive data are most likely to leave, they can further focus their surveillance, reducing the risks that valuable IP follows an employee to a competitor.

Engage the Adversary on the Organization's Network

Cyber-attackers have the advantage of the first move, and a wide array of tools and techniques at their disposal to hide their entry and activities. This makes it extremely challenging to identify malicious actions within the network. To meet this challenge, organizations need to adopt two parallel approaches. The first is to develop hunting teams to identify attackers' actions wherever they occur on the network; the second is to actively manage those attackers rather than just kick them out.

Hunting for Adversaries on the Network   The concept of internal hunting teams is emerging as best practice and is trickling down to midsized and small organizations who recognize the benefits of taking a more active approach to cybersecurity.

Dedicated and experienced cybersecurity operators constantly scour the network to try and spot the attackers they have identified in the intelligence phase of the campaign. The operators need to have a "seek and pursue" mind-set and unearth attacker footholds wherever they may appear on the network.

To hunt successfully, operators have to identify and analyze internal use patterns, access logs, employee behavior and suspicious code. Cybersecurity operators are grappling with big data, just as their counterparts in the business are, but theirs is a world in which every network access request generates a data point, every user keystroke is on record, and every system operation a log. This is big data on steroids. The operators must find ways to make sense of the millions of digital interactions that occur on a network every day, and spot the anomalies from which the team can start hunting down the attackers.

Too few organizations regularly scan applications to detect these anomalies, which can include malicious code or unauthorized access requests. Application development teams may scan code at the development stage—although, as we saw earlier in the book, even this is far from universal—but ongoing scans of live systems are seldom conducted on a regular basis. Cybersecurity teams should also carry out vulnerability assessments (and, ideally, penetration testing to simulate external and internal threats).

To avoid being overwhelmed by data and to make effective decisions, hunting teams need to be able to provide context for all this data. This context comes from three main sources:

1. *Integrated threat intelligence and vulnerability analysis.* This allows hunting teams to develop hypotheses on what the most dangerous intrusion strategies could be. These strategies are often called the cyber "kill chain," a term coined by Lockheed Martin.[8] Each attacker has a standard approach for entering a network, which hunting teams can identify as they begin to see TTPs repeat themselves on the network.

[8] Hutchins, Eric M., Michael J. Cloppert, and Rohan M. Amin, "Intelligence-Driven Computer Network Defense Informed by Analysis of Adversary Campaigns and Intrusion Kill Chains," Lockheed Martin Corporation, March 2011.

2. *An understanding of what constitutes abnormal.* To develop a picture of "normal," companies can create profiles for various job categories that detail what these employees' computer use should look like, and then refine those profiles for certain individuals using machine learning. Compiling a list of "abnormal" (and generally unacceptable) activities, such as massive downloads or printing of sensitive information, will be a continuous process.

3. *An enhanced SOC.* Hunting teams benefit enormously when the SOC is advanced enough to filter out as many false alarms as possible. This allows the teams to focus on actions that are likely to be decisive in meeting and stopping an attacker.

With this knowledge in hand, teams can move rapidly from "seek" to "pursue."

Manage Adversaries on the Network   Once hunting teams identify an attacker on the network, they must decide. Do they evict her and block her route of access, or do they actively manage her within the network. The kneejerk response when an attacker is found is to expel them as fast as possible. However, while this may be a satisfying reaction, and one that is easier to report to management, it is often not the smartest approach.

Removing an attacker has two outcomes. First, the attacker knows that this attempt has failed and therefore will stop wasting time on it. Second, the attacker knows her TTPs have not worked and will adapt them to try again. Neither of these adds to the organization's intelligence about the attacker. In addition, the attacker may have used only one or two tools to gain access and have been saving the most effective tools for later in the kill chain. Suddenly, kicking the attacker out means that the defender does not know what those tools might be and therefore cannot defend against them in the future.

Companies with the right active defense processes in place should therefore resist the urge to expel the attacker. It can, counterintuitively, be more valuable to keep them inside the network. At the most basic level, organizations can deploy honeypots and tar pits with the hope of occupying adversaries and buying time. These static techniques are increasingly prevalent and help at least until the adversary realizes he is caught.

A honeypot is a collection of computers configured to attract hackers and their software (e.g., malware, including botnets), thereby enabling the company to learn their techniques without putting any critical assets at risk. A well-designed honeypot contains nothing of value but looks as if it does. Once it is infected or attacked, the honeypot administrator can log and monitor the actions of the hacker from within a safe controlled environment. This includes assessing the attacker's methods for scanning, gaining access, retaining access, exploiting the target, and, most importantly, covering their tracks as they depart the machines and networks when they have—or think they have—what they want. Such information can then be used to develop countermeasures to protect the real networks. The benefits of honeypots can be enormous relative to their cost, as long as they are used properly (e.g., not appearing fake or operationally irrelevant).[9] Some organizations go so far as to deploy multiple networks of honeypots to continuously monitor and gather intelligence on active threats to their most critical assets.

A tar pit is used to slow down network scans or known malicious actors or code. Tar pits are a collection of network services or servers designed to reduce or deny known or identified malicious network traffic. Normal network traffic has a minor, but expected, delay, and tar pits increase this delay beyond expected thresholds to slow down the traffic for analysis, deterrence or denial. These are less common and require an understating of the network-associated information of known attacks—requiring significant input from the threat intelligence team.

Tar pits are an example of a static approach to engaging adversaries, but the next generation of cybersecurity defenders are dynamically engaging adversaries by using deceptive sandboxes. A deceptive sandbox is a parallel network environment that looks to an attacker exactly like the organization's real network except that it is completely walled off from the real network and there is nothing of value that can be stolen or compromised. A deceptive sandbox is an evolution of the honeypot concept; however, where honeypots are designed as a passive measure to fool attackers into attacking a fake target as a distraction, deceptive sandboxes are designed for the cybersecurity team to actively engage attackers to both occupy them and develop additional intelligence.

---

[9] It is highly recommended that honeypots are established and used by qualified incident handlers in order to ensure efficacy and legality.

Once an attacker is discovered on the actual network, operators guide her into the sandbox. She is then free to deploy the rest of her arsenal of tools, thinking she has not been detected. At this point, the malicious code begins "calling home" for instructions, identifying remote servers that are associated with advanced malware—again, with the assumption that the exploit has not been detected. However, in reality, the sandbox management team is observing the additional tool kits she is using and increasing the intelligence they have on her TTPs and improving their ability to attribute future attacks to her.

One company that employs this technique was able to manage more than 30 attacker campaigns simultaneously, with each hacker thinking he or she was operating undetected and was stealing highly sensitive data. The truth was they were being continuously monitored and were stealing nothing but gibberish that the company planted. The company managed one hacker for five months—that was five months where he was not able to do any damage to the company. It also identified an additional 19 tools beyond that which gave him his initial entry, which it can now defend against on its real network. Had they evicted the attacker when they discovered his first tool, they would have lost all of this advantage—a significant opportunity cost!

Partner to Mitigate External Threats

Although retaliating against attackers by hacking back is risky and often illegal, some companies are partnering with third parties, including security agencies, law enforcement, and the civil courts to increase their defensive capabilities.

Many private-sector companies linked to critical national infrastructure (e.g., aerospace and defense firms, utilities, R&D organizations) are working to improve their relationships with national security organizations who may be able to take action against adversaries. For example, a voluntary effort allows the federal government to provide sensitive and often classified information regarding threats to U.S. Department of Defense (DoD) data that resides on or passes through eligible company networks. The program also allows these companies to take advantage of many elements of the DoD's perimeter defense system, which includes classified threat signatures. Various government departments and agencies have, or are developing, similar efforts to share threat intelligence and protective systems.

Other large companies are actively partnering with national security organizations not just to improve information sharing, but also to deny attackers safe havens. Most large banks, for example, have employees who are solely responsible for engaging with national security agencies with the expectation that the bank can provide information that would allow government agencies to exercise the level of offensive cybersecurity measures that are not available to private-sector organizations.

Facebook worked with local law enforcement agencies to dismantle a malware distribution organization called Lecpetex. Having identified malware that was taking over user accounts, Facebook provided the police with specific information on the adversaries, which led to the servers that propagated the malware being taken offline.[10]

Other organizations have used civil litigation to extend their active cybersecurity defenses. In one of the best-known examples, Microsoft won a court order in 2012 granting it control over an Internet domain that sold pirated versions of Windows PCs that came preloaded with a strain of malware called Nitol that let attackers control the systems from afar in order to engage in theft, fraud, and other malevolent activities. Microsoft was then able to neutralize the botnet's activities at the source.[11]

• • •

All the investments companies make in controls have to be backed up by a robust cybersecurity operational model. Although a well-functioning SOC is critical, the passive defense that traditional SOCs provide cannot rise to the challenge provided by increasingly determined and innovative attackers.

Protecting information assets requires not only basic SOC capabilities but also active defenses that detect, deceive, deter, and manage external and internal attackers. Many companies are still building or refining their SOCs—making sure the basic tool kit of firewalls, IDS, antimalware systems, SIEM platforms, and the cybersecurity analysts to interact with them are all in place. Active defense requires tighter integration of these basic tools, rich analytic platforms, and sophisticated cybersecurity analysts to derive insights and recommend actions.

[10] Kirk, Jeremy, "Facebook Kills 'Lecpetex' Botnet that Turned 250k PCs into Litecoin-Mining Zombies," *PCWorld*, July 9, 2014. www.pcworld.com/article/2452080/facebook-kills-lecpetex-botnet-which-hit-250000-computers.html.
[11] Krebs, Brian, "Microsoft Disrupts 'Nitol' Botnet in Piracy Sweep," *Krebs on Security*, September 13, 2012. http://krebsonsecurity.com/2012/09/microsoft-disrupts-nitol-botnet-in-piracy-sweep.

Implementing an active defense strategy will require significant changes to companies' security management processes and organizational setup. At a minimum, it needs the traditional SOC to integrate with the threat intelligence team to shorten the security decision-making cycle and allow real-time operations against attackers. This may require restructuring of outsourced SOC contracts and process flows. In a more integrated approach, the cybersecurity function may choose to align itself around specific threat campaigns with a supporting operational structure to make decisions and implement changes rapidly.

Given the scarcity and expense of experienced cybersecurity talent, it is essential to automate as many processes as possible so that these people can apply their expertise to the highest-priority issues. Automating the basic triage function, for example, allows cybersecurity professionals to spend their time in the much higher value tasks of hunting and engaging adversaries.

A move to active defense also requires a change of mind-set—one that moves away from detecting and blocking attackers to hunting and managing them. This approach also requires modest changes to the IT infrastructure to allow hunting teams to search for adversaries across network nodes and permit operations teams to manage honeypots, tar pits, and deceptive sandboxes within the network.

While much of the hardest work in building active defenses occurs within cybersecurity, other parts of the organization will have to contribute as well. In particular, IT managers will need to generate the data sets required for sophisticated analytics, and HR managers have to help strike the right balance between protecting employee privacy and identifying activity that indicates an insider threat.

Given all that has to be done, some companies will be tempted to walk before they can run—tempted to get the basic SOC capabilities in place before they think about active defense. Unfortunately, the attackers are already running and will not wait for the defenders to catch up.

7

After the Breach: Improve Incident Response across Business Functions

Companies can protect their critical assets appropriately, they can ensure that cybersecurity is embedded in their culture and systems, and they can step up their defense mechanisms. They can take all the actions we have outlined up to now. But they will still be attacked. Cyberattacks are becoming increasingly sophisticated, more frequent, and their consequences more dire. When determined adversaries set their mind to finding a way inside, every organization with valuable digitized information is at risk of having its critical assets compromised.

Breaches unsurprisingly affect shareholder confidence as investors get spooked by the transgression and often by the slow response of the company to deal with it or even acknowledge it. This impact will be disproportionately heavy for companies trying to exploit new digital business models. CISOs and, increasingly, CEOs are realizing that more business value can be destroyed as the result of a poor response to the breach than by the breach itself. Knowing how to respond to a cyberattack is not a question of having good instincts. It needs to be learned and embedded. Achieving this level of expertise requires developing a robust incident response plan and then—crucially—continuously testing and challenging it through simulations.

Unfortunately, most organizations are not prepared. They are reactive, not proactive. Despite the recognition that breaches will continue to escalate and that they are likely to be attacked, they still do not adequately think through how to respond. They need to know what to do next.

The U.S. Department of Defense (DoD) spends $5 billion a year on cybersecurity,[1] more than anyone else, yet it recognizes that its systems are far from impregnable. Indeed, it assumes that its unclassified network will be penetrated and therefore concentrates on how to maintain day-to-day operations in the event of a breach. Like any good military organization, it has plans in place for all manner of contingencies. It is under no illusion that it can spend its way out of trouble or that technology alone will solve the problem. Instead, its mind-set is one of being prepared to respond when the attack happens.

Companies, which spend far less on protection in the first place, would do well to follow the DoD's lead. There is no such thing as a foolproof system, and the cybersecurity battle is being fought not only at the outer walls but increasingly inside the city gates. Forward-thinking CISOs are therefore adopting an approach of detection, response, and recovery, and companies are being held accountable by the market, customers, and regulators for how they respond to a breach. All three are becoming ever more unforgiving of an unprepared and uncoordinated response.

Tools traditionally used to detect vulnerabilities, such as penetration testing, are now being used to assess security teams' ability to detect a breach. One leading technology company, for example, conducts penetration testing every three weeks, but its goal is not to identify weak spots, but rather to test how well its security team can find the intrusion and respond appropriately. How many traditional companies can say they do this? Only 55 percent of the organizations we surveyed conducted any kind of systematic penetration testing. Of those, almost all of the programs were designed to find the vulnerabilities rather than test the cybersecurity team's skill in detecting breaches.

The IT response is only one aspect of reacting to a breach and often the most advanced. For many organizations, the bigger challenges are coordinating the broader response to a security incident and establishing a culture of continuous learning so their responses improve over time.

---

[1] Some of this is spent on offensive capabilities; see Corrin, Amber, "Defense Budget Routes at Least $5B to Cyber," *Federal Times*, March 5, 2014. www.federaltimes.com/article/20140305/MGMT05/303050005/Defense-budget-routes-least-5B-cyber.

To address these, organizations need to take actions on three fronts. First, they need to draw up an incident response plan that spans business functions. Second, they need to test the plan continuously and embed it into the organization through disciplined practice and war gaming. Third, they need to conduct post-mortems of real breaches to assess the effectiveness of the plan and feed the results back.

DRAW UP AN INCIDENT RESPONSE PLAN

The primary objective of an incident response (IR) plan is to manage a cybersecurity incident in a way that limits damage, increases the confidence of external stakeholders, and reduces recovery time and costs. It achieves this in three ways: clearer decision making, stronger internal coordination and accountability, and tighter third-party collaboration.

Clarify Decision-Making Responsibilities

An insurer's core underwriting system was compromised by malware that was stealing sensitive data. The CISO took the unilateral decision to disconnect the system from the broader network without realizing that this system was a critical piece of the business infrastructure. Taking it offline would cost the company $20 million a day in revenue. After he declared his intent, the head of business operations challenged the CISO's authority to make what amounted to a strategic decision for the company. The two sat at loggerheads not knowing who had the authority to make the call, while data continued to flow out of the compromised system.

By contrast, when the security team at another insurer confirmed that malicious code had infected a core application, there was a consensual decision by management to shut down complete network access. With decision rights already clearly defined, it was relatively straightforward to determine that the risk of continued data loss from this specific application outweighed the associated loss of revenue resulting from downtime. Furthermore, having developed standard procedures for isolating strategic segments of their network, the technology teams followed step-by-step instructions to efficiently quarantine the application.

When an attack happens, managers from across the organization have to make some quick decisions. Identifying as many of those decisions in advance as possible and codifying them in a plan saves time and minimizes loss. But, as we saw in the first example, it is just as important to have clarity over who has the authority to make the decision based on the value at stake. Too often, companies do not anticipate the kinds of decisions that have to be made in the chaotic moments when a breach is discovered.

Strengthen Internal Coordination and Accountability

One institution delayed releasing an important statement to the media about a cyber-attack while executives debated the desired messaging. The delay was due to unclear responsibilities that slowed down the executive group as its members defined a list of external stakeholders, tried to assemble a meeting with internal stakeholders, and debated numerous issues.

Many of these tasks could have been resolved in advance. During the early stages of a data breach crisis at a large retail bank, customer service reps worked from preapproved scripts to handle calls from customers asking about the nature of the breach. Aside from giving a consistent message to the outside world, this also meant that executives and security teams could focus on investigating the data loss without being distracted by having to develop communications on the fly.

However, even having scripts does not guarantee a smooth response. Another financial institution had scripts in place, but the messages they contained had not been coordinated with the regulatory team who were preparing to give regulators messages that differed materially from what service reps were telling customers. Thankfully, managers spotted the inconsistency in time and were spared a potential public relations nightmare.

It is this coordination that gives meaning and structure to the decision making. Fast decisions are important, but not if they are contradictory. In our experience, too many companies try to manage a cybersecurity incident in a decentralized fashion. An effective IR plan establishes clear roles and responsibilities across the organization, but we regularly see that organizations do not have a single leader for all incident response actions. It is a preventable mistake.

An "on-site commander" can coordinate disparate elements of the response. This may seem easy to anticipate and implement, but being able to understand and bring together functions as disparate as technical forensics and social media monitoring is not typically a skill set a single person would have. However, best practice has shown that having a single individual to manage the incident response ensures a much more thorough and consistent set of actions with clear lines of authority. In many organizations, this commander is drawn from the business continuity function, but he or she could easily be a senior IT security executive or a leader from the risk management function. CISOs, however, are often not best suited to the task as they need to concentrate on thinking strategically about the response while the incident commander coordinates the tactical actions.

Effective planning means predetermining how all business functions will work together: corporate communications, regulatory affairs, legal, compliance and audit, and business operations. This coordination, together with easily accessible IR documentation, ensures that the organization can react with greater agility during an incident.

Tighten Third-Party Collaboration

Effective IR plans should help improve an organization's relationships with important third parties, such as law enforcement agencies and breach remediation and forensics experts.[2] Often, a lack of planning or a reticence to air dirty laundry can significantly impede effective incident response. One financial services company had no contract with a third-party forensics firm. During a breach, it lost critical time that ran into days while procurement had to work through a new contract and the forensics vendor familiarized itself with the company's network. These are all tasks that should have been done in advance.

In another example, the legal team at a North American company insisted that a felony had been committed due to a breach. The CISO, however, did not want to contact law enforcement officials for fear that they would delay business continuity operations in favor of preserving forensic evidence for trial. To make matters even worse, managers were not even sure which law enforcement agency to contact.

By contrast, when Hyundai Capital realized it had been breached, it immediately contacted the appropriate law enforcement agencies, who moved swiftly. The perpetrators were tracked down relatively quickly and the extent of the breach was limited.

---

[2] Third-party cybersecurity forensic and remediation experts are often engaged directly after a major incident occurs to provide critical assistance, for example, expediting breach containment to mitigate exposure, obtaining evidence for legal requirements, analyzing attack patterns to understand vulnerabilities and identify potential adversaries, and restoring services.

Overcome the Shortfalls of Existing IR Plans

Many companies have an IR plan already. Indeed, some leading organizations invest serious time, money, and effort in these plans. In one typical organization, the IR plan ran to more than 80 pages and was professionally produced. Between them, team members took the equivalent of 20 months to draw it up.

Unfortunately, few plans are robust enough to truly deliver on the three objectives outlined earlier. They are often too generic when they should be guiding specific activities during a crisis. Key decision makers do not always have access to the plans, and the plan can rely too heavily on one or two go-to experts, who can become a point of failure if they are not available. Worst of all, we sometimes see locally optimized response plans, which can be useful for dealing with targeted attacks on specific business units, but are not effective for managing an incident across the whole business. Developing individual plans in silos also inhibits the sharing of relevant knowledge and best practices.

An effective IR plan addresses these shortfalls but, whether starting anew or building upon an existing effort, creating such a plan requires substantial work and dedicated project resources and should be treated as a formal initiative. Before drawing up the plan itself, best-practice organizations assess the existing response protocols and identify the most critical assets at risk. They also need to know which critical business functions will be called upon in an incident and assign the go-to person and the backup person (who should be just as well prepared) for each function. This group is then the core IR team.

Each primary function owner is responsible for maintaining his or her portion of the IR plan, with the IR team leader (who may be the CISO) ensuring that the plan and the cross-functional linkages are updated continuously. This setup cements the idea that the IR plan is not a special cybersecurity initiative but another business-as-usual practice.

Existing response protocols can be a useful framework from which to develop an IR plan template. Equipped with a solid understanding of the existing environment, organizations can assess how effective previous response efforts have been. For each incident, they should identify any problems that arose with the response, diagnose potential causes for failure, and create an exhaustive list of what can go wrong.

We discussed earlier in the book that organizations need to identify which information assets are most critical to business operations in order to be able to develop the data-specific actions to be taken. The IR team needs to talk to the key people from sales, marketing, operations, IT, security, regulatory affairs, and communications in order to understand the vulnerabilities and potential threats to these assets, the business impact if the asset is compromised, and the response required. This means that when the IR plan is needed, the response will be targeted and not generic. The war-gaming process that we discuss later is another important tool in understanding what is at risk.

Once the team has created the structure of the IR document, it should share the draft with the security team. This not only solicits valuable feedback from an eventual end user but also generates excitement for the tool.

The Components of a Robust IR Plan

There is no set template for an IR plan, though the most effective all contain an incident and asset taxonomy, define responsibilities and the war room setup, and—at their heart—have the playbook, broken down for every plausible scenario.

Incident and Asset Taxonomy   Even beyond the United States, organizations typically follow the incident categorization set by the U.S. National Institute of Standards and Technology. Broadly, this defines incidents as either unauthorized access, malicious code, denial of service, or inappropriate use. Adopting a common taxonomy enables institutions to share security intelligence with each other very easily, as well as standardize their own internal communications. Similarly, developing an internally consistent view on critical information assets will ensure the appropriate response based on the type of information compromised. For example, the response for a breach of personally identifiable customer information will differ from that for a breach of a merger and acquisition (M&A) strategy. Having a validated taxonomy of critical information assets is the starting point for reacting in the right way.

Responsibilities and War Room Setup   The war room is an essential IR tool. It is a well-worn concept for the military but applicable in a cyber-attack. A war room is a physical location with supporting infrastructure (IT connectivity, communications, security, and—importantly—snacks) where the preassigned IR team gathers to share knowledge, speed up decision making, and ensure unity of effort while responding to an incident.

Each member of the team, representing the critical business functions, has decision-making authority, but the on-site commander runs the war room, setting the reporting cadence and managing the decision-making process. It is also vital to have a scribe; someone to capture all the decisions that are made, the assumptions that lead to those decisions, the actions to be taken, and the external communications required. The scribe also logs all the outstanding issues to make sure nothing falls through the cracks. All this information is important evidence for stakeholders and regulators when the time comes to examine why the team made the decisions it did.

IR plans need to specify team structures in the event of an incident, individual roles and responsibilities (based on the assets at risk), escalation processes, and war-room protocols. For example, it is important to specify exactly when to involve executive leadership in the decision processes, when to activate a war room, and at what threshold executives should take decisive measures, such as isolating sections of the network or shutting down core applications. Operating models also document the all-important decision rights, for instance, who authorizes contacting law enforcement and which agencies to contact.

The Playbook   The response playbook itself consists of procedural guides including checklists for containment, eradication, and recovery, as well as guidelines for documenting the response in terms of governance, risk, and compliance. The detailed approaches will vary for each type of data and incident.

Even when incidents are of the same type (e.g., a malicious code breach), organizations will define their responses differently based on the types of information assets they believe are at risk. In other words, the type of data being compromised will determine response efforts because the business impact will be different. This is the most critical element of an IR plan and largely determines the success of the overall response.

For example, a company might have one set of response processes for the loss of confidential customer data and an entirely different set of processes for a loss of critical intellectual property (IP) even if both were caused by the same type of attack. The stakeholders are different in each case, and the resources a company will allocate to mitigation will vary.

For example, the goal when responding to a loss of customer data could be to identify the number of customers affected and the extent of data loss within four hours. Within eight hours the security team should have a good idea of who might be responsible for the theft and an estimate of the business impact. If, instead, the breach compromises sensitive M&A details, then the objective might be to determine the impact of each detail on the deal within 24 hours. This would then trigger a set of activities such as notifying key parties, including regulators, counterparty stakeholders, and investors.

The playbook should also clarify when notification should occur; this will vary by country, and even by state in the United States. By September 2014, 47 states had legislation that requires private and government entities to notify individuals if their personally identifiable information has been compromised. However, these laws differ in terms of who must comply, what "personally identifiable information" specifically means, what "compromised" means, and in terms of notice periods and exemptions. These state-level reporting requirements are in addition to any requirements from federal regulatory agencies.[3]

Even the team setup and operating model will vary by incident type, with roles and responsibilities assigned to specific individuals. Some sophisticated IR teams will assign individuals to deal with a particular jurisdiction or a specific regulatory body. The composition of such a team will therefore have to be flexible, depending on where the compromised records are located.

TEST THE PLAN USING WAR GAMES

An IR plan—even a well-designed one—that sits on the shelf is of limited use if the organization is not well versed in how to use it, and if it is not updated regularly. It is not a static document and should not be buried away in a file but rather woven into the fabric of the organization. The plan needs updating after every incident, and there should be continuous work to identify its weaknesses—that is, where things could go wrong—and to make the necessary adjustments.

Best-practice organizations make sure the plan is distributed widely to all relevant parts of the organization. It should be available in print, in digital formats, and on an internal web-based platform. But what really distinguishes a good IR plan from a great one is having the protocols embedded in the organization's muscle memory

[3] National Conference of State Legislatures, "Security Breach Notification Laws," September 3, 2014. www.ncsl.org/research/telecommunications-and-information-technology/security-breach-notification-laws.aspx.

through regular training and practice. War-gaming techniques are one powerful way of achieving this, though they are not a commitment to make lightly. A large company with multiple business units should seek to run such simulations quarterly, with a different scenario each time. A smaller company might run the exercise enterprise-wide twice a year. This may feel like a big time sink, but it is essential. The impact of responding badly or slowly to an (inevitable) attack is far too great.

The armed forces have long conducted war games to test their capabilities, reveal gaps in plans and build their leaders' ability to make decisions in real time. Leading companies have embraced this concept and conduct cyber war games to help them ensure they have an acceptable answer when the CEO asks, "Are we ready?"

A cyber war game is different from traditional penetration testing, in which companies hire hackers to identify technical vulnerabilities such as unsecured network ports or externally facing programs that share too much information in the browser bar. A cyber war game is far more complex. It can yield insights into which information assets require protection, where there are vulnerabilities that attackers can exploit, and flaws in a corporation's ability to respond to an attack, especially in those crucial areas of communications and decision-making processes.

As we mentioned earlier, the very act of setting up a war game starts a discussion between business and security managers about which types of information assets are most important, who would want to compromise them and what the implications of an attack could be in terms of loss of IP, loss of reputation, or business disruption. One public institution found out through designing a war game that while most of its IT security processes were oriented to preventing online fraud, its biggest risk was actually the loss of confidence associated with a public breach.

The analysis required to ensure that scenarios used in the game are realistic can highlight important security vulnerabilities. In preparing for a war game, a retail brokerage discovered that a large share of its most sensitive data was hosted on applications that had not undergone security reviews and that used out-of-date controls for authenticating users.

How to Run a War Game

The first step in producing a war game is to align on its scope and objectives. It should be organized around a business scenario rather than a purely technical breach and naturally the scenario should be relevant to the particular company in terms of both potential attack and the assets that are at risk. For example, a bank set up a scenario in which cyber-criminals used spear-phishing attacks to target high-net-worth customers in order to defraud them, while a high-tech company built a game based on a sophisticated attacker paying a corporate insider to install malware that enabled the theft of critical IP. Table 7.1 outlines the different decisions needed at different phases of the game.

Companies need to decide how many scenarios to incorporate into the game, how sophisticated those scenarios will be, and how much participation will be required from each business function, especially from those who will design and run the war game. After choosing the scenarios, the team running the game identifies what response failures it needs to test for and creates the detailed script that the facilitators will use.

TABLE 7.1 **A War Game Tests Companies' Processes and Nerve**

Phase	Description	Decisions Required
Initial indication of compromise	Employee reports that hackers have been bragging on underground websites that they **have exfiltrated transaction data for five hedge fund clients** with positions in the oil and gas industry Data from security systems and network logs suggests that there **might have been a breach** but data is inconclusive	Given what you know, do you contact affected customers or do you wait? Do you communicate anything to regulators?
Hacktivists issue ultimatum	Hacktivists initiate contact and claim they have **ability to access weeks of trading data** for bank's largest clients As proof, they transmit one week's transaction data for one client They promise to release all client data online unless bank publicly commits to **cease all trading and "speculation" in the oil and gas sector**	Do you ignore or react to the ultimatum? Do you contact the hacktivists and open a dialogue with them? Do you start cooperation with law enforcement?
Media inquiries	Respected news organization contacts bank and says they are in process of confirming reports that client data has been compromised via a breach in bank's systems	What do you tell external media? Do you confirm reports? What do you communicate internally? Do you make any sort of broader communication to customers?
Initial forensics available	Security team confirms that bank is the source of the compromised data, and believes it has localized breach to 1 to 2 core trading systems CISO recommends shutting down affected systems to complete forensics—this will severely limit trading activity	Do you shut down affected systems?

FIGURE 7.1   **Base War-Game Scenario on High-Risk Events for the Business**

Simplified simulation of events/response

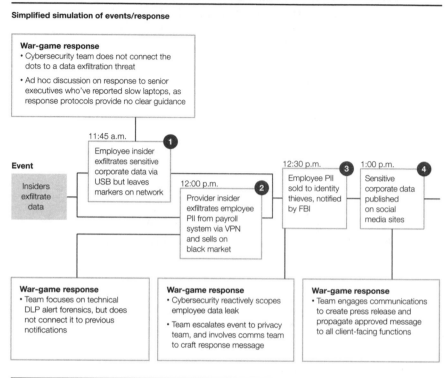

The game should simulate the experience of a real attack: participants receive incomplete information, and objectives may not be fully aligned (Figure 7.1). It should certainly involve participants from beyond information security and indeed beyond IT more broadly. It needs to include customer care, operations, marketing, legal, government affairs, and corporate communications. These sorts of war games happen in real time and can last anywhere from a day to a week or more, depending on the complexity of the scenarios. Throughout the course of the simulation, the facilitator will provide participants with information and what actions they will take. At each turn, the information the players receive depends on the actions they have just taken. Of course, no live systems are involved.

The war game should reveal any flaws in the organization's ability to respond to an attack. Specifically, it looks at three dimensions of the response: the speed of identifying and assessing the breach, the effectiveness of decision making in containing the breach, and the effectiveness of stakeholder communication.

Speed of Identifying and Assessing the Breach   One organization found that the processes used to address a breach were entirely dependent on e-mail and instant messaging. If the attack itself compromised those systems, then the company's ability to respond would be severely hampered.

Effectiveness of Decision Making in Containing the Breach   A large multinational insurer discovered it had no guidelines for deciding when to shut down parts of its IT systems. During the game, senior executives ordered the technology team to sever external connectivity, even though this was not required and, in a real-world situation, would have prevented customers from accessing their accounts. In another example, business managers at a manufacturing company realized they had never thought through the implications if competitors or contractors got access to sensitive information. This meant they were not equipped to change negotiation strategies quickly if proprietary information about their cost structure was disclosed.

Effectiveness of Stakeholder Communication   A war game at the bank testing the spear-phishing scenario revealed that it had no guidelines for communicating with customers whose data had been compromised. In a real attack, the result would have been that those valuable high-net-worth customers would have received an impersonal generic e-mail rather than the tailored personalized communication they would expect.

With the war-game action over and the gaps apparent, the final and most important phase of the process converts the insights generated into actionable steps to improve the organization's ability to respond to an attack. These typically include everything from implementing tools that increase visibility into attacks (such as an advanced analytics engine that detects anomalies that might be indicative of a zero-day attack), clarifying responsibilities, developing guidelines for making high-stakes decisions under pressure, and creating communications protocols that can be pulled off the shelf when required.

Most corporations can plan and conduct a game in 6 to 12 weeks, with an acceptable impact on managers. As we said, they are not a one-off exercise; the cybersecurity landscape is far too dynamic for any company to rest on its laurels. Although conducting this type of war game requires real effort and planning, it remains one of the most effective mechanisms for prioritizing which assets to protect, revealing vulnerabilities, identifying flaws in the ability to respond, and building the type of muscle memory required to make appropriate decisions in real time with limited information.

CONDUCT POSTMORTEMS ON REAL BREACHES TO IMPROVE IR PLAN

War games will not stop a breach occurring. Part of continuously upgrading and refining an IR plan is to incorporate the outcomes of responses to attacks when they do happen. This way, mistakes can be rectified and response protocols improved. Leading organizations already make sure that after a meaningful breach (i.e., one that triggers a response because data is compromised) they take a step back to examine how the IR plan worked. Few, however, conduct a full postmortem. Such a report should analyze the type of incident and determine whether it was categorized correctly (which of course determines the type of response), examine what exactly the attacker did, the specific steps taken by both the security team and other business functions, the degree and success of the response and the level of coordination, and the timeline of events in order to identify inefficiencies, errors, or areas where the IR plan lacked information.

Most companies allocate postmortem responsibility to the security operations team, but they tend to focus almost exclusively on the technical postmortem—that is, what sort of malware was used, which systems it tried to exploit etc. But this ignores how the organization responded, which is so important to stakeholders. Therefore the postmortem needs to be taken out of the hands of the CISO and given to someone with cross-functional responsibilities.

The postmortem team can also conduct what-if analysis to determine how different response actions at each phase might have affected the effectiveness of the attack. All this data then needs to be fed back and incorporated into the IR plan as part of an organization's continuous testing and learning about how to respond to a cybersecurity incident.

• • •

A company can prioritize its information assets and determine the most effective set of defense mechanisms to put in place for each of its important information assets. It can integrate security into core business processes and change the behavior of frontline users. It can build security into its application and infrastructure architectures, and it can engage in active defense. These all make it less likely that a company will suffer a breach, but none can ensure that a company will not be breached. Therefore, achieving digital resilience requires the creation and aggressive testing of IR capabilities to respond to breaches, not only in technology but across all business functions.

Progress in this area requires that senior executives in almost every business area participate in war games to test and enhance response functions. In addition, the general counsel, the chief risk officer and the chief information officer should support the synchronization of the cybersecurity IR plan with other corporate crisis management plans.

8

Build a Program that Drives toward Digital Resilience

Digital resilience will not come from implementing a discrete set of technological or process changes. The levers described in this book are an interrelated, mutually reinforcing system. Putting them in place requires significant behavioral changes not only within the cybersecurity function, but across IT and all major business processes and functions. Change of that scale requires companies to address a set of daunting structural and organizational challenges, including deep-seated mind-set shifts about what cybersecurity aims to achieve and who is responsible for it.

Yet despite the scale of the challenge, even some of the biggest and most sophisticated organizations fail to acknowledge the extent of change required. They try to avoid the problems rather than address them head-on and their security programs remain focused on a series of technical implementations rather than on undertaking a fundamental change in the operating model. The result is often incomplete buy-in from the organization as a whole, which complicates decision making, slows implementation and reduces the chance that the required resources will be available for the program.

Indeed, such a blinkered approach does not just increase the risk of being hacked, it risks slowing down the company's ability to innovate and grow, and will contribute to that $3 trillion shortfall in the value from technology.

Companies must understand what the journey to digital resilience means in practical terms; and they need to be clear on how to get there with a plan that is crystal clear on the priorities all the way from program design to implementation. Crucially, they must ensure that the entire shift remains rooted in long-term business imperatives not technological quick fixes.

WHAT IT TAKES TO GET TO DIGITAL RESILIENCE

Companies face three major challenges in achieving digital resilience. First, they need to get the business engagement and collaboration required to prioritize business risks, make intelligent trade-offs and implement business changes that could help protect information assets. Too often, they conduct mechanistic assessments that do not get to the real issues.

Second, they need to make resiliency a top priority in IT, which has become accustomed to short-term cost and speed objectives.

Finally, they need to improve the skills of the cybersecurity function to make it much more nimble, but most companies find this immensely challenging, especially in a tight labor market.

Drive Business Collaboration and Engagement

Many cybersecurity decisions have far-reaching market and strategic effects and therefore require input from senior business managers. Moreover, many of the ways that companies can better protect information assets require action from outside either cybersecurity or the IT organization more broadly. Success therefore hinges on support from senior business managers. But getting the right level of senior engagement is tough—the language is arcane, the skills required to interact with senior executives are often lacking, and few tools exist to quantify cybersecurity risk or its mitigation.

Companies Need to Accept Risks Given Business Imperatives   Cybersecurity is all-pervasive. It touches every business process and function; but just as business processes rely on valuable information, they also create vulnerabilities that attackers can exploit. For example, product development decisions often can increase the sensitive customer data collected and procurement decisions can lead to new vendors who may not treat sensitive intellectual property with the required care.

Companies need to make sophisticated trade-offs between these risks and competitive imperatives. As one investment banking CISO said, "If I did as thorough a security assessment as I would like before we nailed up a direct connection to a hedge fund, our prime brokerage business would cease to exist."

The questions companies must ask themselves when implementing cybersecurity programs include:

- Will more rigorous password controls for online portals slow customer acquisition?
- Will in-line network controls increase latency and noticeably worsen the customer experience?
- How tightly are we willing to limit access to proprietary intellectual property (IP) used in product development processes?
- How intrusively will we monitor employee activity in order to reduce the risks associated with insider threats?
- How will remediation of insecure applications be prioritized against new business functionality?
- When can data be purged and when should it be retained because of its potential analytic value?
- How much will increasing vendor security requirements reduce the pool of eligible bidders for key services, hurt negotiating power, and therefore increase procured costs?

Action Needed Far Outside the Cybersecurity Function   Most of the critical levers companies must pull to achieve digital resilience extend beyond the cybersecurity team. We have already seen how operations functions have to adopt new business processes; marketing and corporate communications teams need to be primed in the event of a breach; and application development groups have to adopt secure coding techniques and fix insecure applications. There are many more examples. All these actions require new ways of working and thinking in each business function and many of these changes will require substantial one-time project capacity.

Breaking through the noise to spur frontline managers to action can be difficult. Frontline managers often feel overwhelmed by an endless stream of corporate initiatives: Sarbanes-Oxley, Anti-Money Laundering, Six Sigma, organizational restructurings, cost programs—the list goes on. To cut through this, the most senior members of the management team, including the CEO, must be actively engaged in supporting the CISOs and the chief information officers (CIOs). It is only they who can make decisions about the overall level of appetite for cybersecurity-related risk; it is only they who can prioritize information assets and make the trade-offs between risk reduction and operational impact; and it is only they who can prioritize remediation activities over all the other business priorities that fall on the shoulders of frontline staff.

Getting the Right Level of Business Engagement Is Tough   The arcane nature of cybersecurity makes it hard to engage effectively with the senior executive team. Senior business executives already consider IT managers to be a priesthood that uses impenetrable jargon to describe mysterious issues such as software development life cycles, agile development, data architecture, and cloud computing. Cybersecurity is even more confusing. Even those senior executives who feel they have a solid grasp of concepts like applications, data centers, networks, and desktop devices may throw up their hands in frustration when the discussion turns to access controls, machine learning to combat insider threats, and intrusion detection.

The limitations in quantifying cybersecurity risks make it even harder to engage senior executives. They are frustrated by the lack of the type of meaningful metrics they use to assess productivity, quality, or risk in other areas. A banking chief risk officer (CRO) can tell the rest of the management team that the institution has a capital adequacy ratio of 7.5 percent while its peers are in the 7.7 to 7.8 percent range, and the regulator is pushing for 8 percent.[1] A mining CRO can tell her board that the company has averaged two accidents per 10,000 operational full-time equivalents, and that an investment of a few million dollars might reduce that to 1.8.

A CISO does not have these numbers at hand. There is no single metric like value at risk for cybersecurity, and this makes it much harder to communicate the overall level of risk to senior managers and engage them in decisions. Cybersecurity defies this type of precise quantification because it involves so many different types of risks. Some, like cyber-fraud, regulatory fines, legal exposure, and remediation costs, can be directly tied to an immediate financial impact. Others cannot, like the

---

[1] Capital adequacy ratio provides an indication of liquidity risk by measuring the ratio of core capital (i.e., Tier 1 and Tier 2 assets) to overall risk-weighted assets.

reputational impact or the loss of IP. If a foreign competitor steals the plans for a new manufacturing process, how can the company quantify how much of a product's value depends on the new process, let alone the extent to which the competitor could exploit the information. Companies simply cannot answer these questions confidently and precisely.

Quantifying the likelihood of the risks and the impact of remediation can be even more challenging given the paucity of historical data, especially for major breaches that will occur rarely at any one institution. CIOs and CISOs cannot credibly say, "Currently, there is a 22 percent likelihood of a major breach over the next two years and that could go down to 15 percent if we spent an additional $100 million next year."

At one major financial institution, the CISO was asked to come up with three cybersecurity metrics to add to the CEO-level scorecard. Given the scorecard's design criteria, all the options he considered were deemed either less than relevant (e.g., pace of attacks), too narrow (e.g., fraud losses), or too subjective (e.g., qualitative risk assessment). As the chief financial officer (CFO) at another institution told us, "It feels like we're constantly spending more on security, but I have no idea whether that's enough or even what it does."

With all these challenges, it is no surprise that the levels of engagement between senior management and the cybersecurity function vary enormously. We heard about companies where the CISO meets the CEO every few weeks, and we heard about companies where the CISO reports to the CTO (who reports to the CIO, who reports to the CFO) and has never met with the CEO. Even where the C-suite acknowledges the gravity of the issue, CIOs and CISOs still hear the plea, "Just tell me that it can't happen here."

Use the Resiliency Program to Drive Business Engagement   Given the challenges of achieving tighter business collaboration and stronger engagement, companies have to explicitly design their resiliency programs to address this vital issue.

A typical program starts by assessing the state of play and from there developing a perspective on information assets and business risks. Immediately, this helps senior business leaders understand what is at risk and why it's important. Defining an aspiration around business themes rather than technology will also improve the understanding of and commitment to the change required. Providing pragmatic options, with different risk and resource implications, will draw out senior management's implicit risk appetite—and make sure the program as a whole is aligned with it. Building modules into the project plan to engage with each individual business line on differentiated protections will help ensure that business managers take responsibility for making decisions on cybersecurity risks. Finally, governance structures that enable senior managers to weigh in on the dozens of cybersecurity decisions will further emphasize that these issues are owned by the business, not the high priests of IT.

Focus the IT Organization

In many respects, enterprise IT management is a form of risk management. All day, every day, application development and infrastructure managers make risk management decisions. Should they agree to complete a development project in three months, or will it really take four months to do the job right? How many test scripts and test cycles should they plan for? Will they use a traditional piece of packaged software or a new public cloud offering? How quickly should they get a new software patch into production? Should they refresh this outdated infrastructure this year or wait until next? The questions are endless, the answers critical to determining the company's risk exposure.

Enterprise IT organizations are rarely set up to address resiliency systematically. For years, senior managers have focused on budget reductions and the rapid delivery of tactical capabilities over creating sustainable and resilient architectures. In many cases, annual IT budget processes drive resources to short-term efforts that pay for themselves within the year. Partly because of this short-term focus (and partly because they often lack confidence in their own cybersecurity skills), many IT managers believe they can outsource worrying about security implications to the CISO and his team. As a result, companies wind up with application and infrastructure platforms that are not only inefficient and inflexible, but also intrinsically insecure.

A program for achieving digital resilience cannot fix everything in IT, but it can be a powerful force for encouraging changes in the broader IT organization. It can provide an honest account of how shortcomings in the application and infrastructure environments (e.g., outdated business applications, infrastructure software that is no longer supported by vendors, insufficient patching, inflexible network environments) create security vulnerabilities. It can be synchronized with other technology improvement programs to help make the case for change, to ensure that new architectures are built to be secure, and to encourage a priority list that addresses the most important risks fast. It can also put in place operating model changes that increase IT executives' level of ownership and accountability in terms of addressing vulnerabilities in the platforms they manage.

Upgrade Cybersecurity Skills

Achieving digital resilience requires a dramatic improvement in the skills and capabilities of the people in the cybersecurity organization. Each of the seven resiliency levers will stretch the skill and talent models for a cybersecurity organization:

1. *Prioritize information assets based on business risks.* This requires business analysts who can connect business strategies, value chains, and operational processes on the one hand and cybersecurity risks and defense mechanisms on the other.

2. *Provide differentiated protection for the most important assets.* This requires security architects who can stay up to date with the highly fragmented and dynamic vendor landscape for technologies such as identity and access management (I&AM), data loss protection (DLP), antimalware, and a dozen others.

3. *Integrate cybersecurity into enterprise-wide risk management and governance processes.* This requires senior managers who can engage effectively with executives in a range of business functions.

4. *Enlist frontline personnel to protect the information assets they use.* This requires a small number of communications specialists who can translate cybersecurity risks into compelling messages that will change the mind-sets and behaviors of targeted groups of users.

5. *Integrate cybersecurity into the technology environment.* This requires application and infrastructure architects who have deep expertise in secure application development, cloud security, desktop virtualization, mobile security, and software defined networking.

6. *Deploy active defenses to engage attackers.* This requires security intelligence and data analysts who can gather insights and

identify patterns based on external feeds and data from the company's own IT environment.

7. *Test continuously to improve incident response across business functions.* This requires targeted, specialized expertise in war-game development and incident response (IR) planning.

Almost no company's cybersecurity team has all of these skills today, let alone in sufficient quantity to drive toward digital resilience. Moreover, the tight market for cybersecurity talent means companies cannot simply hire the resources they need externally. As a result, companies have to build this capability upgrade explicitly into their programs. Part of this will have to be targeted external hires, and many companies will also outsource some execution activities such as security monitoring in order to free up existing capacity for more value-added tasks. But simply getting the team's hands dirty will be the most important way to improve. The best way to learn how to run a cybersecurity war game is to run a cybersecurity war game, perhaps starting with a simple game in a smaller business unit, but then rapidly increasing the scale and complexity of the exercise. Similarly, the best way to learn how to engage in active defense is to start gathering the data, perform the analysis, and start tracking attackers.

SIX STEPS TO LAUNCH A DIGITAL RESILIENCE PROGRAM

Senior business managers are engaged, the IT function understands what digital resilience means and the cybersecurity team is eager to get started. But the challenges inherent in moving from a basic cybersecurity mind-set to full organizational digital resilience mean that organizations need to take a measured approach.

To launch an effective program, institutions have to first set the agenda, which means understand the full scope of the program, define their goals, and decide how the cybersecurity function should operate. Then they need to set out the plan for how to get there, considering the major risk/resource trade-offs and ensuring that the road map is aligned with both business imperatives and the technology needed to deliver. Finally, they can move to execution ensuring they track progress and have sustained engagement across business functions on cybersecurity issues (Table 8.1).

TABLE 8.1 **Six Steps to Design and Launch a Digital Resilience Program**

Phase	Steps	Key Outputs
Set the agenda	1. Surface the full set of issues	Prioritized information risks and business risks Comprehensive baseline of existing capabilities Comparison to relevant best practices Identification of issues and gaps in addressing business risks
	2. Define an aspirational but specific target state	Strategic themes for future cybersecurity capability Specific actions required to achieve each strategic theme
	3. Determine how to evolve the cybersecurity delivery system	Future cybersecurity organizational structure, operational processes, talent mix, performance management systems, and sourcing arrangements
Create the road map	4. Set out the risk/resource trade-offs for senior management	Major options that provide senior management with a range of risk versus resources trade-offs Business criteria for selecting between options
	5. Develop a plan aligned with both business and technology	Launch charters for all initiatives required Detailed implementation plan for milestones, dependencies, resources, and critical success factors
Launch execution	6. Ensure sustained business engagement on cybersecurity issues	Mechanism to track progress, raise issues, make required decisions and remove barriers Messages and other reinforcing mechanisms from executive team to ensure that managers across business functions play their part in protecting critical information assets

1. Surface the Full Set of Issues

You cannot figure out where to go if you do not know where you're starting from. Get this first stage wrong and you end up with a cybersecurity program that is too narrow, not sufficiently aspirational, and lacks management support. To get the facts required to drive toward digital resilience, a company has to start with the information assets and business risks, understand the relationships between different types of controls, and look at capabilities in a comprehensive way.

Start with Information Assets   There is a natural inclination to want to benchmark cybersecurity. There is, after all, some psychological safety in numbers. However, even institutions in the same industry can have very different risk profiles based on the data they have, the countries they operate in, their public profiles, and the business and technology strategies they pursue.

It is impossible to have an intelligent perspective on how well a cybersecurity function performs without understanding what it needs to protect. A cybersecurity function that makes perfect sense for a mid-market consumer packaged goods company would, for example, be laughably inadequate for a large bank.

Failing to start with information assets and business risks leads to the wrong downstream choices. One financial institution started its program with an assessment of regulatory requirements. Two years later, it had spent a lot of money and made some technical progress but had devoted almost all its efforts to protecting consumers' personal information to the exclusion of other types of important information assets.

Earlier in this book, we laid out a set of principles and an approach for identifying and prioritizing information assets—that should be applied in the earliest days of any cybersecurity program. Depending on the size and complexity of the institution, it may be necessary to prioritize information assets and business risks in phases, starting with a comprehensive prioritization across all business and then drilling in to perform a detailed evaluation of each business in turn.

Assess Risks in an Integrated Way   An attacker does not have to defeat an institution's I&AM or intrusion detection environment—she has to defeat a system of defenses that spans many different types of controls, and she will have a much harder time if those defenses interlock.

Unfortunately, many assessments are structured so that there is a separate score for each element: intrusion detection, I&AM, data protection, incident response, and the like, but no way to look at how these controls combine to protect important information assets. By contrast, looking at how well or badly the combination of password controls, encryption, user training, and DLP currently protects financial transaction data for high-net-worth customers (to take one example) naturally leads to decisions about how to put the right set of differentiated protections in place for such a critically important information asset.

Address the Full Set of Capabilities   We often hear CISOs say, "I want to do a security control assessment." Immediately, that frames the assessment around a tactical set of issues: how good is the intrusion detection or antimalware environment? By excluding strategic alignment, risk management processes, security architecture, and the overall delivery system, the assessment can end up delivering changes only within cybersecurity, when what is needed are changes to business processes much more broadly.

Off-the-shelf accreditations and guidance such as ISO 27001[2] and the U.S. National Institute of Science and Technology's "Framework for Improving Critical Infrastructure Cybersecurity"[3] can be extremely valuable in broadening how organizations think about assessing cybersecurity, but even they have their scope limitations. They underemphasize, for example, product security and many types of third-party risks. In fact, almost all such frameworks focus on technology-related risks at the expense of business process changes like purging sensitive information that is no longer required, creating a secure process for higher-risk transactions, or creating incentives for customers to engage with the company in a more secure way, all of which can have tremendous benefits.

An effective cybersecurity capability assessment must credibly answer the following questions:

- *Strategic.* Is the overall direction of the cybersecurity function consistent with the principles of digital resilience? Are there mechanisms being put in place to prioritize information assets, drive cybersecurity considerations across business processes, enlist frontline users, respond to breaches across business functions, build security into broader IT architectures, and implement active defenses?

- *Governance.* Does the institution have the facts and processes required to make intelligent risk management decisions about

---

[2] ISO 27001 is probably the most common cybersecurity standard. It traces its origins to a code of practice published by the U.K. Department of Trade and Industry in 1992. Since then, it has been adopted and extended first by the British Standards Institute in 1995 and then by the International Organization for Standardization (ISO) and the International Electrotechnical Organization (IEC) as ISO 17799 in 2000 and then as ISO 27001 in 2005.

[3] National Institute of Science and Technology, "NIST Releases Cybersecurity Framework Version 1.0," U.S. Department of Commerce, February 12, 2014. www.nist.gov/itl/csd/launch-cybersecurity-framework-021214.cfm.

cybersecurity policies? Does it understand its assets, attackers, and vulnerabilities? Can it prioritize risks and evaluate potential defense mechanisms objectively?

- *Controls.* What is the level of sophistication and capability across the full range of potential controls (e.g., I&AM, DLP, encryption, application security, network security, infrastructure security)?
- *Security architecture.* To what extent is the technology platform that underpins cybersecurity controls comprehensive, coherent, integrated, and modular and able to incorporate rapidly evolving new tools and vendor offerings?
- *Delivery system.* To what extent does the cybersecurity function have the right structure, processes, capabilities, performance management systems, and sourcing arrangements to operate in a sustainable and efficient way and to continue to improve capabilities?

Many companies have not answered these questions fully, even as they launch their cybersecurity programs. The result is that they do not understand the systemic changes they need to put in place.

2. Define an Aspirational but Specific Target State

There are a thousand directions a company's cybersecurity program could go in: different assets it could focus on, different policies it could define, different technologies it could implement, and different skills it could foster. How, therefore, does a company determine a goal that is both bold and specific to the company's business situation, that is coherent across a wide range of actions, that is sufficiently aspirational, and, crucially, that is simple enough to explain so that it can build organizational support?

The answer is to connect the seven digital resiliency levers to business risks, use business process changes as well as technical controls, and integrate changes into major themes that will communicate intent and galvanize support.

Connect Digital Resiliency Levers to Business Risks   This book has laid out a set of levers that are critical for companies driving toward resiliency. Asking how to use each lever to address high-priority business risks will highlight the capabilities that are needed in the target state.

Let us imagine that a bank's assessment prioritizes the risk that staff—either its own or those from vendors—compromise the confidentiality of the customer information it uses to underwrite loans to corporate customers. Each digital resiliency lever has a role to play in managing this risk.

- *Prioritize information assets based on business risks.* Business managers need to determine what criteria determine whether a particular loan might be especially high risk, for example, whether the loan is related to high-profile merger and acquisition (M&A) activity or is for a controversial business project.
- *Provide differentiated protection for the most important assets.* Use DLP controls to log (and in some cases block) e-mail and printing of documents that are related to highly sensitive transactions, and digital rights management (DRM) controls to prevent unauthorized users accessing them.
- *Integrate cybersecurity into enterprise-wide risk management and governance processes.* Negotiate requirements about how vendor-provided staff handle documents related to sensitive transactions into the vendor contracts.
- *Enlist frontline personnel to protect the information assets they use.* Provide targeted training for underwriting professionals on the value of the data they touch, the impact if it fell into the wrong hands, and the standard procedures for handling sensitive data—and encourage people to speak if they see those procedures being violated.
- *Integrate cybersecurity into the technology environment.* Create a well-functioning document management capability, so underwriting professionals do not have to use e-mail to store and transmit sensitive loan documents.
- *Deploy active defenses to engage attackers.* Build analytics to identify potential risks; for example, an employee who recently had a poor performance review, has been accessing large numbers of files not related to his current projects, and has generated multiple DLP alerts may represent an elevated risk for using sensitive documents inappropriately.
- *Test continuously to improve incident response across business functions.* Develop protocols for communicating with customers and collaborating with law enforcement in the event of a breach.

By looking across each lever for each priority business risk, cybersecurity managers can ask themselves two important questions: (1) will the set of actions, in aggregate, sufficiently address the risk; and (2) are there any duplicate actions that can be removed, given the nature of the risk?

In particular, given many companies' history of focusing on external attackers, CISOs need to make sure a resiliency program fully addresses insider threats.

Use Business Process Changes As Well As Technical Controls   Once cybersecurity managers have applied the seven digital resilience levers to each of the most important business risks in order to identify a broad set of potential actions, they have to make sure they are considering the right mix of controls.

Mechanisms to protect information assets fall into three categories:

1. *Business process controls*. These are changes to end-user behavior and business processes beyond IT. They include actions such as purging data and improving training, creating secure paths for sensitive assets, programs to change customer behavior, vendor policies, M&A/joint venture security processes, war gaming, and business product security architecture.

2. *Broader IT controls*. These are changes to the broader IT architecture and operating model and include secure public and private cloud services, secure coding, secure application architecture, secure infrastructure operations, and secure mobility/end-user devices.

3. *Cybersecurity controls*. These are the technology capabilities and processes focused on protecting information. They include encryption, I&AM, threat management, perimeter security, security analytics, and security operations.

Achieving digital resilience requires using all three types of controls in concert but, given traditional mind-sets, there is a strong tendency in many programs to lean heavily or exclusively on the cybersecurity controls alone. But this can make the cybersecurity program more expensive and intrusive than it needs to be. New cybersecurity controls carry with them the time and cost of implementing a new technology system; business process controls such as purging data or creating secure paths for sensitive data can be implemented more quickly and cheaply. New cybersecurity controls can add complexity to a company's technology architecture, while broader IT controls such as private cloud services and software-defined networking can simultaneously improve security and agility.

Synthesize the Required Changes into Themes   Applying all the digital resilience levers to all the priority business risks will inevitably generate a list of potential actions, but the list will be too long, with too many overlaps, and be too complex for any organization to rally around. Companies find they more readily get organizational buy-in and make faster progress when they synthesize the broad set of improvements they need to make into a short list of major themes.

To develop the themes, cybersecurity managers need to consolidate similar or duplicate actions and then prioritize by scoring the remaining actions in terms of how many priority business risks they address and how much change they will require compared to the current state. Once managers strip out those actions where the reduction is risk is too low given the complexity of implementation, they can aggregate the remaining actions into broader themes.

One health care provider developed nine strategic themes (a typical number), each of which contained specific initiatives and actions. They included:

- Protect personal health information across the entire business system from patient to doctor, through the hospital and, when relevant, to supporting vendors.
- Scrutinize insider activities, both accidental and intentional, at the same level as external activity.
- Minimize corporate "surface area," by rationalizing applications and systems.
- Detect and respond to cyber-events in order to minimize business harm and disruption to care delivery.

These themes enabled managers to describe the program to senior management, rally staff around a program of change, and ultimately track progress.

3. Determine How to Evolve the Cybersecurity Delivery System

Achieving digital resilience will necessarily stress the cybersecurity function. The operational processes, sourcing arrangements, people models, and organizational structures currently in place to operate security as a control function will become increasingly inadequate. There are three issues in particular that cybersecurity managers should pay attention to: streamlining operational processes, revising organizational structures, and upgrading skills.

Streamlining Operational Processes   Cybersecurity includes a set of operational processes, from updating access rights for accounts to assessing vendor security capabilities to reviewing application security architectures. Historically, business and IT managers have seen these processes as slow and cumbersome and as a brake on the rest of the organization's ability to get things done quickly. Many aspects of digital resilience will place additional stress on these processes. For example, as a company starts to place different protections in place for its most important information assets, it will need to be able to implement much more granular policies on passwords and access rights. That could swamp existing processes, reducing business agility and frustrating business and IT managers even more.

Cybersecurity teams may find that applying lean IT mechanisms to drive waste out of security processes would be extremely profitable.[4] An insurance company segmented requests by complexity, eliminated rework, and ran activities in core security processes in parallel, improving both productivity and response time by 30 percent.

Align on the Required Organizational Structure   Not long ago, IT security was just another technology domain in many organizations' IT infrastructure function. Just as the head of IT infrastructure had a manager for the data center, the network, and for desktop domains, he also had an IT security manager responsible for technologies such as remote access, antivirus, and firewalls.

Much has changed since then. Most, but not all, companies have appointed a CISO and expanded the remit of their security organizations. However, the novelty of these changes means that there

---

[4] For more on lean in IT, see McKinsey & Company, "Lean Transformation in IT Maintenance." www.mckinsey.com/client_service/business_technology/case_studies/lean_transformation_in_it_maintenance.

is still a lot of variation and often fragmentation in cybersecurity organizational models, which can minimize the effectiveness of a digital resilience program. As they put such programs in place, companies need to consolidate cybersecurity resources, determine the right reporting and role for the CISO, and create structures that facilitate interactions with business units on security strategy.

Cybersecurity is a technologically sophisticated domain that depends heavily on tools, and companies need to use both their expertise and the tools across businesses rather than fragment them. Yet some companies still have substantial cybersecurity activity in each business unit. One bank found that it had as many cybersecurity personnel embedded in the businesses as in its central security organization, with as much as 15 percent redundant through overlaps. Leading companies are starting to consolidate cybersecurity strategy, architecture, management of technologies, operations, and I&AM and vendor governance, while continuing to maintain a much smaller number of decentralized staff to perform business-specific activities such as project governance. This setup yields both capability and efficiency benefits.

Deciding to consolidate is relatively straightforward, but selecting the right role and reporting relationship for the CISO's organization is much more complicated. There are four fairly common models:

1. *Traditional.* The CISO has organizational ownership for all aspects of cybersecurity and reports to the head of infrastructure.
2. *Mainstream.* The CISO has organizational ownership for all aspects of cybersecurity and reports directly to the CIO.
3. *IT risk.* The head of IT risk has organizational ownership of all aspects of cybersecurity plus responsibility for other IT risk issues (e.g., disaster recovery, quality, IT compliance) and reports directly to the CIO, possibly with a dotted line to the CRO.
4. *Strategic.* The CISO has organizational ownership for strategy, policy, and governance and reports to the CRO; operational aspects of cybersecurity are typically owned by the head of infrastructure.

Fewer and fewer companies that are serious about cybersecurity use the traditional model, in which the CISO reports into the head of infrastructure. The structure simply does not provide the seniority and visibility that the security team needs to drive resiliency. It underscores a company's view of cybersecurity as a "technology" rather than a "business" issue, and makes it much harder to recruit high-quality cybersecurity talent.

Most companies use some variant of the mainstream model, with the CISO reporting to the CIO, sometimes with a dotted line to the CRO. This gives the CISO more visibility and seniority without the complexity of developing a common approach across different IT risk domains or teasing apart the cybersecurity team into its strategic and operational components. This option tends to work well for organizations that are further behind in terms of cybersecurity maturity and need to pick up speed.

Both the IT risk and strategic models require additional organizational sophistication. Getting full value from the IT risk model requires developing common approaches for managing risk across cybersecurity, vendor risk, disaster recovery, and compliance. Obviously, this can be enormously powerful and allows the CISO to look at issues across a variety of domains, but success requires some degree of maturity in each individual IT risk domain.

Likewise, the strategic model can be powerful in that it can ensure that short-term operational imperatives do not crowd out risk prioritization, strategy development, and governance. Having the CISO (or head of IT risk) report directly to the CRO also emphasizes that cybersecurity is a business risk just like any other risk. However, it also requires splitting out the operational aspects of cybersecurity from the strategy and keeping them firmly in IT—no CIO can afford to let staff from risk, or indeed from anywhere outside his organization, touch IT operations directly.

A major health care company decided that creating a strategic CISO would enhance its focus on protecting the confidentiality and integrity of patient data. It had already invested for several years to get to a basic level of cybersecurity maturity and felt comfortable breaking apart the cybersecurity organization, with the more technical and operational activities remaining in the infrastructure function. Naturally, the CISO and the senior IT team invested in real-time mapping out the links between the new cybersecurity group and the IT organization in order to ensure that the strategies and policies the new group developed continued to be relevant.

Upgrade Skills and Resources   As noted earlier, achieving digital resilience will require new types of skills. The cybersecurity labor market is tight, so improving the function's skills and resources may be both one of the most challenging and most important aspects of a digital resilience program. There are four techniques that leading organizations use to upgrade the capabilities of their cybersecurity teams.

First, they focus relentlessly on retention, given that every employee who leaves represents one more slot the CISO has to fill. Basic managerial hygiene matters a lot, especially when high performers have so many options. In addition, some companies place a sharp focus on exposure, career paths, and community participation. They deliberately give high performers the opportunity to interact with senior business leaders and sometimes the board. They create well-articulated career paths for security professionals, sometimes including the opportunity to rotate through application development, infrastructure, and business functions. They also provide the time and space for high performers to participate in industry and technology forums focused on cybersecurity.

Second, they draw from nontraditional talent pools. Not only do they recruit relatively young professionals from the military and intelligence communities to specialize in security intelligence and data analytics, but they also poach intrinsically strong problem solvers from elsewhere in the IT organization and sometimes from business functions as well. Realizing that they have to take a long-term view, they establish relationships with colleges and universities (and, in a few cases, high schools) to create a pipeline of technical talent in the areas they operate.

Third, they minimize the time devoted to lower-value activities by automating wherever possible. As we saw in the chapter on active defense, they are building arrangements with managed security service providers who can perform operational activities such as security monitoring or basic triage, thereby releasing internal staff for more value-added tasks.

Fourth, and most importantly, leading cybersecurity organizations build capabilities by doing. The best way to build capabilities in war gaming is to conduct a war game. The best way to understand how to prioritize information assets is to pick a line of business and work with its leadership team to assess those information assets and business risks. Cybersecurity organizations that are lagging behind let the absence of a capability stand in the way of developing that capability. Leading organizations aggressively push themselves to advance their capabilities in business engagement, security architecture, war gaming, active defense, and other areas.

4. Set Out the Risk/Resource Trade-offs for Senior Management

Everyone in cybersecurity agrees that risk appetite is important but different companies have different tolerances for risk based on their sector, culture, and overall business strategy. A digital resilience program must deliver an overall level of risk that is in line with this risk appetite.

The challenge, as we have already mentioned, is that there is no simple metric for quantifying cybersecurity risk. This means rather than trying to formulate some highly abstract (and therefore largely meaningless) statement of risk appetite, CIOs and CISOs should instead present managers with three or four pragmatic options that represent different levels of risk reduction and resource commitment and use this to gauge their risk appetite.

For example, the cybersecurity team at a North American bank laid out an ambitious goal that would be an enormous change from where it stood. They argued that some of the actions required were essential to reach a minimum standard of responsible practice. Many other actions were standard practice for their peers and also provided additional protection for their most important information assets. A final set of actions was more cutting edge and relevant to more sophisticated attackers.

Based on this, the team developed three options with progressive levels of protection and resource commitment: (1) the minimum standard, (2) protect priority assets, and (3) defend against sophisticated attackers. More importantly, the team also calculated a rough costing for each option and described which types of business risks each option would protect the institution against (Table 8.2).

Although the work that went into this was time consuming, the benefit of being able to present senior managers with such a digestible set of options was immeasurable. It allowed for a robust discussion about how much additional capital investment, operating expense, and management attention the company could afford to devote to the cybersecurity program and how much risk reduction that would buy.

Unsurprisingly, the bank's senior management decided that it had a responsibility to go beyond the bare minimum of basic practice. However, because it did not have the public profile and global footprint of the largest banks, they also decided that the investment required to deliver cutting edge protection against the most sophisticated attackers did not make sense given their challenging financial constraints. Instead, the bank settled on the middle option of making sure it had differentiated protection for its most important information assets.

TABLE 8.2 **Options for Risk Reduction/Resource Commitment Trade-offs**

	Meet Minimum Standard	Protect Important Information Assets	Defend against Sophisticated Attackers
Themes and Related Initiatives			
Enhance business engagement	Implement metrics to track progress, capabilities, and future design	Establish business-unit aligned cybersecurity points of contact Create targeted training for key user groups	Integrate cybersecurity metrics in goals and objectives for senior business managers
Implement "fit for purpose" control model	Establish ownership for business information and assets Classify information assets based on sensitivity Implement tiered I&AM model, with multifactor authentication for priority systems Align new vendor contracts with new security requirements	Expand use of encryption at rest Review backlog of contracts to identify gaps to security requirements and address Apply use of DLP to structured data	Move sensitive unstructured data to document management systems Extend DLP to unstructured data
Enhance application and infrastructure security	Move engagement with security team earlier in the software development life cycle	Train every developer on secure coding practices Implement one-time passwords for privileged access	Accelerate migration of private cloud and virtual desktops Segment network to reduce lateral movement
Create enhanced SOC and improve incident response	Create SOC that links intelligence to operations Codify IR plans and establish links to other crisis management plans	Expand and advance independent technical security assessments to verify security posture Conduct ongoing regime of cybersecurity war games	Implement deep packet inspection and malware detection and detonation Implement advanced server and endpoint analytics
Selected Risks Addressed by Scenario			
Significant distributed denial of service attack could interfere with payment systems	√	√	√
Insider could accidentally release customer information		√	√
Insider could take underwriting practices when he left for competitor			√
Sophisticated attacker could corrupt financial transactions			√
...			

177

5. Develop a Plan Aligned with Both Business and Technology

Once companies have assessed existing cybersecurity capabilities, defined where they want to be given the risk appetite, and aligned on an organizational model, they need to develop a plan for making all the necessary changes. To develop and launch an effective plan, companies must not only apply traditional program management rigor but also sequence the plan based on business risks, integrate it with a broader set of IT change programs, and create top-down program oversight.

Apply Traditional Program Management Rigor   All the practices critical to the success of any major business-technology program are equally important for a cybersecurity program. A company must appoint a single a responsible leader for the overall program, in this case typically the CISO. It must define work streams with specific actionable initiatives. Each initiative must have a manager who will be accountable and devote real effort to the initiative, a charter that lays out expected outcomes, and a work plan that articulates milestones, dependencies, and resource requirements. The initiatives must be synthesized into an overall road map that provides insight into resource requirements and the interdependencies across initiatives.

Sequence the Plan Based on Business Risks   Traditionally, cybersecurity plans have been based on the different types of controls that need to be implemented or upgraded. However, to truly integrate cybersecurity into business processes and strategies, a full digital resilience plan would include initiatives aligned by business as well as by technology controls. For example, an insurance firm originally designed its cybersecurity program around regulatory requirements and developed a plan to implement a series of technology controls. As a result, the program did not focus on the most important assets and did not drive change in individual business units—most senior executives barely knew what it did.

After the insurer invested the time to think through its most important information assets and business risks, it redesigned and resequenced its plan. In addition to putting in place new technology capabilities, it also laid out initiatives to roll through each business in its portfolio over 18 months to assess their information assets, identify business process changes that would protect critical information, and implement differentiated controls. It tackled these actions in order of

FIGURE 8.1 **Phased Rollout Plan to Protect the Most Critical Areas First**

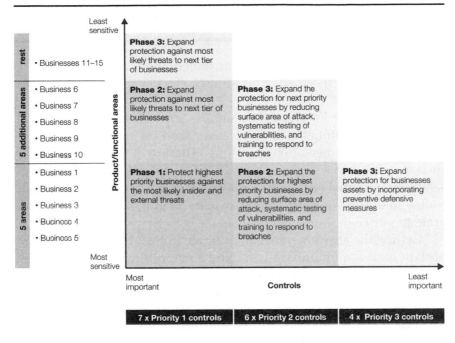

risk impact. Phase 1 applied the highest impact controls to the businesses with the most important information assets. Phase 2 applied the second tier of controls to the first tranche of businesses and the first tier of controls to the second tranche of businesses. That way, the insurer could both ensure real change at the individual business level and accelerate risk reduction impact, even in the face of constraints that prevented the company from trying to do everything in parallel (Figure 8.1).

Integrate Cybersecurity Program with a Broader Set of IT Programs   As noted in Chapter 5, many potential IT improvements, such as the private cloud, desktop virtualization, software-defined networking, and enhanced application development have contributed mightily to reducing vulnerabilities and improving companies' overall security posture.

None of these initiatives will live on the cybersecurity road map, yet the program leadership must invest time with the leaders of these other technology programs to understand existing plans, influence them to maximize security impact, and ensure they are in line with the broader cybersecurity program. In some cases, there may be opportunities to shape these programs to accelerate risk reduction, for example, by prioritizing applications with sensitive information that run on out-of-date infrastructure for remediation so that they can be migrated to a private cloud environment.

Create Top-Down Program Oversight   Any cybersecurity program for a sizeable institution will involve hundreds of individual granular design and implementation decisions. These will include questions such as what types of data should DLP tools stop employees from sending to external recipients; what types of documents must be controlled in document management systems; and which users must migrate to virtual desktop environments?

Getting the answers right can mitigate vulnerabilities, protect important data, and improve a company's risk position. However, they can also affect employees' and customers' experiences in using technology, which can mean a lot of additional energy is absorbed by requests for more analysis and more stakeholder consultation. Putting in place senior, cross-functional program oversight that can cut through disagreements between different organizations will accelerate decision making and enhance the cybersecurity program overall.

One health care company estimated that taking a consensus-driven approach to implementing cybersecurity changes could add several hundred million dollars to the overall program by slowing implementation and demanding the use of less than optimal solutions. To overcome this, the company put in place an executive steering committee comprising the CIO, CISO, CFO, and a couple of business unit executives and gave it a mandate to accelerate decision making. The committee created a fast-track process for decisions that would have a large business or security impact but where the required investment was less than $10 million. So while the decision whether to restrict sending health records via external e-mail and strengthening employee password controls was fast-tracked, the decision whether and how to implement network access control was not, as it had a significantly larger investment budget and therefore had to be addressed in a more traditional decision-making process (Table 8.3).

For each fast-track decision, the relevant managers took up to two weeks to put together a simple business case that laid out the situation, the proposed change, the rationale, and the high-level implications.

TABLE 8.3 **Decision Process Aligned with Impact and Cost**

Traditional Decision Making	Fast-Track Approach
Six- to eight-week decision-making cycle for all types of decisions	Fast paced decision cycle of two weeks specifically for decisions with cybersecurity program impact
Significant preparations with detailed data collection, analysis, and business case presentation	Focused business case with lean yet sufficient data to make informed decisions
Decisions require multiple executive touch-points	Decision imperatives/outcomes decided in a single meeting
Consensus driven approach involving key stakeholders and other nonkey entities	Decisions driven by the responsible/accountable stakeholders
Standard process, does not vary based on decision impact or cost	

This made it much easier for the steering committee to make a fact-based and final decision. In the preceding example, they agreed to establish a policy that no personal health information should be transmitted via external e-mail, that DLP should be used to block large numbers of personal health records from leaving the company via external e-mail, and to invest in collaboration tools that made it easier to share health records with outside parties such as specialist physician groups and diagnostic labs.

6. Ensure Sustained Business Engagement on Cybersecurity Issues

Cybersecurity is a high-stakes topic; therefore, it is a CEO-level topic. Given the way cybersecurity touches all functions and the challenging decisions it required, progress toward digital resilience can be achieved only with active engagement from the CEO and other senior members of the management team.

Based on the survey we conducted, senior management time and attention was the single biggest driver of maturity in managing cybersecurity risks. It was more important than company size, company sector, and even more than the size of the budget. Yet senior management has often failed to give it sufficient attention; some CISOs do have frequent access to the senior management, but roughly two thirds in the companies we spoke to have no regular interaction with the CEO at all.

The launch (or relaunch) of a cybersecurity program is the perfect opportunity for the senior management team to set and clarify its expectations of how each member will help make sure that the business can protect its important information assets. Each has an important role to play (Table 8.4).

TABLE 8.4 **Clarify Cybersecurity Roles and Responsibilities throughout the Organization**

Role	Responsibilities
CEO	Set overall expectations on institutional risk appetite Reinforce behavior changes in senior management team (e.g., how to handle sensitive business material) Ensure appropriate funding
Business unit operating executives	Give input for prioritizing information assets and making trade-offs between data protection and operational impact Incorporate cybersecurity considerations into product, customer, and location decisions Communicate need for behavioral change at the frontline Back up security team in enforcing important polices
Enabling function executives (e.g., Finance, HR, etc.)	Synchronize cybersecurity strategy with corporate policies (e.g., HR, procurement) Integrate cybersecurity into quality/compliance programs Incorporate cybersecurity into regulatory and public affairs agenda
CRO	Ensure enterprise risk methodology accommodates the idiosyncrasies of cybersecurity risks Incorporate prioritized cybersecurity risks into enterprise risk report In some cases, provide governance and oversight for cybersecurity function
CIO	Ensure cybersecurity program supports institution's risk appetite and that business strategy is in place and on plan Drive required changes across IT organization Conduct effective dialog with the board

This is undoubtedly additional work for the executive team, and will require a set of mutually reinforcing actions. They will need to provide the senior management team with credible, specific information about the risks their business or function faces and with highly targeted information about the specific actions they need to take to help the company protect its important information assets. The CEO and chief operating officer need to signal with both their time and their attention the importance they attach to protecting the institution's information assets, and the company should build high priority cybersecurity objectives (e.g., major program milestones) into the goals and objectives of management team members.

• • •

Achieving digital resilience—where a company has a cybersecurity operating model that protects a company's information assets from ongoing attacks, while still enabling continued innovation—is hard. Cybersecurity touches every business process and function and depends on the quality of the application and infrastructure environments, so success hinges on taking actions far outside the security organization itself. Taken together, the resiliency levers described in this book represent a fundamental change in how business organizations interact with IT, how IT addresses security, and how the cybersecurity organization runs itself.

Many companies run cybersecurity programs that avoid the challenges rather than address them, which leads to a lack of buy-in from the organization as a whole, painful decision making, slower implementation, and, in many cases, insufficient resources. An effective program for getting to digital resilience has to be designed from the very start to integrate with the rest of the business, reorient the IT function toward resiliency and create a much more nimble and responsive cybersecurity organization.

9

Creating a Resilient
Digital Ecosystem

In order to protect the information assets that the world economy depends on, companies have to prioritize information assets, implement differentiated protections, build cybersecurity into business processes, change user behavior, create resilient technology platforms, engage in active defense, and learn how to respond to breaches across business functions.

However, the digital ecosystem that companies operate in can be an accelerant or a barrier to digital resilience. If technology vendors build products to facilitate security, that makes it easier for companies to create resilient technology platforms, and if industry associations can pool and distribute threat intelligence, that makes it easier for companies to move from passive to active defense.

Putting in place the practices required for digital resilience will be challenging for individual companies, but getting such a supportive ecosystem will be at least as complex given the wide range of actors involved. In addition, cybersecurity is a global issue, so actors in different parts of the world will have different views on how to make trade-offs, for example, between security and privacy. All this means that there is far less consensus on the specifics of how to develop the broader digital ecosystem than there is on how individual companies should protect themselves.

Even in the face of all this complexity, there are still potential avenues of action and detailed discussion in the areas of public policy, community action, and system-wide structures. Continued collaboration between public, private, academic multilateral, and nongovernmental organizations will be especially important.

THE DIGITAL ECOSYSTEM

While each company must protect itself, it does so in the context of a broader digital ecosystem that shapes its risks, constraints, and options. Attackers may have greater or lesser fear of discovery and prosecution. Vendors may pay greater or lesser attention to how their products affect their customers' ability to protect themselves. Educational institutions may produce more or fewer graduates trained in cybersecurity. Peer institutions may be more or less open to sharing best practices and intelligence.

The digital ecosystem represents the full set of actors that drive confidence in the integrity of information assets and therefore the confidence that consumers and businesses have in the digital economy—and the avenues for interaction or collaboration among them.

- Many types of suppliers handle sensitive data and therefore affect the overall level of risk but two types of suppliers are especially important. Technology vendors have a disproportionate impact on the overall digital ecosystem depending on the extent to which their products and services can be used in a secure way. Insurance carriers could, over time, help companies manage the risk of cyber-attack in a more predictable and transparent way.

- The public sector is taking an increasingly visible and active role in cybersecurity, but "the government" is far less monolithic than a single corporation. Even within a single jurisdiction, a panoply of ministries or agencies may aim to protect consumer privacy, prosecute criminal behavior, safeguard critical national infrastructure, discourage espionage, and promote economic development. In pursuing these objectives, ministries and agencies use a variety of tools, including regulation, criminal law, intelligence gathering, civil law, subsidies, development of state-owned capabilities, and collaboration with private or nongovernmental organizations.

- Academic institutions are an important source of cybersecurity research, not only in their computer science departments but, increasingly, also in business schools, public policy schools, political science departments, and multidisciplinary institutes. Equally importantly, academic institutions educate and train the next generation of cybersecurity professionals.
- Standards-setting bodies (e.g., the Internet Engineering Task Force or the Cloud Security Alliance) can develop protocols for private actors to interact in a secure way and technical standards that encourages them to eliminate vulnerabilities from their products and services.
- Advocacy groups (e.g., the Electronic Frontier Foundation) seek to influence how private companies and government agencies address important issues they perceive as related to their primary mission in civil liberties, privacy or human rights.
- Industry associations (e.g., the Information Sharing and Analysis Centers, or ISACs, in the United States) provide forums for companies to debate best practices, coordinate responses to common threats, and share intelligence.
- Multilateral organizations (e.g., the Organization of American States) provide forums for different governments to work through complicated issues like legal jurisdiction, cooperation in law enforcement, and regulatory harmonization.

These stakeholders come together in a variety of ways to build a more resilient ecosystem. Some of the most important types of collaboration will be cross-industry, public-private, and multistate. Cross-industry collaboration can be the informal exchange of ideas among peers, more structured cooperation in the form of an industry association, or a commercial arrangement for shared capabilities. In public-private collaboration, the government shares intelligence, technologies, and best practices with companies on a voluntary basis. In multistate collaboration, different governments come together to address points of contention across borders.

These are only some of the types of collaboration possible within digital ecosystems. For example, individual companies or industry associates can collaborate with academic institutions to accelerate and improve the education of cybersecurity professionals.

THE POWER OF A RESILIENT DIGITAL ECOSYSTEM

Earlier in this book we laid out three scenarios—three ways in which the risk of cyber-attacks could affect the digital economy. In the "muddling into the future" scenario, both attackers and private companies improved their capabilities incrementally, resulting in a world in which cyber-attacks were an inconvenience but did not prevent companies from taking advantage of the digital economy. In the "digital backlash" scenario, attackers' skills improved much faster than companies' skills, reducing confidence in the digital economy and slowing the pace of technology innovation. In the "digital resilience" scenario, companies dramatically improved their cybersecurity capabilities, allowing the digital economy to develop quickly and robustly.

Collaboration among private companies, government agencies, and nongovernmental organizations could accelerate and expand the impact of the digital resilience scenario by creating the conditions that enable and encourage companies to implement sophisticated cybersecurity capabilities.

June 15, 2020

One of the things Elizabeth liked most about her job was its diversity. As CISO for one of the world's largest and best-known petroleum and energy companies, no two days were ever the same. Even so, as she drove into the office today, she knew she was entering very new territory.

Her team had just discovered malware in the pipeline control and monitoring system in their two-year-old operation in Surulan. There was a growing middle class in Surulan, and it was rapidly being recognized more as an emerging economy than a developing one; nevertheless, it still suffered from security concerns, and the strength of its institutions varied greatly. No one was quite sure what the malware did, but it was definitely communicating back to a host. This was doubly concerning. The systems sensors tracked commercially sensitive information about the oil flows. More significantly, the system's actuators controlled multiple physical systems and valves throughout the network—in the wrong hands these could not only stop the flow of oil but cause severe damage to the physical infrastructure. Some of the control points passed through residential areas and through larger processing plants; any explosion from too much pressure at these points would be far more damaging and could involve human casualties.

Elizabeth pondered her next move. She had led the team in its risk strategy when the system was deployed and connected to the enterprise TCP/IP network last year. All the right processes had kicked in immediately: the malware was immediately isolated and the server quarantined. Backup servers and data kicked in seamlessly. The malware was feeding a stream of simulated data so the attackers were not alerted to the fact that they had been detected, giving the team time to assess the situation, coordinate with law enforcement, and decide on the next steps.

The typical attackers for this global petroleum brand were variations of the politically driven hacktivist, sometimes leaning toward cyber-terrorism. Elizabeth had built strong relationships with the law enforcement community in all the major developed countries where the company had operations, as well as in some states that dealt with terrorism within their borders. At home, the company was considered part of the critical infrastructure, and there were protocols in place for situations where attacks appeared to be state sponsored. In this case, however, the malware seemed to be sending data to a local IP address within Surulan. Perhaps it was being relayed on from there to another site, but that was not visible from Elizabeth's system. She knew her colleagues had dealt with the police and army in Surulan regarding the physical security of their infrastructure, but she had no idea of their cyber capabilities or who to contact.

Arriving at the office, she sent a note to her operational security colleagues and to her informal multi-industry network of fellow CISOs—peers that met a few times a year and kept in touch online in between. Could anyone offer any guidance? Her internal colleagues said they could forward the request through the appropriate channels, but warned that in the absence of a physical emergency there would be some bureaucratic drag in response times. One of her fellow CISOs, however, suggested she might be able to help and suggested they speak.

Lisa worked for a large retailer and was part of a multistakeholder group that provided capacity-building assistance to Surulan. Three years ago, her company had started to see a sharp increase in spam, phishing, and high-volume/low-value fraud out of Surulan. She had joined a group that comprised a number of international and regional organizations, academic institutions, and tech and nontech firms from around the world that invested in building cyber capabilities in developing and emerging economies. Lisa stressed her choice of words: this was an investment, not a donation. The Surulan government had made the program a priority after it saw the rise of crime originating from within its borders (and its inability to deal with it through the criminal justice system) was starting to negatively affect foreign direct investment. The program was personally sponsored by the minister for justice and the prime minister himself.

Just last summer, some of Lisa's team had been on the ground in Surulan providing cyber forensic training to a newly created team within the

Department of Justice. Other parts of the group had provided other services: assisting with the policy framework, the legal code, frontline officer training, police forensic capabilities, and so on.

Lisa put Elizabeth in touch with the leading civil servant in the Department of Justice and the appointed cyber lead in the police force. They worked together and shared the relevant information that enabled local law enforcement to get the warrant required to search the property linked to the IP address the malware was communicating with. The owner was a local businessman whose server had also been co-opted by the malware. Local law enforcement specialists and Elizabeth's own team were able to trace the origins of the attack back to a third country source, which Elizabeth's team was already very familiar with.

Interpol recognized the TTPs of the attack from other recent cases and, together with Elizabeth's team, established a honeypot operation to gather further information about the attackers and their intended targets. This meant they were able to identify other targets who were unaware they were victims-in-waiting.

In parallel, Elizabeth made the business case internally for her company to contribute resource and funding to these international efforts. With operations in countries at all stages of development, the board quickly understood the win-win in continued investment in the rule of law and cyber capabilities in all countries. The company became a regular contributor to the multistakeholder group's efforts and continued to gain advantage and critical insights through its growing network of increasingly sophisticated partners.

Elizabeth's experience is becoming more common. As cyberattacks proliferate, organizations need to reach out beyond their walls. Every organization sits in the center of its own ecosystem and needs to develop resilience across the board. This ecosystem thinking is fundamental to the core business strategy for most organizations in their journey to become digital enterprises—cybersecurity is no different.

Many organizations already engage in collaborative activities, from formal and informal networks in which to share common challenges and experiences to more structured networks that share intelligence and threat data. Beyond this, however, all stakeholders need to be aware of and contribute to the broader digital environment in terms of shared business practices, the role of government, and academic and private-public partnerships. Furthermore, serious proposals have been advanced to make some systemic changes that would change the nature of the operating environment significantly.

TABLE 9.1 **Actions to Build a Digital Resilience Ecosystem**

Theme	Areas for Action
Public and international policy	National cybersecurity strategy
	Domestic policy and incentives
	Foreign policy
	End-to-end criminal justice system
	Public goods
Community action	Research
	Information sharing
	Knowledge transfer
	Community self-governance
	Shared resources for capacity building
	Mutual aid
Systemic action	Risk markets
	Embedded security/changes to the Internet

WHAT'S REQUIRED TO CREATE A RESILIENT DIGITAL ECOSYSTEM

Discussions with business executives, technology managers, regulators, law enforcement, civil society leaders, and others yielded a framework of potential areas for action across three themes (Table 9.1). Stakeholders can use this as a guide to help them develop a consensus view of their capabilities, define the precise next steps, and discuss roles and responsibilities. A much fuller version of this framework is shown at the end of this chapter (see Figure 9.3 and Table 9.2).

Further discussions made clear that these levers have been applied only in a relatively incomplete or immature way in many countries or regions. Why? Making use of the levers above is even harder than implementing best practices in individual companies, especially given the variety of private actors, government agencies, and nongovernmental organizations, each with its own set of constraints and priorities.

Some of the issues related to cybersecurity can be highly emotional and politicized. Cybersecurity is not an isolated issue; inevitably, it touches issues like intelligence gathering, economic competitiveness, and consumer privacy that cannot be addressed as factually and dispassionately as how to segment a network or what practices to use in coding applications.

Given the multifaceted nature of cybersecurity, public dialogue on the topic remains fragmented. Issues such as intellectual property (IP) enforcement, national security, consumer fraud, terrorism, and organized crime may all be addressed in a discussion on cybersecurity, yet in the predigital environment, we evolved different institutions and mechanisms to deal with them even if they may be interrelated.

There is a fundamental disconnect between the global nature of cybersecurity as an issue and the national scope of many institutions. How can national governments effectively formulate policies to enable digital resilience when attackers and their targets may be separated by a dozen time zones. In many cases, global enterprises experience this disconnect most acutely. CISOs at the largest banks, manufacturers, and pharmaceutical companies point out how difficult it is to work with local enforcement to address a crime that may have touched assets on three continents or how challenging it can be to explain to regulators how they will secure a single global network. Of course, different countries may have not only different regulatory regimes and law enforcement practices, but also vastly different culture norms, for example, about employee privacy.

As a result, there are significant disagreements about how to proceed in the areas of collaboration and policy development. Almost everyone agrees that companies should share intelligence about attacks more extensively. Some CISOs said this could be accomplished within existing legal regimes. Others disagreed and argued that companies would not share more intelligence unless immunized from legal liability. Almost everyone agreed that more research on cybersecurity techniques and practices would be valuable. Some CISOs suggested that the public sector could play a valuable role in setting and funding a research agenda. Others argued that governments could not set intelligent research priorities in as dynamic a space as cybersecurity.

Attitudes toward regulation provide a good example of the absence of consensus. Forty percent of technology executives said that, on balance, cybersecurity regulation encouraged companies to be more secure in a helpful way. Conversely, 46 percent said it either requires a lot of time and effort but does not make companies more security, or that it actively makes companies less secure. There were pronounced differences by sector. Only a quarter of banking executives expressed positive views about cybersecurity regulation. They said regulations were cumbersome and locked into place outdated practices. In many cases, they said regulators lacked the expertise to

FIGURE 9.1 **Executives' Perspective on Cybersecurity Regulation Varies Widely by Sector, with Banking Most Skeptical**

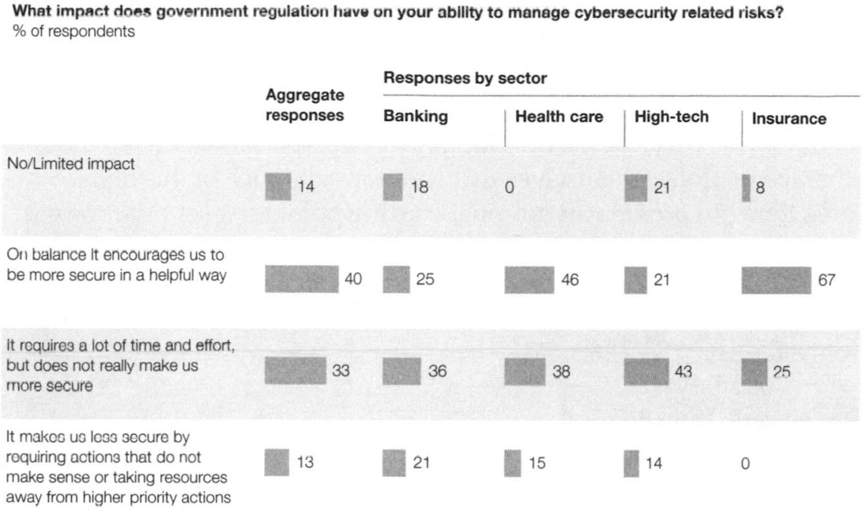

What impact does government regulation have on your ability to manage cybersecurity related risks?
% of respondents

	Aggregate responses	Responses by sector			
		Banking	Health care	High-tech	Insurance
No/Limited impact	14	18	0	21	8
On balance it encourages us to be more secure in a helpful way	40	25	46	21	67
It requires a lot of time and effort, but does not really make us more secure	33	36	38	43	25
It makes us less secure by requiring actions that do not make sense or taking resources away from higher priority actions	13	21	15	14	0

make the right judgments about cybersecurity practices. By contrast, nearly half of health care technology executives, and about two thirds of their insurance counterparts had positive views of cybersecurity regulation. They said that while might regulation might be suboptimal, it could encourage senior management to devote the required resources and attention to cybersecurity (Figure 9.1).

Such debates can feel distant for many companies, but there are costs and risks associated with not proactively shaping the broader ecosystem. For example, in November 2012, a motion to effectively hand control of the Internet over to national governments was narrowly defeated at the world congress of a technical standards body of the United Nations. Many feared that, if passed, the result would have been the fragmentation and militarization of the Internet, creating an extreme version of the digital backlash scenario described earlier in the book.[1] Yet most businesses leaders were not even aware that this vote was taking place.[2]

[1] Arthur, Charles, "Internet Remains Unregulated after UN Treaty Blocked," *The Guardian*, December 14, 2012. http://www.theguardian.com/technology/2012/dec/14/telecoms-treaty-internet-unregulated.

[2] Jones, Rory, "Nations Meet to Discuss Web Rules," *Wall Street Journal*, December 3, 2012. http://www.wsj.com/news/articles/SB10001424127887323401904578157592874176534.

COLLABORATION FOR A RESILIENT ECOSYSTEM

Back in 2011, the World Economic Forum developed a set of Principles for Cyber Resilience that focused on recognizing the interdependence of actors within the ecosystem, the role of leadership, risk management, and promoting uptake along the value chain. These principles served as a critical backdrop for the development of the specific actions companies can take to protect themselves that run through much of this book. Similarly, they can provide an essential starting point for a set of actions that companies, governments, and other institutions can take in collaborating to build a more resilient ecosystem. Taken together, they highlight the opportunity for collaboration among the different participants in the digital ecosystem.

Recognize Interdependence   Every actor in the digital ecosystem depends on other actors. Companies depend on suppliers to protect sensitive information assets, on academic institutions to develop cybersecurity talent, on their peers for knowledge sharing, and so forth. Governments depend on companies to protect privately owned critical infrastructure. Governments also depend on each other to track cyber-criminals across national borders. As a result of this interdependence, all the participants in the digital ecosystem have to experiment with different types of collaboration to achieve goals that they could not achieve individually.

Understand the Role of Leadership   In previous chapters, we described the importance of senior leadership implementing the changes required for digital resilience. Given the cross-functional nature of cybersecurity and the complicated choices involved, only senior management can ratify the decisions and marshal the organizational commitment required for sustained progress. This is even more true in creating a resilient ecosystem. The diversity of the actors, the conflicting agenda, and the complexity of the issues require involvement from the senior-most business, public, academic, and nongovernmental leaders.

Focus on Risk Management   Recognizing that cybersecurity is about economics—that it involves optimizing choices about risk and economic return—provides a fundamentally different context, language, and set of objectives than arise when discussing it through a political or technological lens. It forces the question, "What is it we are trying to protect?" After all, the most digitally secure environment is one that is disconnected from the Internet, but at what cost?

In its 2011 Cyber Security Strategy, the U.K. government stated: "Our vision is for the UK in 2015 to derive huge economic and social value from a vibrant, resilient and secure cyberspace, where our actions, guided by our core values of liberty, fairness, transparency, and the rule of law, enhance prosperity, national security and a strong society." To achieve this, the government's first objective was to "be one of the most secure places in the world to do business in cyberspace." The U.K. government clearly understood the economic benefits from digital resilience and driving economic prosperity for all is a political goal that all leaders can rally around.

All nations compete against each other in the global economy while simultaneously collaborating on a common set of rules that enable such competition. The recognition of the huge potential economic gains or opportunity costs outlined in our scenarios earlier in the book should provide a clear incentive for all governments to ensure that they do not allow an inadequate or fragmented approach to hamper collective opportunities.

Promote Uptake along the Value Chain   As noted elsewhere in the book, cybersecurity plays an increasingly important role in commercial transactions. Criminals can steal important information from a company's suppliers, or they can use network connections among business partners as avenues for cyber-attacks. Increasingly, many of the actors in the digital ecosystem can take a value chain view, in which they create standards and contractual terms that facilitate more sophisticated cybersecurity practices.

Despite the challenges moving forward, working sessions with many stakeholders confirmed that the Principles for Cyber Resiliency highlighted a set of important and feasible actions, many of which involve voluntary cooperation rather than state mandates. Governments could use national cyber strategies to increase alignment across agencies and with private and nongovernmental stakeholders. They could improve the skills and capabilities of the end-to-end criminal justice system, and use multilateral organizations to improve cooperation across borders. Companies could deepen and expand their efforts shared intelligence, best practices and capabilities, and also build more effective markets for valuing and transferring risks associated with cyber-attacks.

Domestic and International Policy

Two actions came to the fore in terms of domestic and international policy: using national cyber strategy and improving the capabilities of the end-to-end criminal justice system.

National Cybersecurity Strategy Working sessions highlighted the value in each country having a comprehensive, transparent national cybersecurity strategy that is harmonized with the strategies and procedures across all domestic and international policy. At the time of writing, only 36 countries have published or announced the development of such a strategy, half of them within the European Union (Figure 9.2).[3] The United States has focused on cybersecurity since the 1990s and has published a number of cybersecurity documents, but has no overarching strategy. Compare this to Estonia, which is one of the most digitally dependent societies and has a cybersecurity strategy that is integrated into the national defense strategy. Elsewhere in Europe, France and Germany's strategies both give their respective governments a relatively active role, while the Dutch and Finnish plans focus on collaboration as the bedrock of the strategy. Without

FIGURE 9.2 **OECD Countries Are Starting to Put Cybersecurity Strategies in Place**

2003	2004	2005	2006	2007	2008	2009	2010	2011	2012	2013
										USA
										UK
										SWE
										ESP
										POL
										NZL
										NL
					USA			LUX		USA
					SVK	UK		GER	SWI	HUN
					EST	JAP	EU	FRA	NOR	FIN
USA	CAN		JAP		AUS	AUS	CAN	CZE	NL	EU

[3] ENISA (EU Agency for Network and Information Security), "National Cyber Security Strategies in the World." http://www.enisa.europa.eu/activities/Resilience-and-CIIP/national-cybersecurity-strategies-ncsss/national-cyber-security-strategies-in-the-world.

dedicated strategies, activities become overlapping, fragmented, and, at worst, conflicting in terms of investment, programs, and policy and legislative measures, all of which in turn hinders economic growth.

In developing and executing a national strategy, governments should incorporate the perspectives and requirements of the widest range possible of public and private bodies. The very process of developing such a strategy can be the catalyst to start the conversation between leaders in different sectors.

Active business involvement will be especially critical. In our discussions, most governments recognized the driving role that business has in achieving their goal of protecting citizens and ensuring digital resilience at the society level. Governments also recognized the economic benefits that the Internet has brought and have no wish to hinder businesses in creating economic value through digitization. As such, many governments are actively keen to engage business and understand the private sector needs in this space. However, a challenge we heard expressed in many of our discussions with policymakers was that consultation with the private sector does not always yield clarity. A common reaction was, "If we ask 30 different companies about their views on what policies are required in a particular space, we get 30 different responses."

Businesses often talk about the need for policy alignment. However, they have a responsibility to develop a clear alignment on policy needs. Some disparity is inevitable—it may well be the case that the role of government cybersecurity policy is different for health than it is for automotive, but even this level of clarity is currently lacking.

A rapidly growing number of countries are actively looking at what kind of policy and regulatory steps they should be taking to deal with cyber-risks. Many are seeking input from the private sector. However, if the business community cannot align on defining its key policy needs in a globally connected digital environment, the risk of a highly fragmented landscape increases.

Finally, given the range of stakeholders involved in the process, one competent agency may need to be responsible for the strategy's successful implementation and rollout to avoid challenges over ownership and purpose. This also gives stakeholders transparency into the process and a clear accountable point of contact. Just as governments struggled with diverging viewpoints across the business community, businesses and nongovernmental organizations struggle to understand agendas and actions of different government agents.

End-to-End Criminal Justice System   Law enforcement agencies need both the ability and resources to investigate cybercrimes, and a comprehensive and agile legal code to back them up in their investigations and prosecutions. As the chief information officer (CIO) of a financial services organization said, "Institutions can take all the actions they want on their own. However, if there is no law enforcement mechanism to pursue and prosecute perpetrators, then our actions are meaningless." There is a whole set of actions governments can take, without compromising privacy, to enhance the enforcement of laws and the prosecution of criminals in the digital realm.

- *Modernize and clarify laws governing cyber-crime.* The pace of innovation has created gaps in the legal code that need to be addressed. For example, the U.S. Electronic Communications Privacy Act (ECPA) is the main law governing communication privacy, but it was developed in 1986 before e-mail was in common use and before social networks had even been conceived. There may also be a meaningful disparity between the sentencing guidelines given for cyber-crimes versus their "real-world" equivalents.
- *Continue to invest in specialist units and capabilities.* Cyber-crime is an arcane discipline, requiring technical depth to address. Specialist forensic capabilities to identify wrongdoers is especially important.
- *Expand basic digital competency in nonspecialist units.* The ability to prosecute and defend an alleged criminal can depend on judges and lawyers having sufficient knowledge and understanding to process cases. Prosecutors and judges do not need to be cybersecurity experts, but they do need a basic level of digital literacy, for example, an understanding of how the Internet works. Similarly, it may be necessary to provide basic-level training in selected law enforcement agencies so that officers know how to handle reports of cyber-criminal activities and can follow the correct processes when a cyber-crime is reported.
- *Enhance collaboration with the private sector.* Real tension can exist between companies suffering cyber-crime and law enforcement agencies. At times, each side has accused the other of being secretive, uncooperative, and only concerned with its own institutional interests. Confidence-building measures, like briefings

from law enforcement on emerging threats, make it easier for companies and law enforcement agencies to work together effectively after a breach.

- *Invest in data gathering and analytics.* Reporting crime gives the police data from which they can identify patterns. This helps both in terms of resource planning as well as in tackling organized crime. While true for all types of crime, it is especially useful in cyber-crime given the geographically dispersed nature of cyber-crime networks and rapid evolution of cyber-crime techniques. The ability to aggregate and analyze data on individual crimes would therefore be an enormous help.

- *Establish mechanism for cross-border law enforcement cooperation.* Given the global nature of cyber-crime, dedicated units to coordinate with peers in other countries can be critical in bringing cyber-criminals to justice. These mechanisms are especially important where they may be policy differences between countries—countries that disagree on the extent of cyber-espionage can still cooperate in fighting fraud or disruption of online markets.

Effective criminal justice in this area will become even more important as the range of potential cyber-crimes expands. As our lives become ever more connected to the Internet, the range of risks that individuals face from products being compromised will increase, and there will not always be an obvious incentive for the provider of a hacked product to assume that risk. Questions are already being asked about the liabilities around driverless cars, or web-controlled household appliances, all of which have the potential to cause significant damage if corrupted.

Community Action

There are a whole set of actions that communities of countries and communities of companies can take together. Shared research includes pooling resources to invest in developing new techniques and technologies. Information sharing includes aggregating intelligence about attackers and attack paths they use. Knowledge transfer includes sharing best practices in how to operate cybersecurity organizations. Shared capability building includes creating shared utilities for activities such as vendor assessments or incident response. Mutual aid involves a commitment to provide assistance when a community member is under attack. Community self-government involves creating forums to align on priorities, for example, when providing input to governments as they develop national cybersecurity strategies.

Both countries and private entities can benefit from community action, which can help address complicated issues in a flexible way that incorporates the varying interests of the parties involved.

Assistance among Countries   There are opportunities for countries to assist one another in creating a resilient digital ecosystem, sometimes via multilateral organizations. For example, the Organization of American States (OAS) works to ensure political cohesion among member states, allowing the formulation and implementation of cybersecurity policies throughout the region. Over the years, the OAS Cyber Security Program evolved to address the challenges in a multifaceted and tailored way, establishing lines of action that can be adapted to best fit a country's specific needs.

The OAS Cyber Security Program undertakes several initiatives with member states to develop their cybersecurity capabilities, for example, it has a program that develops national Computer Security Incident Response Teams (CSIRTs). Since 2006, the number of CSIRTs in the Americas has risen from 5 to 18. To ensure better communication between CSIRTs at the regional level, the OAS has developed a network that serves not only as a communication platform but as a tool where teams can perform incident response processes.

The program has also successfully mentored member states in developing national cybersecurity strategies. In 2011, after extensive collaboration with the OAS, Colombia became the first country in the region to officially adopt a national strategy, followed by Panama (2012) and Trinidad and Tobago (2013). The OAS Cyber Security Program also carries out technical assistance missions designed to address countries' cybersecurity requirements, including technical incident response courses and crisis management exercises. In recent years, the program has also worked with the private sector to produce comprehensive reports on the state of cybersecurity in the Americas. These reports aim to detail the experiences member states have had in mitigating cyber-risk and to produce knowledge that brings Latin American and Caribbean perspectives on cybersecurity matters.

The OAS's initiative here may provide a template for other community action among governments, especially in transferring capabilities from developed to less developed countries. For some countries, it may be difficult (especially in the initial stages) for spending on cybersecurity to become a priority when it has to compete with basic services such as health or education or even paying down national debt. Global enterprises and richer states can help by providing resources for capacity building—this can be in their own interest, in that it creates a safer and more stable digital economy.

Academic institutions, regional and international organizations, and civil society organizations can all play a critical role in identifying and promoting opportunities for countries to engage in community action. They can act as honest brokers to enable cooperation on research, information sharing, or knowledge transfer.

Community Building among Companies   Again and again, technology executives within a given industry will say, "When it comes to cybersecurity, we're all on the same side." This perspective drives active collaboration by some companies within some industries. Historically, CISOs at the largest banks have compared notes and shared intelligence informally, but only with peers they knew personally and trusted. More recently, some of the ISACs, especially those for financial services and the defense sector, have become effective forums for collaboration across a sector. For example, CISOs at smaller banks credit the intelligence received via the financial services ISAC with their ability to withstand a campaign of serious DDoS attacks in late 2012 and early 2013.

CISOs and other senior cybersecurity executives from 40 of the most important health care institutions in North America have met periodically since 2012 to share intelligence, exchange tangible best practices, debate issues with public policy implications, and develop strategies for improving the National Health ISAC. When the Heartbleed and Bash vulnerabilities came to light, members shared remediation tactics. Most recently, the group has started to plan a shared utility to perform common cybersecurity activities. All this collaboration has helped companies protect themselves more effectively.

There is still much to do in terms of community building among companies within sectors. Not every sector has the collaboration model that exists in financial services or health care. Across sectors, there are opportunities to broaden and deepen community action. In addition to shared utilities, collaboration across companies to develop more standard industry models for the risks from cyber-attacks could be very powerful.

As noted earlier in this book, most companies lack effective, repeatable mechanisms for assessing cybersecurity risks. A robust, standard risk model would immediately change the nature of the discussion. Rather than speaking in broad risk terms, which already makes the dialogue more business-like, a robust method of risk assessment would result in the cybersecurity discussion being fully incorporated into business decisions. Just as a new investment proposal would consider country risk, currency risk, operational risk, and competitive challenges, it would include a confident measure of cybersecurity risk. Similarly, a new product or service proposal would include the associated digital risks. This would enable what many cybersecurity experts struggle to achieve: getting security considered at the beginning of development or investment cycles rather than as an after-the-fact addition. It would enable "security by design," whether for investments, new business opportunities, new product or service developments, or simply changes to the information or operational environment. The endorsement of industry groups would greatly increase credibility and facilitate adoption within individual companies.

Systemic Action

Some ideas for getting to a resilient ecosystem are fundamental and systemic. For example, in recent years, there have been various proposals to reshape the inherently open architecture of the Internet for security, but nobody has yet been able to lay out a practical approach for doing so—either in terms of a technical model that preserves the flexibility that makes the Internet so valuable or a political model for getting alignment to do such a thing.[4] In contrast, using better and more standardized risk assessment techniques to enable deeper and more liquid markets for transferring the risks associated with cyberattacks would greatly facilitate the emergence of a resilient ecosystem.

Certainly, companies can buy insurance against the risk of cyberattack—premium revenue has been growing at about 13 percent per annum[5]—but the market is limited. Insurance executives will admit

[4] Whitsitt, Jack, "'Cart before the Horse': Re: Another Set of Suggestions to Re-architect the Whole Internet (or Vast Parts of It) for Better Security," *Art and Security in Washington, DC*, February 20, 2009. http://sintixerr.wordpress.com/2009/02/20/cart-before-the-horse-re-another-set-of-suggestions-to-re-architect-the-whole-internet-or-vast-parts-of-it-for-better-security.

[5] IbisWorld, "Cyber Liability Insurance in the US: Market Research Report," August 2014. www.ibisworld.com/industry/cyber-liability-insurance.html.

that they are in the early days of cyber-insurance, which lacks the data and models that they have relied on for decades in underwriting other types of risks. Given this, insurance carriers will cover notification costs, legal defense, forensics, and remediation costs, but will not cover third-party liability,[6] reputational damage, or loss of IP or trade secrets.[7] Almost all carriers limit coverage to $25 million, so some companies have recouped only a small percentage of the cost of a breach even when they have had coverage. As a result, the total cyber-insurance premiums amount to only about $2 billion[8] out of a total market of $4.9 trillion across insurance products globally[9] and only about a third of companies find it worthwhile to buy cyber-insurance.[10]

A more mature cyber-risk insurance market would change the landscape for both companies and potentially society more broadly. It would offer companies an important additional tool and would be a significant step in normalizing their treatment of cyber-risks. From different types of stakeholders we heard that pricing the risk of a cyber-attack via insurance would help senior executives engage more effectively on the issue. Even the debate about whether a company should buy coverage amounting to $500 million or $700 million would provide a useful framing for discussing the overall level of risk. Even more specifically, a CISO might be able to make the case that spending $5 million to put differentiated protections in place would be worthwhile because it would reduce insurance premiums by $7 million, just as facilities managers often justify fire suppression systems based on reduced insurance premiums. Better insurance markets could also reduce the turbulence that cybersecurity concerns are already introducing in the supply chain. For example, many potential purchasers of IT outsourcing services ask for unlimited liability related to loss of customer data, which providers are naturally reluctant to provide. Several IT outsourcing executives told us they could do business more effectively if they could ask potential

[6] Matthews, Christopher M., "Cybersecurity Insurance Picks Up Steam, Study Finds," *Wall Street Journal*, August 7, 2013. http://blogs.wsj.com/riskandcompliance/2013/08/07/cybersecurity-insurance-picks-up-steam-study-finds.

[7] National Protection and Programs Directorate, "Cybersecurity Insurance Workshop Read-out Report," US Department of Homeland Security, November 2012. https://www.dhs.gov/sites/default/files/publications/cybersecurity-insurance-read-out-report.pdf.

[8] IbisWorld, 2014.

[9] Aon Benfield, "*Insurance Risk Study: Growth, Profitability, and Opportunity*," Ninth edition, 2014. http://thoughtleadership.aonbenfield.com/Documents/20140912_ab_analytics_insurance_risk_study.pdf.

[10] Matthews, 2013.

customers how much liability they wanted the supplier to assume, and then buy the appropriate insurance and price it into the deal. Making the cost of liability explicit would smooth negotiations.

Small and medium-sized enterprises could be even bigger beneficiaries. Large corporations may be able to afford their cybersecurity spend, take out large policies, and manage losses as a part of doing business. Typically, SMEs cannot support the same level of investment in expertise, resources, and private-public partnerships, and while retail banking customers are reimbursed for any losses caused by cyber-fraud, the same protections do not extend to small businesses, who must carry the losses themselves. Verizon's Data Breach Report found that 71 percent of cyber-attacks target companies with 100 employees or less.[11]

Transferring risks requires an agreed methodology for measuring those risks and data about breaches and their impact. Developing any model to measure cyber-risk for an individual enterprise is challenging. Many companies have programs to try to integrate their security and risk practices, and a variety of models are emerging. Naturally, there will be limitations and caveats as there are for other risks, and practices will focus on the pragmatic and the measurable. For example, the disclosure of embarrassing activities by the CEO—whether revealed through a cybersecurity breach or not—cannot be fully predicted in advance. Just because the disclosure was possible through a cyber-attack does not mean it should be dealt with in the same way that the company deals with the theft of customer data or intellectual property.

One key challenge, however, will be how to develop common measurement models—or models that are common *enough*—to be able to share risk information between organizations and across markets. This will require not just harmony among different enterprise models, but will also need to integrate accounting, audit, and insurance perspectives. That is challenging but not impossible, and a smaller number of organizations are already engaging in informal dialogue with partners to share models. The other key challenge will be the development of granular and comprehensive data sets about cyber-attacks. Companies are obviously reluctant to disclose breaches unless they absolutely have to,[12] but more openness to sharing data, even in disguised form, will greatly help the development

[11] Verizon, "2014 Data Breach Investigations Report," 2014. www.verizonenterprise.com/DBIR/2014/reports/rp_Verizon-DBIR-2014_en_xg.pdf.

[12] Yadron, Danny, "Executives Rethink Merits of Going Public with Data Breaches," *Wall Street Journal*, August 4, 2014. www.wsj.com/articles/a-contrarian-view-on-data-breaches-1407194237.

of insurance markets. The more insight carriers have into historical losses, the more aggressively they will underwrite policies.

Companies may be tempted to keep their proprietary models to themselves, but there would be enormous benefits to sharing at least components of such models. They can collectively develop best-of-breed practices and standardized models, both of which should rapidly accelerate the emergence of a robust cyber-risk market, which would benefit everyone.

• • •

As much as companies might do to protect themselves, and as much as they might put in place operating models designed for digital resilience, they still exist in a broader digital ecosystem of suppliers, customers, many types of governance agencies, academic institutions, and nongovernmental organizations. How these actors work with or against each other can be a tremendous accelerant or barrier to achieving digital resilience and maximizing the potential of the online economy.

As hard as it might be to put in place cutting-edge practices that drive resilience within a single company, it is even harder to build a resilient digital ecosystem. There is a wide variety of actors, with different objectives, constraints, and governance models, and the issues are complicated and sometimes politically charged.

That said, there is a path forward. A large majority of stakeholders we interviewed emphasized the importance of collaboration: between governments and the private sector in developing national cybersecurity strategies, among many types of actors in enhancing the ability of criminal justice systems to address cyber-crime, among states to disseminate cybersecurity capabilities to developing countries, across industries so that companies can help each other, and among many types of companies to create robust markets for cyber-insurance.

Just as senior executives must engage to ensure that companies make progress in protecting themselves, senior leaders of all types must engage to ensure progress toward a resilient digital ecosystem. For example, ministers and agency heads must drive national cybersecurity strategies, and senior business executives have to make sure that companies provide effective input. Building the right set of capabilities to investigate and prosecute cyber-crimes will require attention from the most senior law enforcement and justice officials. Likewise, senior business managers have to emphasize the importance of a resilient digital ecosystem and help their companies engage in the collaboration required to get there.

FIGURE 9.3   **Maturity Curve for the Pillars of a Digital Resilience Ecosystem**

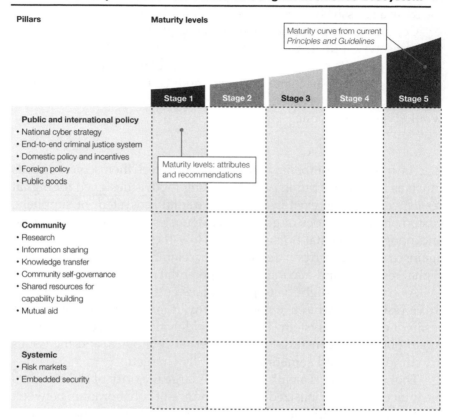

TABLE 9.2 **Recommendations for Building an Enabling Ecosystem for Digital Resilience**

Institutional Readiness	Public and International Policy	Community	Systemic
Governance	*National cybersecurity strategy*	*Research*	*Risk markets*
• Prioritize information assets based on business risks	• Have a comprehensive and transparent national cybersecurity strategy integrated with the strategies and procedures of all policy domains	• Increase education and awareness	• Expand reach and breadth of cybersecurity insurance markets
• Integrate cybersecurity into enterprise-wide risk management and governance processes	• Incorporate private and civil sectors and economic and security issues	• Encourage research on enterprise and macroeconomic impact of cybersecurity to prioritize and focus policies	
• Lead in practice and policy from most senior executives	• Establish a competent institution for the national strategy implementation and rollout	• Create an atmosphere in which white-hat research is encouraged	
Program/network development	*End-to-end criminal justice system*	*Shared resource for capability building*	*Embedded security*
• Provide differentiated protection for the most important assets	• Ensure law enforcement has the capability and resources to investigate cyber crimes	• Foster partnerships between governments and universities and private sector for skills development	• Explore ways to create a more secure Internet
• Enlist frontline personnel to protect the information assets they use	• Draw up an appropriate, comprehensive, and agile legal code for investigating and prosecuting cyber crimes		• Develop a methodology for quantifying the impact of cyber-risks
• Integrate cybersecurity into the technology environment	• Ensure legal advocates understand the cybersecurity ecosystem well enough to carry out due process		
• Deploy active defenses to engage attackers			
• Continuous testing to improve incident response			

(continued)

207

TABLE 9.2 *(continued)*

Institutional Readiness	Public and International Policy	Community	Systemic
	Domestic policy and incentives • Start private, public, and civil dialogue to develop appropriate coherent mix of policy and market mechanisms • Create governmental mechanisms that support law enforcement's efforts and are appropriately agile *Foreign policy* • Establish a national cybersecurity doctrine • Identify persons at the local, state, and national level responsible for cybersecurity • Establish formal and informal channels of communication between law enforcement entities • Create interoperability among national-level entities responsible for cybersecurity • Work to harmonize national and international policies surrounding the prosecution of cybercrime • Establish a multistakeholder approach toward governance on this issue *Public good* • Ensure evolving and robust incident response capability • Increase investments in cybersecurity technical education • Fund a cybersecurity research agenda • Provide "safe harbor" protection for limited sharing of information among and between companies and government	*Information sharing* • Where legally feasible, find mechanisms for information sharing between institutions • Improve the quality of the ISACs/Computer Emergency Response Teams and other information-sharing venues • Promote an interoperable, extensible and automated system for sharing • Provide common protocols for information regarding cybersecurity events	

Conclusion

During our research for this book, we shared our interim findings about the economic implications of cyber-attacks and the importance of getting to digital resilience with a reporter for a national business publication.

We discussed that the risk to the global economy and the imperative for action is clear. He said he understood that companies were not protecting themselves effectively but he had one probing question. If it was so clear that companies needed to move beyond cybersecurity as a control function and focus protection on the most important assets, so obvious that they needed the help of their staff, so beneficial to embed security into IT more broadly, then why haven't they just gone ahead and done it?

Stephen Biddle wrestled with a similar quandary in his book *Military Power: Explaining Victory and Defeat in Modern Battle*. Biddle convincingly demonstrated that the way armies used their forces overwhelmingly outweighed the size of those forces or their technological sophistication in determining who had won battles over the past century. In particular, he laid out a "modern system" of force deployment—a tightly interrelated complex of cover, concealment, dispersion, suppression, small-unit independent maneuver, combined arms, depth, reserves, and differential concentration—that had succeeded in every major clash of arms since World War I.[1]

[1] Biddle, Stephen, *Military Power: Explaining Victory and Defeat in Modern Battle*. Princeton, NJ: Princeton University Press, 2006.

However, despite the dramatic success of this system, relatively few armed forces have adopted it. Why? Biddle explained that building the skills required to employ the modern system is difficult and is also organizationally threatening for many in the military. For example, generals serving autocrats may not be comfortable empowering noncommissioned officers to make independent decisions.

The situation in cybersecurity is similar. More resources do not necessarily yield better protection. No single technology, no matter how hyped, can provide protection alone. Instead, as we have set out in this book, there is a set of tightly interrelated, mutually reinforcing levers that can be applied to achieve digital resilience.

Understanding business risks and information assets gives companies the ability to put differentiated protections in place. Integrating cybersecurity considerations into business processes and enlisting frontline users to make security more robust complement each other in making business models more resilient. Building cybersecurity into the application and infrastructure environments creates transparency that is critical for putting in place active defense. Using continuous testing to improve incident response processes across business functions backstops the other levers. Taken together, the seven levers are a way of making companies more resilient in the face of attack—as opposed to the traditional practice of locking down technology environments ever more tightly, putting control processes in place, and making it harder to use enterprise technology in innovative and value-creating ways.

Why have companies not done more in terms of putting these levers in place and making progress toward digital resilience? Because, like changing the culture of the military, it is difficult and organizationally challenging. Getting to resiliency requires three things:

1. Collaborative engagement between the cybersecurity team and its business partners to prioritize risks, make intelligent trade-offs, and, where appropriate, change business processes and behaviors, rather than implement technology solutions to manage risks.

2. A focus on resiliency in the broader IT organization, to facilitate the convergence of security, efficiency, and agility—and to make sure that IT managers design technology platforms from the outset to be resilient and secure.

3. A dramatic uplift of the skills and capabilities of the cyber-security team so its managers can understand business risks, collaborate effectively with business partners, navigate a rapidly changing technology environment, influence application and infrastructure environments, and implement active defense tactics.

Unfortunately, many companies fail to design their cybersecurity programs with the right level of ambition. They assume that they can proceed step by step, first putting in place basic cybersecurity capabilities and worrying about more sophisticated activities later on—unfortunately, their attackers do not have as much patience. Senior leaders at many companies do not give the time and attention required to foster the collaboration between cybersecurity teams and business managers; they continue to accept outdated and opaque application and infrastructure environments that are simultaneously inflexible, inefficient, and intrinsically insecure.

The value promised by the digital economy is apparent: it should deliver radically more efficient business processes, profoundly more intimate customer relationships, and exponentially better fact-based decision making.

Senior business leaders and policymakers can continue to let cybersecurity be a bureaucratic control function and see the value inherent in the digital economy diminished by $3 trillion in 2020. Or they can recognize that cybersecurity is one of this century's critical social and economic issues, and demand that their organizations drive the transition to digital resilience. Specifically, senior business leaders can make sure that business, IT, and cybersecurity managers collaborate to adopt the resiliency levers in their organizations. Technology vendors can make sure they build their products and services for security. And regulators can design policies that enable forward-looking cybersecurity strategies rather than lock in the outdated methods of the past.

The choice is clear: We must move beyond cybersecurity to digital resilience.

Acknowledgments

This book benefited from the work of and input from a range of people, whom we gratefully acknowledge here.

Jonathan Turton provided invaluable editorial assistance. His previous experience writing such books was deeply appreciated.

From McKinsey we received help and insights from a range of experts including Andrea del Miglio, Wolf Richter, Jim Boehm, Andreas Schwarz, Dimitris Economou, Venky Anant, Roshan Vora, Maya Kaczorowski, Jim Miller, Suneet Pahwa, Kacper Rychard, Paul Twomey, Charles Barthold, and Hil Albuquerque. All put in hours way beyond their normal heavy workload and cheerfully responded to e-mails late at night and on weekends. In addition, we would like to recognize Joseph Hubback, J. R. Maxwell, Paul Yoo, Mike Connolly, Ryan Leirvik, Blair Kessler, Ritesh Argawal, Ryan Van Dyk, and Kamayani Sadhwani for their contributions.

As always, Steffi Langner's patience, perseverance, and flawless coordination proved essential.

We also want to thank Allen Weinberg, David Chinn, Steve van Kuiken, Michael Bender, and Michael Bloch from McKinsey, who provided us with the support and resources to accomplish this project.

The team we worked with at Wiley, Bill Falloon and Meg Freeborn, was an important part of getting this book off the ground and providing us with timely and wise counsel.

About the Authors

JAMES M. KAPLAN

James M. Kaplan is a partner in McKinsey & Company's Business Technology and Financial Services practices. He co-leads McKinsey's IT infrastructure and cybersecurity practices globally and serves banks, health care providers, technology companies, insurance carriers, and manufacturers in maximizing the value from business technology. He has contributed articles on business technology to the *McKinsey Quarterly*, *McKinsey on Business Technology*, *Financial Times Connected Business*, the *Wall Street Journal*, and the *Harvard Business Review* blog network. James holds an AB in history from Brown University and an MBA from the Wharton School of the University of Pennsylvania. He lives in New York with his wife, Amy, and their two sons, Adam and Matthew.

TUCKER BAILEY

Tucker is a partner in the Washington, D.C., location of McKinsey's Business Technology Office, where he focuses principally on defense, security, and IT issues. He has served multiple Fortune 500 and public-sector clients across a range of IT issues and leads McKinsey's cybersecurity practice in North America. Prior to working for McKinsey, Tucker served as an Information Dominance Warfare Officer with the U.S. Navy and as a special agent with the Naval Criminal Investigative Service. Tucker holds a BSE from Duke University with majors in civil engineering and political science, and has an MBA from Harvard Business School.

CHRIS REZEK

Chris Rezek is a senior expert consultant with McKinsey & Company in Boston and is part of the firm's Risk Management and Business Technology practices. He is a core leader of McKinsey's cybersecurity practice serving banks, manufacturers, and other enterprises managing information risk as well as investors and technology companies on cybersecurity product-market strategy. Chris has helped define best practices on cloud risk management with the Cloud Security Alliance and risk technology and operations with the Institute of International Finance. He has a BS from MIT and an MBA from Yale. Chris lives near Boston with his family.

DEREK O'HALLORAN

Derek is the head of Information Technology Industries at the World Economic Forum, responsible for the CEO-led community of the world's leading IT companies and for shaping the technology agenda for the broader organization. Derek manages the Global Agenda Councils on the Future of the Software and Society and on the Future of Electronics, which convene leaders and thought leaders across the industry ecosystem. Derek holds an MPA in international finance and economic policy from the School of International and Public Affairs at Columbia University and an MA Hons in philosophy from the University of Edinburgh and is a graduate of the Global Leadership Fellows Programme at the Forum.

ALAN MARCUS

Alan is senior director and head of Information Technology and Telecommunications Industries at the World Economic Forum. Previously, he held senior management positions in engineering, marketing, and market development in Asia-Pacific, North America, and Europe and the Middle East. He holds a BSc in computer science and computer engineering from Rutgers University, New Jersey and a graduate diploma in telecommunications engineering from the University of California, Berkeley.

Index